AEPA 22 Special Education: Cross-Category

Teacher Certification Exam

By: Sharon Wynne, M.S
Southern Connecticut State University

"And, while there's no reason yet to panic, I think it's only prudent that we make preparations to panic."

XAMonline, INC.
Boston

Copyright © 2008 XAMonline, Inc.
All rights reserved. No part of the material protected by this copyright notice may be reproduced or utilized in any form or by any means, electronic or mechanical, including photocopying, recording or by any information storage and retrievable system, without written permission from the copyright holder.

To obtain permission(s) to use the material from this work for any purpose including workshops or seminars, please submit a written request to:

XAMonline, Inc.
21 Orient Ave.
Melrose, MA 02176
Toll Free 1-800-509-4128
Email: info@xamonline.com
Web www.xamonline.com
Fax: 1-781-662-9268

Library of Congress Cataloging-in-Publication Data

Wynne, Sharon A.
    Special Education: Cross-Category 22: Teacher Certification / Sharon A. Wynne. -2nd ed.
    ISBN 978-1-58197-770-7
    1. Special Education: Cross-Category 22   2. Study Guides.   3. AEPA
    4. Teachers' Certification & Licensure.   5. Careers

Disclaimer:
The opinions expressed in this publication are the sole works of XAMonline and were created independently from the National Education Association, Educational Testing Service, or any State Department of Education, National Evaluation Systems or other testing affiliates.

Between the time of publication and printing, state specific standards as well as testing formats and website information may change that is not included in part or in whole within this product. Sample test questions are developed by XAMonline and reflect similar content as on real tests; however, they are not former tests. XAMonline assembles content that aligns with state standards but makes no claims nor guarantees teacher candidates a passing score. Numerical scores are determined by testing companies such as NES or ETS and then are compared with individual state standards. A passing score varies from state to state.

Printed in the United States of America   œ-1

AEPA: Special Education: Cross-Category 22
ISBN: 978-1-58197-770-7

ACKNOWLEDGEMENTS
Special Education

XAMonline recognizes the hard work and professionalism that has made our study guides possible. The insight and subject expertise of our authors and editors ensures that we meet, and exceed, the high standards expected of us. Our study guides aim to uphold the integrity and pride represented by modern educators who bear the name
TEACHER.

Providers of Foundational Material:

Founding authors 1996	Kathy Schinerman
	Roberta Ramsey
Pre-flight editorial review	Paul Sutliff
Pre-flight construction :	Brittany Good
	Harris
	Brooks
	Hughes
Authors 2006	Paul Sutliff
	Beatrice Jordan
	Marisha Tapera
	Kathy Gibson
	Christi Goddard
	Carol Moore
	Twya Lavender
Sample test rational	Sidney Findley

Editorial and Production Staff:

Project Manager	Sharon Wynne
Project Coordinator	Twya Lavender
Senior Editor	Zakia Hyder
Series Editor	Mary Collins
Editorial Assistant	Virginia Finnerty
Marketing Manager	John Wynne
Marketing support	Maria Ciampa
Cover design	Brian Messenger
Sales	Justin Dooley
Production Editor	David Aronson
Typist	Julian German
Manufacturing	Chris Morning/Midland Press
E-Books	Kristy Gipson/Lightningsource

TEACHER CERTIFICATION STUDY GUIDE

Table of Contents

About the Test...vi

Introduction...vii

Pre-test..1

Rigor Table..54

DOMAIN I.	**UNDERSTANDING STUDENTS WITH SPECIAL NEEDS**
Competency 1.0	Understand typical learning processes and the significance of various disabilities for learning...............55
Competency 2.0	Understand types and characteristics of emotional disabilities...66
Competency 3.0	Understand the effects of emotional disabilities on human development and learning.............................70
Competency 4.0	Understand types and characteristics of specific learning disabilities...79
Competency 5.0	Understand the effects of specific learning disabilities on human development and learning.................85
Competency 6.0	Understand types and characteristics of mild, moderate, and severe mental retardation.........................86
Competency 7.0	Understand the effects of mild, moderate, and severe mental retardation on human development and learning..89
Competency 8.0	Understand types and characteristics of orthopedic (physical) and other health impairments........................90
Competency 9.0	Understand the effects of orthopedic (physical) and other health impairments on human development and learning..91

SPECIAL EDU. CROSS-CATEGORY

TEACHER CERTIFICATION STUDY GUIDE

DOMAIN II.	ASSESSING STUDENTS AND DEVELOPING INDIVIDUALIZED EDUCATION PROGRAMS (IEPs)
Competency 10.0	Understand types and characteristics of assessment instruments and methods 92
Competency 11.0	Understand assessment procedures of the multidisciplinary evaluation team for evaluating individual differences and making placement and programming decisions for students with disabilities 102
Competency 12.0	Understand procedures and criteria for evaluating and identifying the educational strengths and needs of students with emotional disabilities 110
Competency 13.0	Understand procedures and criteria for evaluating and identifying the educational strengths and needs of students with specific learning disabilities 110
Competency 14.0	Understand procedures and criteria for evaluating and identifying the educational strengths and needs of students with mental retardation 110
Competency 15.0	Understand procedures and criteria for evaluating and identifying the educational strengths and needs of students with orthopedic (physical) or other health impairments 110
Competency 16.0	Understand the uses of ongoing assessment in the education of students with special needs 111
Competency 17.0	Understand procedures for developing and implementing Individualized Education Programs (IEPs) for students with special needs 115

TEACHER CERTIFICATION STUDY GUIDE

DOMAIN III.	PROMOTING STUDENT DEVELOPMENT AND LEARNING
Competency 18.0	Understand how to establish a positive and productive learning environment for all students............ 121
Competency 19.0	Understand approaches and techniques used to improve students' reading skills 133
Competency 20.0	Understand strategies and techniques used to promote students' written expression 143
Competency 21.0	Understand strategies and techniques used to promote students' math skills 151
Competency 22.0	Understand strategies and techniques used to promote students' acquisition of academic skills 156
Competency 23.0	Understand strategies and techniques used to promote students' acquisition of functional skills 159
Competency 24.0	Understand strategies and techniques used to improve students' independent learning skills 163
Competency 25.0	Understand the development and implementation of behavior interventions 166
Competency 26.0	Understand strategies and techniques used to improve students' transition to adult life roles........... 192
Competency 27.0	Understand principles of and procedures for supporting students' transition from school to employment and/or post-secondary education and training........ 193

SPECIAL EDU. CROSS-CATEGORY

TEACHER CERTIFICATION STUDY GUIDE

DOMAIN IV. WORKING IN A COLLABORATIVE LEARNING COMMUNITY

Competency 28.0   Understand how to establish partnerships with other members of the school community to enhance learning opportunities for students with special needs 197

Competency 29.0   Understand how to promote strong school-home relationships 215

Competency 30.0   Understand how to encourage school-community interactions that enhance learning opportunities for students with special needs 227

Competency 31.0   Understand the history and philosophy of special education, key issues and trends, roles and responsibilities, and legal and ethical issues 243

Post-Test 258

Rigor Table 288

Answer Key 289

Rationales for Post-Test Sample Questions 290

References 344

TEACHER CERTIFICATION STUDY GUIDE

ABOUT THE TEST

The Arizona Educator Proficiency Assessments (AEPA) is a required examination of anyone who seeks to become an educator in Arizona. The purpose of this test is to ensure that each person seeking a career as an educator in Arizona has the necessary knowledge to practice effectively in Arizona public schools.

The tests are criterion-referenced and objective-based. Each test has a section of selected-response questions.

Domain #	Approximate Percentage of Selected-Response Items on Test Form
1. Understanding Students with Special Needs	29%
2. Assessing Students and Developing Individualized Education Programs (IEPs)	26%
3. Promoting Student Development and Learning	32%
4. Working in a Collaborative Learning Community	13%

Scores
Test results range from 100 to 300, with 240 representing the passing score.

Location and cost

Please go to www.aepa.nesinc.com for up-to-date information about cost, location, and dates.

TEACHER CERTIFICATION STUDY GUIDE

INTRODUCTION

This one-volume study guide was designed for professionals preparing to take a teacher competency test in special education or in any field in which the principles of special education are a part of the test content. Objectives specific to the field of special education were obtained from state departments of education and federal territories and dependencies across the nation. Educators preparing to take tests in the various areas of special education should find the manual helpful, for the objectives and the scope of the discussions concerning each objective cover a wide range of the field.

The study guide offers many benefits to the person faced with the necessity of making a qualifying score on a competency test in special education. A large number of source materials must be covered in order to study the conceptual knowledge reflected by the objectives listed in each state study guide. These objectives encompass the major content of the special education field. The term "objective" may be called "competency" in some states. These terms are synonymous and refer to an item of professional knowledge for mastery.

Many prominent textbooks used by pre-service teacher training programs nationwide were researched for the content of this book. Other important resources (e.g., books, journal articles, and media) were included in the discussions about the objectives. The compilation of this research alleviates the hardship imposed on a teacher who attempts to accumulate, as one individual preparing for an examination, the vast body of professional material. This one-volume study guide highlights the current knowledge and accepted concepts of the field of special education, thus reducing the massive amount of material that would need to be assembled if one did not have it between a single set of covers.

The book is organized by major topical sections. These topics often correspond with course titles and textbooks in pre-service teacher training programs. The objectives and discussions about them comprise the main content within each section. The discussions feature important information from textbooks in the field of special education, reported in the books in a synthesized and summarized form. Specific references have been given for charts and quoted materials, which were included to enhance understanding of conceptual discussions. Complete reference citations can be located in the reference listings.

TEACHER CERTIFICATION STUDY GUIDE

Finally, questions specific to the discussion of each objective have been written to help determine if the reader understands that material. Correctness of responses to questions can be checked for immediate accuracy in the Answer Key section. Test questions are written as teaching mechanisms and appear in the style and format to cover those used on tests by any state.

Though this manual is comprehensive, it in no way purports to contain all the research and applied techniques in every area of exceptionality. Research generates new applications, and continuing in-service education is a requirement for all special education professionals. This manual gives the reader a one-volume summary of the fundamentals known and practiced at the time of writing.

TEACHER CERTIFICATION STUDY GUIDE

Great Study and Testing Tips!

What to study in order to prepare for the subject assessments is the focus of this study guide, but equally important is *how* you study.

You can increase your chances of truly mastering the information by taking some simple, but effective steps.

Study Tips:

1. Some foods aid the learning process. Foods such as milk, nuts, seeds, rice, and oats help your study efforts by releasing natural memory enhancers called CCKs (*cholecystokinin*) composed of *tryptophan*, *choline*, and *phenylalanine*. All of these chemicals enhance the neurotransmitters associated with memory. Before studying, try a light, protein-rich meal of eggs, turkey, or fish. All of these foods release the memory enhancing chemicals. The better the connections, the more you comprehend.

Likewise, before you take a test, stick to a light snack of energy-boosting and relaxing foods. A glass of milk, a piece of fruit, or some peanuts all release various memory-boosting chemicals and help you to relax and focus on the subject at hand.

2. Learn to take great notes. A byproduct of our modern culture is that we have grown accustomed to getting our information in short doses (e.g., TV news sound bites or *USA Today* style newspaper articles).

Consequently, we've subconsciously trained ourselves to assimilate information better in neat little packages. If your notes are scrawled all over the paper, it fragments the flow of the information. Strive for clarity. Newspapers use a standard format to achieve clarity. Your notes can be much clearer through use of proper formatting. A very effective format is called the *"Cornell Method."*

Take a sheet of loose-leaf lined notebook paper and draw a line all the way down the paper about 1-2" from the left-hand edge.

Draw another line across the width of the paper about 1-2" up from the bottom. Repeat this process on the reverse side of the page.

Look at the highly effective result. You have ample room for notes, a left-hand margin for special emphasis items or inserting supplementary data from the textbook, a large area at the bottom for a brief summary, and a little rectangular space for just about anything you want.

SPECIAL EDU. CROSS-CATEGORY

3. **Get the concept, then the details.** Too often we focus on the details and don't gather an understanding of the concept. However, if you simply memorize only dates, places, or names, you may well miss the whole point of the subject. A key way to understand things is to put them in your own words. If you are working from a textbook, automatically summarize each paragraph in your mind. If you are outlining text, don't simply copy the author's words.

Rephrase them in your own words. You remember your own thoughts and words much better than someone else's, and subconsciously tend to associate the important details to the core concepts.

4. **Ask Why?** Pull apart written material paragraph by paragraph and don't forget the captions under the illustrations.

Example: If the heading is "Stream Erosion," flip it around to read "Why do streams erode?" Then answer the questions.

If you train your mind to think in a series of questions and answers, not only will you learn more, you will lessen your test anxiety because you are used to answering questions.

5. **Read for reinforcement and future needs.** Even if you only have 10 minutes, put your notes or a book in your hand. Your mind is similar to a computer; you have to input data in order to have it processed. *By reading, you are creating the neural connections for future retrieval.* The more times you read something, the more you reinforce the learning of ideas.

Even if you don't fully understand something on the first pass, *your mind stores much of the material for later recall.*

6. **Relax to learn, so go into exile.** Our bodies respond to an inner clock called biorhythms. Burning the midnight oil works well for some people, but not everyone.

If possible, set aside a particular place to study that is free of distractions. Shut off the television, cell phone, and pager and exile your friends and family during your study period.

If you really are bothered by silence, try background music. Light classical music at a low volume has been shown to aid in concentration over other types.

Music that evokes pleasant emotions without lyrics is highly suggested. Try just about anything by Mozart. It relaxes you.

SPECIAL EDU. CROSS-CATEGORY x

TEACHER CERTIFICATION STUDY GUIDE

7. Use arrows, not highlighters. At best, it's difficult to read a page full of yellow, pink, blue, and green streaks.

Try staring at a neon sign for a while and you'll soon see the point—the horde of colors obscure the message.

A quick note, a brief dash of color, an underline, or an arrow pointing to a particular passage is much clearer than a horde of highlighted words.

8. Budget your study time. Although you shouldn't ignore any of the material, allocate your available study time in the same ratio that topics may appear on the test.

TEACHER CERTIFICATION STUDY GUIDE

Testing Tips:

1. <u>Get smart, play dumb.</u> Don't read anything into the question. Don't make an assumption that the test writer is looking for something else than what is asked. Stick to the question as written and don't read extra things into it.

2. <u>Read the question and all the choices *twice* before answering the question.</u> You may miss something by not carefully reading, and then re-reading, both the question and the answers.

If you really don't have a clue as to the right answer, leave it blank on the first time through. Go on to the other questions, as they may provide a clue as to how to answer the skipped questions.

If later on, you still can't answer the skipped ones . . . ***Guess.***
The only penalty for guessing is that you *might* get it wrong. Only one thing is certain; if you don't put anything down, you will get it wrong!

3. <u>Turn the question into a statement.</u> Look at the way the questions are worded. The syntax of the question usually provides a clue. Does it seem more familiar as a statement rather than as a question? Does it sound strange?

By turning a question into a statement, you may be able to spot if an answer sounds right, and it may also trigger memories of material you have read.

4. <u>Look for hidden clues.</u> It's actually very difficult to compose multiple-foil (choice) questions without giving away part of the answer in the options presented.

In most multiple-choice questions you can often readily eliminate one or two of the potential answers. This leaves you with only two real possibilities and automatically your odds go to fifty-fifty for very little work.

5. <u>Trust your instincts.</u> For every fact that you have read, you subconsciously retain something of that knowledge. On questions that you aren't really certain about, go with your basic instincts. **Your first impression on how to answer a question is usually correct.**

6. <u>Mark your answers directly on the test booklet.</u> Don't bother trying to fill in the optical scan sheet on the first pass through the test.

Just be very careful not to mismark your answers when you eventually transcribe them to the scan sheet.

7. <u>Watch the clock!</u> You have a set amount of time to answer the questions. Don't get bogged down trying to answer a single question at the expense of 10 questions you can more readily answer.

SPECIAL EDU. CROSS-CATEGORY

TEACHER CERTIFICATION STUDY GUIDE

Pre-Test Sample Questions

1. A child may be classified under the special education "umbrella" as having traumatic brain injury (TBI) if he/she does not have which of the following causes? *(Competency 1) (Rigorous)*

    A. Stroke
    B. Anoxia
    C. Encephalitis
    D. Birth trauma

Answer: D. Birth trauma

According to IDEA and Part 200, a child may not be labeled as having traumatic brain injury if the injury is related to birth

2. Children with ADHD are often medicated with stimulants. These drugs can have many side effects. Which of the following is not one of them: *(Competency 1) (Rigorous)*

    A. Tremors.
    B. Confusion
    C. Aggressive behavior
    D. Headaches

Answer: B. Confusion

Confusion is a known side effect of most tranquilizers, not that of stimulants. However, they do share the side effects of tremors.

3. A developmental delay may be indicated by a: *(Competency 1.0) (Rigorous)*

    A. A 4th Grader that has difficulty understanding conservation of number.
    B. Stuttered response
    C. Kindergartner not having complete bladder control
    D. Withdrawn behavior

Answer: A. A 4th Grader that has difficulty understanding conservation of number.

Conservation of number is generally mastered by the age of 7. A typical 4th Grader is approximately 8 to 9 years old While many children have full bladder control by age four, it is not unusual for "embarrassing accidents" to occur.

SPECIAL EDU. CROSS-CATEGORY

TEACHER CERTIFICATION STUDY GUIDE

4. **According to IDEA, a child whose disability is related to being deaf and blind may and has been diagnosed as being mentally retarded may be classified as:** *(Competency 1.0) (Rigorous)*

    A. Multiple disabilities
    B. Other health impaired
    C. Having mental retardation
    D. Visually Impaired

Answer: A. Multiple Disabilities

The only stated area where deaf-blindness is not accepted is in multiple disabilities. However, the additional element of mental retardation will allow for the classification of multiple disabilities

5. **A student who has issues with truancy, gang membership, low school performance, and drug use is displaying:** *(Competency 2.0) (Average Rigor)*

    A. Emotionally disturbed behaviors
    B. Symptoms of self-medication
    C. Average adolescent behavior
    D. Warning signs of crisis

Answer: D. Warning signs of crisis

The student is acting out by using aggression. This gives him or her a sense of belonging.

6. **Normality in child behavior is influenced by society's _____.** *(Competency 2.0) (Average Rigor)*

    A. Attitudes and cultural beliefs
    B. Religious beliefs
    C. Religious and cultural beliefs
    D. Attitudes and Victorian era motto

Answer: A. Attitudes and cultural beliefs

People are the product of their environment. Cultures outside of America may not have the same expectations. A child that comes from a culture where looking an adult in the eyes is considered being disrespectful, may have difficulty here as we see not looking a person in the eye as a sign of disrespect.

7. **Parents are more likely to have a child with a learning disability if:** *(Competency 2.0) (Average Rigor)*

   A. They smoke tobacco
   B. The child is less than five pounds at birth
   C. The mother drank alcohol on a regular basis until she planned for a baby
   D. The father was known to consume large quantities of alcohol during the pregnancy

Answer: B. The child is less than five pounds at birth

Babies that are born weighing less than five pounds at birth are more likely to have a form of learning disability. The reasoning is that the babies may not have fully developed before birth.

8. **Janelle is a new student in your 12:1:1 class. You begin to note that she laughs at inappropriate times, and responds to questions with answers that have absolutely nothing to do with the topic. You note that when she is not looking at you that her lips appear to be moving. You are concerned because you think Janelle may be exhibiting symptoms of:** *(Competency 2.0) (Easy)*

   A. Sensory perceptual disorder
   B. Mental illness
   C. Depression
   D. Tactile sensory deprivation

Answer: B. Mental illness

Janelle may be demonstrating delusional or hallucinogenic symptoms. These symptoms may indicate a need for psychiatric treatment within a more restrictive environment.

TEACHER CERTIFICATION STUDY GUIDE

9. Julio is a quiet regular education student, and has some difficulty learning in an inclusive classroom. He gets in trouble a little more than the average boy. He appears exhausted throughout the day, and becomes more withdrawn. When you walk by his desk during free time, you note that he has drawn a violent picture. What should you be concerned about? *(Competency 2.0) (Average Rigor)*

    A. Possible depression
    B. Central processing disorder
    C. Possible emotional disturbance
    D. Both a and c

Answer: D. Both a and c

Julio may be exhibiting signs of depression and/or emotional disturbance. Reporting these observations to your colleague who is responsible for the child, and your thoughts about what the child's educational needs may truly be are a responsibility of yours.

10. Modeling of a behavior by an adult who verbalizes the thinking process, overt self-instruction, and covert self-instruction are components of: *(Competency 3.0) (Rigorous)*

    A. Rational-emotive therapy
    B. Reality therapy
    C. Cognitive behavior modification
    D. Reciprocal teaching

Answer: C. Cognitive behavior modification

Neither A, B, nor D involves modification or change of behavior.

11. What is the most important skill a teacher can help a student learn? *(Competency 3.0) (Average Rigor)*

    A. Reading
    B. Budgeting
    C. Cooking
    D. Self-advocacy

Answer: D. Self-advocacy

The skill of self-advocacy creates the road to independence, with an understanding of personal limits and needs to find success in his or her endeavors.

SPECIAL EDU. CROSS-CATEGORY

TEACHER CERTIFICATION STUDY GUIDE

12. A person who has a learning disability: *(Competency 4.0) (Easy)*

    A. Has an IQ two standard deviations below the norm
    B. Has congenital abnormalities
    C. Is limited by the educational environment
    D. Has a discrepancy between potential and achievement.

Answer: D. Has a discrepancy between potential and achievement.

13. Spatial relationship difficulties become evident when a child demonstrates: *(Competency 4.0) (Average Rigor)*

    A. Letter confusion
    B. Dyslexia
    C. Hesitant expression
    D. Difficulty measuring

Answer: A. Letter confusion

Students with a spatial relationship disability may not be able to differentiate between similar letters such as "b" and "p."

14. A person with Autism is generally diagnosed by what age? *(Competency 4.0) (Rigorous)*

    A. 2
    B. 3
    C. 4
    D. 5

Answer: C. 3

When a child has difficulty interacting with a parent, they will generally take the child to the doctor out of concern. When a child fails to participate in parallel play additional red flags raise. These observations note basic developmental concerns.

15. Which of these factors relate to eligibility for learning disabilities? *(Competency 4)* *(Easy Rigor)*

    A. A discrepancy between potential and performance
    B. Sub-average intellectual functioning
    C. Social deficiencies or learning deficits that are not due to intellectual, sensory, or physical conditions
    D. Documented results of behavior checklists and anecdotal records of aberrant behavior

Correct answer is "A."

Tests need to show a discrepancy between potential and performance. Classroom observations and samples of student work (such as impaired reading ability) also provide indicators of possible learning disabilities. Eligibility for services in behavior disorders requires documented evidence of social deficiencies or learning deficits that are not due to intellectual, sensory, or physical conditions. Any student undergoing multidisciplinary evaluation is usually given an intelligence test, diagnostic achievement tests, and social and/or adaptive inventories. Answers b, c, and d are symptoms displayed before testing for eligibility. Some students who display these symptoms do fail the tests and are not categorized as eligible to receive services.

16. A child that reads a sentence and has difficulty interpreting its meaning has difficulty with? *(Competency 4.0)* *(Rigorous)*

    A. Working memory
    B. Short-term memory
    C. Visual perception
    D. Spatial perception

Answer: A. Working memory

Working memory, the active processing of a thought may be a concern when it appears evident that a student has either a delay in interpreting what is going on around them, or reading simple passages.

17. Which of the public perceptions listed below many with disabilities do not appreciate is that_____. (Competency 5.0) (Easy Rigor)

    A. You must make laws to grant public access
    B. People with disabilities cannot contribute to society.
    C. People with disabilities need access to public assistance
    D. People with physical disabilities may need preferred seating on a bus.

Answer: B. People with disabilities cannot contribute to society.

Several people with disabilities lead normal lives, hold jobs, and contribute to society in various ways. This is considered an insult today.

18. Persons with mental retardation have an IQ below: (Competency 6.0) (Average Rigor)

    A. 70
    B. 80
    C. 60
    D. 90

Answer: A. 70

Mental retardation exists when a persons IQ is below 70; two standard deviations below the norm.

19. Women who drink alcoholic beverages excessively during pregnancy or more likely to have children who: (Competency 6.0) (Easy)

    A. have Fetal Alcohol Syndrome.
    B. are below 5 lbs. at birth.
    C. learning disabled.
    D. all of the above.

Answer: D. All of the above

Alcohol usage during pregnancy can be detrimental to the brain's natural development, as well as other physical factors.

20. People who have physical impairments have disabling conditions directly related to: (Competency 8.0) (Average Rigor)

    A. the musculoskeletal system
    B. cardiopulmonary system
    C. social isolation
    D. all of the above

Answer: A. the musculoskeletal system

People with physical disabilities may have additional health impairments, but this is not always this case.

21. Which of these would be the least effective measure of behavioral disorders? *(Competency 10.0) (Average Rigor)*

    A. Alternative assessment
    B. Naturalistic assessment
    C. Standardized test
    D. Psychodynamic analysis

Answer: C. Standardized test

These tests make comparisons, rather than measure skills.

22. Safeguards against bias and discrimination in the assessment of children include: *(Competency 10.0) (Easy Rigor)*

    A. The testing of a child in standard English
    B. The requirement for the use of one standardized test
    C. The use of evaluative materials in the child's native language or other mode of communication
    D. All testing performed by a certified, licensed psychologist

Answer: C. The use of evaluative materials in the child's native language or other mode of communication

The law requires that the child be evaluated in his or her native language or mode of communication. The idea that a licensed psychologist must evaluate the child does not meet the criteria if it is not done in the child's normal mode of communication.

23. Which is characteristic of group tests? *(Competency 10.0) (Average Rigor)*

   A. Directions are always read to students
   B. The examiner monitors several students at the same time
   C. The teacher is allowed to probe students who almost have the correct answer
   D. Both quantitative and qualitative information may be gathered

Answer: "B." The examiner monitors several students at the same time

In group tests, the examiner may provide directions for children up to and including fourth grade. Children write or mark their own responses. The examiner monitors the progress of several children at the same time. He or she cannot rephrase questions or probe or prompt responses. It is very difficult to obtain qualitative information in group tests. Group tests are appropriate for program evaluation, screening, and some types of program planning (such as tracking). Special consideration may need to be given if there is any motivational, personality, linguistic, or physically disabling factors that might impair the examinee's performance. When planning individual programs, individual tests should be used.

24. For which of the following uses are individual tests most appropriate? *(Competency 10.0) (Easy Rigor)*

   A. Screening students to determine possible need for special education services
   B. Evaluation of special education curricular
   C. Tracking gifted students
   D. Evaluation of a student for eligibility and placement, or individualized program planning, in special education

Answer: D. Evaluation of a student for eligibility and placement, or individualized program planning, in special education

See previous question.

TEACHER CERTIFICATION STUDY GUIDE

25. Which of the following is an advantage of giving individual, rather than group tests? *(Competency 10.0) (Easy Rigor)*

    A. The test administrator can control the tempo of an individual test, giving breaks when needed
    B. The test administrator can clarify or rephrase questions
    C. Individual tests provide for the gathering of both qualitative and quantitative results
    D. All of the above

Answer: D. All of the above

26. Mrs. Stokes has been teaching her third-grade students about mammals during a recent science unit. Which of the following would be true of a criterion-referenced test she might administer at the conclusion of the unit? *(Competency 10.0) (Average Rigor)*

    A. It will be based on unit objectives
    B. Derived scores will be used to rank student achievement.
    C. Standardized scores are effective of national performance samples
    D. All of the above

Answer: A. It will be based on unit objectives

Criterion-referenced tests measure the progress made by individuals in mastering specific skills. The content is based on a specific set of objectives rather than the general curriculum. Criterion-referenced tests provide measurements pertaining to the information a given student needs to know and the skills that student needs to master. Norm-referenced tests have a large advantage over criterion-referenced tests when used for screening or program evaluation. Norm-referenced tests provide a means of comparing a student's performance to the performance typically expected of others of his or her age.

27. For which of the following purposes is a norm-referenced test least appropriate? *(Competency 10.0) (Average Rigor)*

    A. Screening
    B. Individual program planning
    C. Program evaluation
    D. Making placement decisions

Answer: B. Individual program planning

If you plan to create an individual program, using a norm referenced test will not provide you with the knowledge you need to do so.

SPECIAL EDU. CROSS-CATEGORY

28. **Criterion-referenced tests can provide information about:**
    (Competency 10.0) (Easy Rigor)

    A. Whether a student has mastered prerequisite skills
    B. Whether a student is ready to proceed to the next level of instruction
    C. Which instructional materials might be helpful in covering program objectives
    D. All of the above

Answer: A. Whether a student has mastered prerequisite skills

In criterion-referenced testing, the emphasis is on assessing specific and relevant behaviors that have been mastered. Items on criterion-referenced tests are often linked directly to specific instructional objectives.

29. **Which of the following purposes of testing calls for an informal test?**
    (Competency 10.0) (Average Rigor)

    A. Screening a group of children to determine their readiness for the first reader
    B. Measuring the content of a social studies unit prepared by the classroom teacher covering one aspect of the general curriculum
    C. Evaluating the effectiveness of a fourth-grade math program at the end of its first year of use in a specific school
    D. Determining the general level of intellectual functioning of a class of fifth graders

Answer: B. Measuring the content of a social studies unit prepared by the classroom teacher covering one aspect of the general curriculum

Formal tests are commercially prepared standardized tests. Formal tests may be categorized as norm-referenced or as criterion-referenced. Informal tests are usually teacher-prepared. These are usually criterion referenced. Answer b is the only teacher-made test.

TEACHER CERTIFICATION STUDY GUIDE

30. Which of the following is not a true statement about informal tests? *(Competency 10.0) (Average Rigor)*

   A. Informal tests are useful in comparing students to others of their age or grade level
   B. The correlation between curriculum and test criteria is much higher in informal tests
   C. Informal tests are useful in evaluating an individual's response to instruction
   D. Informal tests are used to diagnose a student's particular strengths and weaknesses for purposes of planning individual programs

Answer: A. Informal tests are useful in comparing students to others of their age or grade level

Informal or teacher-made tests are usually criterion-referenced. Norm-referenced tests are usually group tests given to large populations.

31. For which situation might a teacher be apt to select a formal test? *(Competency 10.0) (Average Rigor)*

   A. A pretest for studying world religions
   B. A weekly spelling test
   C. To compare student progress with that of peers of the same age or grade level on a national basis
   D. To determine which content objectives outlined on the student's IEPs were mastered

Answer: C. To compare student progress with that of peers of the same age or grade level on a national basis

See previous question.

32. The extent to which a test measures what its authors or users claim that it measures is called its: *(Competency 10.0) (Rigorous)*

   A. Validity
   B. Reliability
   C. Normality
   D. Acculturation

Answer: A. Validity

Validity is the degree or extent to which a test measures what it was designed or intended to measure. Reliability is the extent to which a test is consistent in its measurements.

SPECIAL EDU. CROSS-CATEGORY

TEACHER CERTIFICATION STUDY GUIDE

33. **If a scholastic aptitude test is checked against predictive success in academic endeavors, which type of validity is being established?** *(Competency 10.0) (Rigorous)*

   A.   Content
   B.   Criterion-related
   C.   Construct
   D.   Confirmation

Answer: B. Criterion-related

There are different kinds of evidence to support a particular judgment. If the purpose of a test is to measure the skills covered in a particular course or unit, then it is hoped that there will be test questions on all the important topics and not on extraneous topics. If this condition is met, then there is content validity. Some tests, like the SAT, are designed to predict outcomes. If SAT scores correlate with academic performance in college, as measured by GPA in the first year, then there is criterion-related validity. Construct validity is probably the most important. It is gathered over many years and is indicated by a pattern of scores (e.g., older children can answer more questions on intelligence tests than younger children). This fits with the general construct of intelligence.

34. **Which of the following is a factor in determining test validity?** *(Competency 10.0) (Rigorous)*

   A.   The appropriateness of the sample items chosen to measure a criterion
   B.   The acculturation of the norm group as compared to that of the population being tested
   C.   The reliability of the test
   D.   All of the above

Answer: D. All of the above

Validity can be affected by:
- The appropriateness of the sample items chosen to measure a criterion
- The cultural, environmental, and linguistic background of the norm group as compared to that of the population being tested
- The accuracy with which a person's performance on a criterion can be predicted from his or her test score on that criterion
- The consistency in administration and scoring of the test
- The reliability of the test

SPECIAL EDU. CROSS-CATEGORY

35. To which aspect does fair assessment relate? *(Competency 10.0) (Easy Rigor)*

    A. Representation
    B. Acculturation
    C. Language
    D. All of the above

Answer: D. All of the above

All three aspects are necessary and vital for assessment to be fair.

36. Acculturation refers to the individual's: *(Competency 10.0) (Average Rigor)*

    A. Gender
    B. Experiential background
    C. Social class
    D. Ethnic background

Answer: B. Experiential background

A person's culture has little to do with gender, social class, or ethnicity. A person is the product of his or her experiences. Acculturation is basically the differences in experiential background.

37. Youngsters in regular classrooms receive regular testing primarily related to: *(Competency 10.0) (Easy Rigor)*

    A. Eligibility for special education
    B. Promotion by grade level
    C. IEP program planning
    D. All of the above

Answer: B. Promotion by grade level

Promotion by grade level is the only reason for testing regular students in regular classrooms.

TEACHER CERTIFICATION STUDY GUIDE

38. **Which of the following statements reflects true factors that affect the reliability of a test?** *(Competency 10.0) (Rigorous)*

    A. Short tests tend to be more reliable than long tests
    B. The shorter the time length between two administrations of a test, the greater the possibility that the scores will change
    C. Even if guessing results in a correct response, it introduces error into a test score and into interpretation of the results
    D. All of the above

Answer: C. Even if guessing results in a correct response, it introduces error into a test score and into interpretation of the results

The reliability of a test is concerned with the extent to which the person tested will receive the same score on repeated administrations of that test. When a person's score fluctuates randomly, the test lacks reliability.

39. **Mrs. Freud administered a personality traits survey to her high school psychology class. She re-administered the same survey two weeks later. The method which she used to determine reliability was that of:** *(Competency 10.0) (Rigorous)*

    A. Test-retest
    B. Split half
    C. Alternate form
    D. Kuder-Richardson formula

Answer: A. Test-retest

The test-retest reliability is accomplished by administering the same test on a second occasion.

40. **Children who write poorly might be given tests that allow oral responses unless the purpose for giving the test is to:** *(Competency 10.0) (Average Rigor)*

    A. Assess handwriting skills
    B. Test for organization of thoughts
    C. Answer questions pertaining to math reasoning
    D. Assess rote memory

Answer: A. Assess handwriting skills

It is necessary to have the child write if the test is assessing his or her skill in that domain.

41. Which of the following types of tests is used to estimate learning potential and to predict academic achievement? *(Competency 10.0)* *(Average Rigor)*

   A. Intelligence tests
   B. Achievement tests
   C. Adaptive behavior tests
   D. Personality tests

Answer: A. Intelligence tests

An intelligence test is designed to measure intellectual abilities like memory, comprehension, and abstract reasoning. IQ is often used to estimate the learning capacity of a student and to predict academic achievement.

42. Which skills are typically assessed by an intelligence test? *(Competency 10.0)* *(Rigorous)*

   A. Abstract reasoning, comprehension
   B. Interest, capacity
   C. Math computation, math-reasoning skills
   D. Independent functioning, language development

Answer: "A." Abstract reasoning, comprehension

See previous question.

43. A test that measures students' skill development in academic content areas is classified as an _____ test. *(Competency 10.0)* *(Average Rigor)*

   A. Achievement
   B. Aptitude
   C. Adaptive
   D. Intelligence

Answer: A. Achievement

Achievement tests directly assess students' skill development in academic content areas. They measure the degree to which a student has benefited from education and/or life experiences compared to others of the same age or grade level. They may be used as diagnostic tests to find strengths and weaknesses of students. They may be used for screening, placement progress evaluation, and determining curricular effectiveness.

TEACHER CERTIFICATION STUDY GUIDE

44. A good dynamic assessment requires: *(Competency 11) (Rigorous)*

    A. Both a pre and post test
    B. Portfolios
    C. Long-range planning
    D. Diverse responses

Answer: A. Both a pre and post test

Dynamic assessments measure possible impediments to learning by testing prior knowledge. The test then evaluates both the student and the manner in which he/she was taught.

45. Chang-tsu is a new in your class on politics from China. You have students working on a group project and discussing what they should do. Chang-tsu comes to you in private and asks to work on his own, this happened after the group has made a decision on what the project will look like. You tell Chang-tsu that this is a group project and he cannot work on his own. He returns to the group and does not participate. His grades in all other areas are As. What should you do first? *(Competency 11) (Rigorous)*

    A. Complain to the principal
    B. Ask for a parent-teacher conference
    C. Check to see if this is a cultural norm in his country
    D. Create a behavior contract for him to follow

Answer: C. Check to see if this is a cultural norm in his country

While A, B, and D are good actions, it is important to remember that Chang-tsu comes from a culture where publicly criticizing a person's concept is not looked on as acceptable behavior. Learning this information will enable the school as a whole to address this behavior.

TEACHER CERTIFICATION STUDY GUIDE

46. **When a child has been fully evaluated, and the IEP team meets to discuss classification eligibility, what should happen if the team decides the student does not qualify?** *(Competency 11) (Average Rigor)*

    A. Refer the parental interventions to the 504 Plan
    B. Inform the parent with their due process rights with the committee
    C. Recommend to the parent possible resources outside of the committee for which the child may qualify
    D. All of the above

Answer: D. All of the above.

A parent of a child who does not qualify to be labeled as needing special education services should be shown other possibilities that they can seek to find the assistance they believe their child needs.

47. **An administrator has asked that you observe a student that is not yours in another classroom. The child's teacher recently recommended a change in placement. Why would the principal seek your input?** *(Competency 11) (Average Rigor)*

    A. Your observation skills
    B. Your objectivity
    C. Your assessment knowledge
    D. Your easy rapport with students

Answer: B. Your objectivity

Presenting a case for change of placement to your supervisor does not require parental permission. It requires your ability to objectively analyze the needs of the student versus current placement.

SPECIAL EDU. CROSS-CATEGORY

TEACHER CERTIFICATION STUDY GUIDE

48. **Which of the following statements was not offered as a rationale for inclusion?** *(Competency 11) (Average Rigor)*

    A. Students with special needs are generally not identified until a severe need is noted.
    B. Placement in an inclusive classroom lowers monetary need to meet student services.
    C. Segregated classroom placements are stigmatizing.
    D. There are students with learning or behavior problems who do not meet special education requirements but who still need special services.

Answer: B. Placement in an inclusive classroom lowers monetary need to meet student services.

All except lack of funding were offered in support of inclusion.

49. **A student is in your self-contained class, you have noted that the student appears able to do grade level material with little support. What placement change should you recommend?** *(Competency 11) (Average Rigor)*

    A. Special class (self-contained)
    B. Full-time inclusive setting with Special Education Co-Teacher throughout the day.
    C. Full-time inclusive setting with Consult Teacher.
    D. Part-time inclusive setting with Special Education Co-Teacher, limited to one current area of success.

Answer: D. Part-time inclusive setting with Special Education Co-Teacher, limited to one current area of success.

When one or more levels of delivery of Special Education services is skipped when promoting students to a less restrictive setting than they are currently in can be setting a child up for failure.

TEACHER CERTIFICATION STUDY GUIDE

50. **NCLB in 2004, changed the testing requirement of students with Limited English Proficiency (LEP) how?** *(Competency 11) (Rigorous)*

    A. State reading tests were no longer required IF the student was enrolled in US school for less than one year.
    B. State assessments are now to be given in the student's native language.
    C. English reading proficiency levels have to be met by LEP students before giving state tests in English.
    D. Supplemental services for students who do not speak and/or read English may now be discontinued after 1 year in a US based school.

Answer: A. State reading tests were no longer required IF the student was enrolled in US school for less than one year.

The policies for LEP students and students with disabilities under the No Child Left Behind legislation was changed in February 2004. One change was that schools were no longer required to give students with limited English proficiency their state's reading test if the students were enrolled in a U.S. school for less than a year. Schools are still required to give those students the state's math test, but they may substitute an English-proficiency test for the reading test during the first year of enrollment.

51. **MissTone is teaching a special class on Shakespeare. She has the group divide into four groups of three to discuss how they would rewrite the ending of Macbeth. She then demonstrates how she would change the play acting out her own concept. The groups are informed this is what they need to develop as a group. What teaching methods were employed?** *(Competency 16.0 (Average Rigor)*

    A. KWL
    B. Lecture
    C. Peer tutoring
    D. Modeling

Answer: D. Modeling

Miss Tone modeled the assignment she wanted the students to create.

TEACHER CERTIFICATION STUDY GUIDE

52. Ms. Greco's students are slated to give their oral presentations today. She hands out forms for the students to provide their own thoughts about each presentation. This is an example of: *(Competency 16.0) (Average Rigor)*

   A. Peer nomination
   B. Peer rating
   C. Peer assessment
   D. Sociogram

Answer: C. Peer assessment

Students are asked to provide input—while they might not contribute to a grade, they do provide a sense of assessment.

53. Mychal will be graduating soon. He has an occupational therapy 3 times a week. What most likely has the therapist worked on to assist in Mychal's independence after graduation? *(Competency 17.0) (Rigorous)*

   A. Training Mychal exercises to allow him to walk better.
   B. Teaching Mychal how to use adaptive equipment to clean his teeth.
   C. Teaching Mychal the importance of not missing his medication.
   D. Independent study skills that utilize his specific learning styles.

Answer: B. Teaching Mychal how to use adaptive equipment to clean his teeth.

Occupational Therapists work towards brining their clients to independence outside of an institutional environment as best as possible. The adaptive equipment used to brush Mychal's teeth most likely would have been created by his occupational therapist.

SPECIAL EDU. CROSS-CATEGORY

TEACHER CERTIFICATION STUDY GUIDE

54. Mrs. Pritchard was meeting with her principal and an irate parent. The parent insists that the teacher's notations of her child are prejudicial and insists on seeing all of her records on the child. Which record will Mrs. Pritchard not be required to provide? *(Competency 17.0) (Average Rigor)*

    A. her notes that are presently in the child's cumulative file.
    B. the child's grades from the grade book.
    C. her notes on student work.
    D. her personal notes on the child's behavior and needs, etc.

Answer: D. her personal notes on the child's behavior and needs, etc.

Anything in a cumulative file is considered accessible by a parent. The parent may look only at the grades of their own child, so a way to maintain confidentiality must be made when sharing the grades from the grade book. A teacher's personal notes are her own and it is the teacher's choice whether or not to share any personal notes with a parent.

55. Which of the following is not required on an IEP? *(Competency 17.0) (Average Rigor)*

    A. Test modifications.
    B. Annual goals
    C. Short-term objectives
    D. Assistive technology needs.

Answer: C. Short-term objectives.

IDEA 2007 removed the requirement of short-term objectives.

56. Which of the follow is most likely to provide a distraction to students in your classroom? *(Competency 18.0) (Rigorous)*

    A. Lighting adequacy
    B. The color of the room
    C. Window placement
    D. Emergency poster placement

Answer: B. the color of the room

Neutral colors such as a light tan, off white, are the standard in school environments because they are less distracting than cool colors such as blue, green, purple, or some combination of these.

SPECIAL EDU. CROSS-CATEGORY

TEACHER CERTIFICATION STUDY GUIDE

57. **Cooperative learning utilizes:** *(Competency 18.0) (Average Rigor)*

   A. Student leadership
   B. Small groups
   C. Independent practice
   D. Prior relevant knowledge

Answer: B. small groups

Cooperative learning focuses on group cooperation; it allows for the sharing of student expertise and provides some flexibility for creative presentation of the students as they share with others.

58. **Word attack skills specifically enable a child to?** *(Competency 19.0) (Average Rigor)*

   A. Decode unknown words
   B. Recognize previously known words
   C. Increase comprehension
   D. Understand contextual clues

Answer: A. Decode unknown words

The knowledge a child has when seeing a word for the first time will enable them to understand how to approximately pronounce it first. This may lead to a recognition of an orally known word and increase comprehension.

59. **Bloom's Taxonomy includes all of the following EXCEPT?** *(Competency 19.0) (Average Rigor)*

   A. Comprehension
   B. Synthesis
   C. Integration
   D. Analysis

Answer: C. Integration

Benjamin Bloom's taxonomy includes knowledge, comprehension, application, analysis, synthesis, and evaluation.

SPECIAL EDU. CROSS-CATEGORY

60. When teaching a student who is predominantly auditory to read, it is best to: *(Competency 19.0)* *(Average Rigor)*

   A. Stress sight vocabulary
   B. Stress phonetic analysis
   C. Stress the shape and configuration of the word
   D. Stress rapid reading

Answer is B. Stress phonetic analysis

Sensory modalities are one of the physical elements that affect learning style. Some students learn best through their visual sense (sight), others through their auditory sense (hearing), and still others by doing, touching, and moving (tactile-kinesthetic). Auditory learners generally listen to people, follow verbal directions, and enjoy hearing records, cassette tapes, and stories. Phonics has to do with sound, an auditory stimulus.

61. When teaching writing the introduction should be written when? *(Competency 20.0)* *(Rigorous)*

   A. In the Pre-writing stage
   B. When you enter the writing stage it should be the first thing written
   C. When you have all the information needed to "sell" the paper.
   D. When the paper is completed

Answer: D. When the paper is completed

When you are done with the body of your written piece, it is easier to put in the "zinger" that tells someone to read what you have written.

62. Antonia is working on a report about cats. She uses MS Word cut and paste to rearrange sections and paragraphs. She then prints the paper so she can continue writing. Which stage of the writing process is Antonia working on? *(Competency 20.0) (Easy)*

   A. Final draft
   B. Prewriting
   C. Revision
   D. Drafting

Answer: C. Revision

Antonia is revising and reordering before final editing.

63. Mrs. Sepulveda is leading her class by constructing a web diagram of ideas to use for a writing activity. Which stage of writing does this activity take place? *(Competency 20.0 (Easy)*

   A. Revision
   B. Drafting
   C. Prewriting
   D. Final draft

Answer: C. Prewriting

Organizing ideas come before drafting, final draft, and revision.

64. "The girl in row three and the boy next to her were passing notes across the aisle." This sentence is an example of? *(Competency 20.0) (Easy)*

   A. Simple sentence with compound subject.
   B. Simple sentence with compound predicate.
   C. Compound sentence with compound subject.
   D. Compound sentence with compound predicate.

65. Children generally begin school with all of the following math concepts EXCEPT? *(Competency 22.0) (Average Rigor)*

   A. Comparing
   B. Ordering
   C. Equalizing
   D. Describing

Answer: C. Equalizing

Conservation of amount is normally not attained until age 7, which would be in Grade 2 or 3.

66. Which of the following is an example of the math learning state "semi-concrete? *(Competency 22.0) (Average Rigor)*

   A. Using a worksheet with pictures to add and subtract.
   B. Using manipulatives to check previously given answers.
   C. understanding place value
   D. Adding 3+4 = 7 in your head.

Answer: A. Using a worksheet with pictures to add and subtract.

The semi-concrete stage is followed by the abstract stage, the usage of pictures not manipulatives is a medium ground between abstract and concrete.

67. Which of the following is considered to be the primary area of mathematical difficulty for students? *(Competency 22.0) (Average Rigor)*

   A. Logic
   B. Algebra
   C. Problem solving
   D. Application to life skills

Answer: C. Problem solving.

Problem solving skills require a level of analytical thought, and an ability to see the problem as well as knowing the methodology to reach the solution.

68. The purpose of a "Functional Curriculum" is to: *(Competency 23.0) (Rigorous)*

   A. Ensure that students are able to meet their state IEP diploma requirements.
   B. Prepare students for functioning in society as independently as possible as adults.
   C. Concentrate on daily living skills rather than academics.
   D. All of the above

Answer: B. Prepare students for functioning in society as adults.

The purpose of the functional curriculum is to center on personal-social skills, daily living skills, and occupational readiness. The emphasis is for students to learn those skills needed to prepare them to function in society as independently as possible.

SPECIAL EDU. CROSS-CATEGORY

TEACHER CERTIFICATION STUDY GUIDE

69. Kenny, a 9th grader enrolled in Wood Shop, is having difficulty grasping fractions. You know that Kenny has difficulty with abstract concepts. What would be a good method to teach this concept? *(Competency 23.0) (Rigorous)*

    A. Pie blocks that proportionately measure whole, half, 1/4, 1/8, etc.
    B. Strips of paper that proportionately measure whole, half, 1/4, 1/8, etc.
    C. One-on-one review of the worksheet
    D. Working in the wood shop, privately showing him how to measure

Answer: B. Strips of paper that proportionately measure whole, half, 1/4, 1/8, etc.

Strips of paper can be used to teach the concept by cutting a whole sheet into proportionate pieces. The strips of paper can be used like a tape measure to measure a length of wood. This concrete manipulative tool would assist Kenny in transferring knowledge on a more concrete level.

70. Functional curriculum focuses on all of the following EXCEPT: *(Competency 23.0) (Rigorous)*

    A. Skills needed for social living
    B. Occupational readiness
    C. Functioning in society.
    D. Remedial academic skills

Answer: D. Remedial academic skills

Remedial academics may be applied but are not a focus. The primary goal is to achieve skills for functioning in society on an independent basis, where possible.

SPECIAL EDU. CROSS-CATEGORY

71. Which of the following is a good example of generalization? *(Competency 23.0) (Average Rigor)*

   A. Jim has learned to add and is now ready to subtract.
   B. Sarah adds sets of units to obtain a product.
   C. Bill recognizes a vocabulary word on a billboard when traveling.
   D. Jane can spell the word "net" backwards to get the word "ten".

Answer: C. Bill recognizes a vocabulary word on a billboard when traveling.

Generalization is the occurrence of a learned behavior in the presence of a stimulus other than the one that produced the initial response. It is the expansion of a student's performance beyond the initial setting. Students must be able to expand or transfer what is learned to other settings (e.g., reading to math word problems, resource room to regular classroom).

72. Transfer of learning occurs when: *(Competency 23.0) (Rigorous)*

   A. Experience with one task influences performance on another task
   B. Content can be explained orally
   C. Student experiences the "I got it!" syndrome
   D. Curricular objective is exceeded

Answer: A. Experience with one task influences performance on another task.

Positive transfer occurs when the required responses and the stimuli are similar. Negative transfer occurs when the stimuli remain similar, but the required responses change.

TEACHER CERTIFICATION STUDY GUIDE

73. Marissa is a fourth grader with a learning disability. She attends a general education classroom with support from the consultant teacher. One of the learning strategies the general education uses in her classroom is cooperative grouping. The general education teacher noted that Marissa does not actively participate in the group, but allows the other students to do her work for her. The general education approaches the special education consultant teacher for strategies to encourage Marissa to be more independent within the cooperative group setting. What would be the most appropriate suggestion for the special education consultant teacher to make? *(Competency 24.0) (Rigorous)*

    A. Make sure that Marissa is assigned a specific role and the necessary modifications have been made to enable Marissa to complete that role.
    B. Grade the students on the basis on their level of participation in the group.
    C. Assign a "buddy" to assist Marissa within the group
    D. Allow the students to assess the level of participation within the group and grade according to participation.

Answer: A. Make sure that Marissa is assigned a specific role and the necessary modifications have been made to enable Marissa to complete that role.

Marissa should be given a specific responsibility within the group. Assigning a student "buddy" may be a helpful strategy, but does not promote her independence. The consultant teacher should make sure that appropriate modifications are being made.

SPECIAL EDU. CROSS-CATEGORY

74. Sam is working to earn half an hour of basketball time with his favorite P.E. teacher. At the end of each half hour, Sam marks his point sheet with an X if he reached his goal of no call-outs. When he has received 25 marks, he will receive his basketball free time. This behavior management strategy is an example of: *(Competency 24.0) (Average Rigor)*

   A. Self-recording
   B. Self-evaluation
   C. Self-reinforcement
   D. Self-regulation

Answer: A. Self-recording.

Self-management is an important part of social skills training, especially for older students preparing for employment. Components for self-management include:

1. *Self-monitoring:* choosing behaviors and alternatives and monitoring those actions.
2. *Self-evaluation:* deciding the effectiveness of the behavior in solving the problem.
3. *Self-reinforcement*: telling oneself that one is capable of achieving success.

75. Mark, a student with a learning disability, receives math instruction in a general education classroom. The general education teacher states that Mark is capable of doing the work but is concerned that Mark does not always complete his classwork without several reminders. What would be a good starting point in helping Mark to become more independent? *Competency 24.0) (Rigorous)*

   A. Have Mark bring his classwork for you to check before he turns it in.
   B. Suggest that the teacher check with Mark periodically during the class period to make sure he is working.
   C. Set up a charting system with Mark where he checks off the assigned tasks as he has completed them.
   D. Suggest that the teacher grade Mark according to the amount of work he completes, not the entire assignment.

Answer: c Set up a charting system with Mark where he checks off the assigned tasks as he has completed them.

One strategy to foster independence is to make Mark responsible for completing his work. The charting system provides him with a visual reminder and is a self-management strategy. Although a,b, and d may be appropriate in some situations, they do not encourage independence.

TEACHER CERTIFICATION STUDY GUIDE

76. Mr. Solis is working with a small group of students in a general education high school science classroom. Before the students begin a lab experiment, Mr. Solis reviews the vocabulary for the lesson with the students. He then reviews the basic safety rules for the lab and asks the students to walk through the steps for completing the experiment before actually beginning to perform the experiment. What strategy is Mr. Solis using to assist his students to become more independent? *(Competency 24.0) (Rigorous)*

    A. Priming
    B. Partial participation
    C. Cooperative grouping
    D. Collaborative teaching

Answer: A. Priming

Priming (or prepractice) entails previewing information or activities that a student is likely to have problems with before they begin working on that activity.

77. An effective classroom behavior management plan includes all but which of the following? *(Competency 25.0) (Average Rigor)*

    A. Transition procedures for changing activities
    B. Clear consequences for rule infractions
    C. Concise teacher expectations for student behavior
    D. Strict enforcement

Answer: D. Strict enforcement

There are always situations where rules must be flexible. Not all of the rules need to be flexible, but allowing a student to stop a behavior with a reminder of the rule is a good way to avoid strict enforcement.

78. Which of the following should be avoided when writing goals for social behavior? *(Competency 25.0) (Average Rigor)*

    A. Non-specific adverbs
    B. Behaviors stated as verbs
    C. Criteria for acceptable performance
    D. Conditions where the behavior is expected to be performed

Answer: A. Non-specific adverbs

Behaviors should be specific. The more clearly the behavior is described, the less the chance for error.

SPECIAL EDU. CROSS-CATEGORY

79. Which of the following is NOT an assumption of Assertive Discipline as outlined by Canter and Canter? *(Competency 25.0)* (Rigorous)

   A. Students with emotional disabilities cannot control their behavior.
   B. Consequences for not following rules are natural and logical, not a series of threats or punishments.
   C. The focus is on the behavior and the situation, not the student's character.
   D. Positive reinforcement occurs for desired behavior.

Answer: A. Students with emotional disabilities cannot control their behavior.

Assertive discipline, developed by Canter and Canter, is an approach to classroom control that allows the teacher to constructively deal with misbehavior and maintain a supportive environment for the students. Along with b, c, and d above, one of the assumptions of Assertive Discipline is that behavior is a choice.

80. Which of the following is NOT the best way to encourage and strengthen a social skill? *(Competency 25.0)* *(Easy)*

   A. Role playing
   B. Field trips
   C. Student story telling
   D. Reading a book on the topic

Answer: D. Reading a book on the topiC.

All of the other answers are interactive and involve student input on possible ethical dilemmas.

81. Distractive behavior, verbal outbursts, and passive aggressiveness should be addressed using: *(Competency 25.0)* (Rigorous)

   A. Time-outs
   B. Response cost
   C. Planned ignoring
   D. Rule reminders

Answer: C. Planned ignoring.

Planned ignoring takes away the attention the student may be seeking to receive. It is also a good way to model appropriate responses to the behavior for the other students in the room.

SPECIAL EDU. CROSS-CATEGORY

82. Ms. Watkins teaches students with multiple disabilities. One of her students, Briana, has a goal to learn to brush her teeth with minimal assistance. Ms. Watkins goes through the tooth brushing sequence herself, carefully noting each step in the process. She then breaks each step down into smaller components. Which of the following instructional strategies is Ms. Watkins using? *(Competency 25.0) (Rigorous)*

   A. Behavior Modification
   B. Task Analysis
   C. Proactive Planning
   D. Behavior Assessment

Answer: B. Task Analysis

When using Task Analysis, the successful learning of a skill depends on the presentation of skills in a logically sequenced curriculum, with the sequence extending from lower to higher order concepts and skills.

83. Jeremiah is a student who has been diagnosed with Autism. He has been exhibiting emotional outbursts in the classroom on a regular basis. The teacher has not been able to pinpoint what triggers Jeremiah's outbursts. What would be the most appropriate first step for the special education teacher to take?
(Competency 25.0) (Rigorous)

   A. Conduct a functional behavioral assessment to determine the antecedents of the tantrums and what consequences may be reinforcing the behavior.
   B. Ask the school administration to remove Jeremiah from the classroom when he begins a tantrum.
   C. Call Jeremiah's mother and ask her to come pick him up.
   D. Create a Behavior Intervention Plan for Jeremiah including goals, interventions, and a timeline for implementation.

Answer: A. Conduct a functional behavioral assessment to determine the antecedents of the tantrums and what consequences may be reinforcing the behavior.

The first step in addressing the behavioral concern is to perform a Functional Behavioral Assessment. The information obtained from the FBA will be utilized in developing the Behavior Intervention Plan (BIP).

TEACHER CERTIFICATION STUDY GUIDE

84. Which is NOT included by Henley, Ramsey, and Algozzine (1993) as steps teachers use to establish cooperative learning groups in the classroom? The teacher: *(Competency 25.0) (Rigorous)*

   A. Selects members of each learning group
   B. Directly teaches cooperative group skills
   C. Assigns cooperative group skills
   D. Has students self-evaluate group efforts

Answer: D. Has students self-evaluate group efforts.

According to Henley et al, there are four steps to establish cooperative learning groups:
1. The teacher selects members of each learning group.
2. The teacher directly teaches cooperative group skills.
3. The teacher assigns cooperative group activities.
4. The teacher evaluates group efforts.

85. Leslie is a 12 year old with mental retardation and a visual impairment. She has been attending a general education Physical Education class with an aide. The teacher noted that each day when Leslie enters the PE classroom, she begins to make loud noises and continues to make noise until the aide takes her back to her special education classroom. The special education teacher analyzes the situation using the Behavior Modification concept of ABC. What does ABC stand for? *(Competency 25.0) (Rigorous)*

   A. Antecedent, Behavior, Controlling Factor
   B. Analysis, Behavior, Consequence
   C. Antecedent, Behavior, Consequence
   D. Assessment, Behavior, Competency

Answer: c Antecedent, Behavior, Consequence

The ABCs of behavior modification are specified as the antecedent, the behavior, and the consequence. Stimuli that precede the behavior are referred to as antecedents; stimuli that follow the behavior are known as consequential events. All three are interactive components.

TEACHER CERTIFICATION STUDY GUIDE

86. **When would proximity control not be a good behavioral intervention? *(Competency 25.0) (Easy)***

    A. Two students are arguing
    B. A student is distracting others
    C. One student threatens another
    D. Involve fading and shaping

Answer: C. One student threatens another.

Threats can break into fights. Standing in the middle of a fight can be threatening to your ability to supervise the class as a whole or to get the help needed to stop the fight.

87. **Which of the following is NOT a feature of effective classroom rules? *(Competency 25.0) (Easy)***

    A. They are about four to six in number
    B. They are negatively stated
    C. Consequences are consistent and immediate
    D. They can be tailored to individual teaching goals and teaching styles

Answer: B. They are negatively stated.

Rules should be positively stated, range from four to six in number, result in immediate and consistent consequences, and should be tailored to individual teaching goals and teaching styles.

88. **Teaching children skills that will be useful in their home lives and neighborhoods is the basis of: *(Competency 27.0) (Average Rigor)***

    A. Curriculum-based instruction
    B. Community-based instruction
    C. Transition planning
    D. Academic curriculum

Answer: B. Community-based instruction.

Transitional training is a standard for all students labeled as having special needs after age 14. For example, students can learn how to balance a checkbook, shop, and understand how to use mass transit.

SPECIAL EDU. CROSS-CATEGORY 35

89. Social maturity may be evidenced by students': *(Competency 27.0)* *(Easy)*

    A. Recognition of rights and responsibilities (their own and others)
    B. Display of respect for legitimate authority figures
    C. Formulation of a valid moral judgment
    D. Demonstration of all of the above

Answer: D. Demonstration of all of the above.

Some additional evidence of social maturity:
- The ability to cooperate
- Following procedures formulated by an outside party
- Achieving appropriate levels of independence

90. Transition planning was included in: *(Competency 27.0)* *(Rigorous)*

    A. Americans with Disabilities Act
    B. IDEA (Public Law 101-476).
    C. Public Law 95-207
    D. Public Law 940142

Answer: B. IDEA (PL 101-476)

Transition planning is mandated in the Individuals with Disabilities Education Act (IDEA). The transition planning requirements ensure that planning is begun at age 14 and continued through high school.

91. A student's transition plan must address each of the following EXCEPT: *(Competency 27.0)* *(Easy)*

    A. Test Scores
    B. Instruction
    C. Community Experiences
    D. Objectives related to employment and other post-school areas.

Answer: A. Test Scores

The transition activities that have to be addressed, unless the IEP team finds it uncalled for, are: instruction, community experiences, and the development of objectives related to employment and other post-school areas.

TEACHER CERTIFICATION STUDY GUIDE

92. **An effective transition plan is characterized by which of the following?** *(Competency 27.0) (Easy)*

    A. Student-centered
    B. Flexible
    C. Collaborative Effort
    D. All of the Above

Answer: D. All of the Above

Transition planning and services focus on a coordinated set of student-centered activities designed to facilitate the student's progression from school to post-school activities. Transition planning should be flexible and focus on the developmental and educational requirements of the student at different grades and times.

93. **Michael's Individual Transition Plan (ITP) addresses the following objectives: "sort and organize objects by size and color", "identify functional sight words", and "follow a picture schedule". The long-term goal for Michael is most likely:** *(Competency 27.0) (Rigorous)*

    A. Work at a semi-skilled job.
    B. Attend a technical training school.
    C. Work in a sheltered workshop setting.
    D. Live independently.

Answer: C. Work in a sheltered workshop setting.

The goals identified for Michael indicate that he will need to be employed in a supervised work setting such as a sheltered workshop.

94. As a special education teacher, you can support your students in developing self-advocacy skills. Which of the following would be LEAST likely to support the student to develop self-advocacy skills?
(Competency 27.0) (Rigorous)

   A. Listen to problems and ask the student for input.
   B. Talk about solutions, pro and cons of a situation.
   C. Make a list of the student's preferences, likes and dislike for the ITP meeting.
   D. Structure role-playing activities.

Answer: C. Make a list of the student's preferences, likes and dislike for the ITP meeting.

The student should be encouraged to speak for himself at the ITP meeting regarding his preferences, likes, and dislikes. While it is appropriate for the teacher to assist the student, the teacher should encourage the student to speak for him/herself.

95. Which is NOT a goal of collaboration for a consultant special education teacher?
(Competency 28.0) (Average Rigor)

   A. To have the regular education teacher understand the student's disability
   B. Review content for accuracy
   C. Review lessons for possible necessary modifications
   D. Understanding of reasons for current grade

Answer: B. Review content for accuracy.

In the consultant teaching model, the general education teacher conducts the class after planning with the special educator about how to differentiate activities so the needs of the student with a disability are met.

TEACHER CERTIFICATION STUDY GUIDE

96. Parents of children with disabilities may seek your advice on several aspects regarding their children. A mother calls you and complains she can't keep her son on task and she has to keep sending her son back to the bathroom until he finishes getting prepared for the day. What advice should you give her? *(Competency 28.0)* *(Average Rigor)*

   A. Request an educational evaluation
   B. Recommend close supervision until he does all tasks together consistently
   C. Create a list of tasks to be completed in the bathroom
   D. Ask for outside coordination of services advocacy that can assist with this type of issue

Answer: C. Create a list of tasks to be completed in the bathroom.

This requires the child to be independent on each task. Calling outside resources is a good idea, but it does not address the issue. The student may simply have a short-term memory loss, and may need a reminder to keep on task.

97. Which of the following is a responsibility that can NOT be designated to a classroom aide? *(Competency 28.0)* *(Average Rigor)*

   A. Small group instruction
   B. Writing lesson plans
   C. Coordination of an activity
   D. Assist in BIP implementation

Answer: B. Writing lesson plans

Classroom aides are invaluable in the classroom and may provide a variety of services for the teacher as well as the students. However, the daily planning of classroom activities is the responsibility of the teacher, not the aide.

SPECIAL EDU. CROSS-CATEGORY 39

98. You are having continual difficulty with your classroom assistant. A good strategy to address this problem would be: *(Competency 28.0) (Rigorous)*

    A. To address the issue immediately
    B. To take away responsibilities
    C. To write a clearly established role plan for discussion
    D. To speak to your supervisor

Answer: C. To write a clearly established role plan for discussion.

If you are having difficulty with your classroom assistant, it is most likely is over an issue or issues that have happened repeatedly, and you have attempted to address them. Establishing clear roles between the two of you will provide a good step in the right direction. It may also provide you with the ability to state you have made an attempt to address the issue/issues to an administrator should the need arise.

99. By November, Annette's 7th grade teacher is concerned with her sporadic attendance. What action should take place next? *(Competency 28.0) (Average Rigor)*

    A. Notify Children's Protective Services
    B. Notify the police of non-compliance with compulsory attendance
    C. Contact parents about the absences
    D. Notify the administrator

Answer: C. Contact parents about the absences.

The parents should be contacted initially, the may have a rational reason for the absences. The next step would be to consult with your school administration.

100. A Behavior Intervention Plan (BIP) is written to teach positive behavior. Which element listed below is NOT a standard feature of the BIP? *(Competency 28.0) (Rigorous)*

    A. Identification of behavior to be modified
    B. Strategies to implement the replacement behavior
    C. Statement of distribution
    D. Team creation of BIP

Answer: C. Statement of distribution.

School personnel determine the method of distribution appropriate for a campus. Each teacher who deals with the student must receive a copy of the student's BIP in order to be able to implement it in his/her classroom. Often the student's case manager or consultant teacher is responsible for distributing copies of the BIP.

101. You have a group of 8th grade students in an English class. Sheryl sits in the back of the room by choice and rarely answers questions. You believe that she has a learning disability and begin to modify her worksheets. You are: *(Competency 28.0)) (Average Rigor)*

    A. Planning for success of the student
    B. Creating a self-fulfilling prophecy
    C. Developing a student-centered curriculum
    D. Testing her ability

Answer: B. Creating a self-fulfilling prophecy.

If Sheryl does not answer questions orally, she may simply not be as expressive as those around her, or she is may not be a fluent English speaker, but it does not necessarily mean that she has a learning disability. The phenomenon of a *self-fulfilling prophecy* is based on the attitude of the teacher and means that what one expects to happen is usually what ends up happening.

TEACHER CERTIFICATION STUDY GUIDE

102. **Students with disabilities develop greater self-images and recognize their own academic and social strengths when they are:** *(Competency 28.0) (Easy)*

    A. Included in the mainstream classroom
    B. Provided community-based internships
    C. Socializing in the hallway
    D. Provided 1:1 instructional opportunity

Answer: A. Included in the mainstream classroom.

When a child with a disability is included in the regular classroom, it raises the expectations of the child's academic performance and his or her need to conform to "acceptable peer behavior."

103. **The ability to supply specific instructional materials, programs, and methods and to influence environmental learning variables are advantages of which service model for exceptional students?** *(Competency 28.0) (Rigorous)*

    A. Regular classroom
    B. Consultant teacher
    C. Itinerant teacher
    D. Resource room

Answer: B. Consultant teacher.

In the consultant teaching model, the general education teacher conducts the class after planning with the special educator about how to differentiate activities so the needs of the student with a disability are met.

TEACHER CERTIFICATION STUDY GUIDE

104. The key to success for the exceptional student placed in a regular classroom is: *(Competency 28.0) (Average Rigor)*

    A. Access to the special aids and materials
    B. Support from the special education teacher
    C. Modification in the curriculum
    D. The mainstream teacher's belief that the student will profit from the placement

Answer: D. The mainstream teacher's belief that the student will profit from the placement.

The attitude of the teacher can have both a positive or negative impact on student performance. A teacher's attitude can impact the expectations that the teacher has toward the student's potential performance, as well as how the teacher behaves toward the student. This attitude, combined with expectations, can impact a student's self-image as well as his or her academic performance.

105. Diversity can be identified in students by: *(Competency 29.0) (Average Rigor)*

    A. Biological factors
    B. Socioeconomic status (SES)
    C. Ethnicity
    D. All of the above

Answer: D. All of the above.

Diversity in a classroom can encompass a variety of factors including: biological, sociological, ethnic, socioeconomic, psychological, and learning styles.

106. Parent contact should first begin when: *(Competency 29.0) (Easy).*

    A. You are informed the child may become your student
    B. The student fails a test
    C. The student exceeds others on a task
    D. An IEP meeting is scheduled and the parent has not responded to the notice of the meeting.

Answer: A. You are informed the child will be your student.

A best practice is for student contact to begin as a "getting to know you" piece, which allows you to begin on a non-judgmental platform. It also allows the parent to receive a view that you are a professional who is willing to work with them.

SPECIAL EDU. CROSS-CATEGORY

107. You have documented proof that Janice performs better when allowed to use a computer on both class work and tests. Which kind of IEP Meeting should be held? *(Competency 29.0) (Easy)*

    A. Manifestation determination
    B. Post-school transition to insure provision of a laptop by outside services
    C. Amendment; change of program/placement
    D. Annual

Answer: C. Amendment; change of program/placement.

The amendment IEP meeting should be held to add or remove services. Adding a test modification or service is a change in program.

108. Which of the following must be provided in a written notice to parents when proposing a child's educational placement? *(Competency 29.0) (Average)*

    A. A list of parental due process safeguards
    B. A list of current test scores
    C. A list of persons responsible for the child's education
    D. A list of academic subjects the child has passed

Answer: A. A list of parental due process safeguards.

Written notice must be provided to parents prior to a proposal or refusal to initiate or make a change in the child's identification, evaluation, or educational placement. Notices must contain:
- A listing of parental due process safeguards
- A description and a rationale for the chosen action
- A detailed listing of components (e.g., tests, records, reports) that were
- the basis for the decision
- Assurance that the language and content of the notices were understood by the parents

109. **Mrs. Valdez, the mother of your student, Suzie, sends a note to school requesting an IEP meeting to review Suzie's goals. You should:** *(Competency 29.0) (Rigorous)*

   A. Contact the mother and ask her to wait until the next annual IEP meeting.
   B. Call the mother and assure her that the meeting will be scheduled as soon as possible.
   C. Contact Mrs. Valdez and ask her about her concerns.
   D. Begin the process to schedule an IEP meeting.

Answer: D. Begin the process to schedule an IEP meeting.

While b and c would promote good communication with the parent, the parent has a right to request an IEP meeting at any time. You should begin the process established by your campus for scheduling IEP meetings without delay.

110. **The integrated approach to learning advocates utilizing all resources available to address student needs. Which of the following might these resources include?** *(Competency 30.0) (Average Rigor)*

   A. The student and his parents.
   B. The teacher(s) and educational support team.
   C. Community resources.
   D. All of the Above.

Answer: D. All of the above.

In the integrated approach to learning, teachers, parents, and community support members become the integral apexes to student learning. The focus and central core of the school community is triangular as a representation of how effective collaboration can work in creating success for student learners.

111. Mr. Jackson teaches a class of twelve to fourteen year old students, all of whom have mild to moderate mental disabilities. A local community organization invited his classroom to participate in their annual Easter egg hunt. Mr. Jackson politely declined the invitation. On what basis did he decline the invitation? *(Competency 30.0) (Rigorous)*

A. The students were scheduled for testing on the day of the activity.
B. He could not find a parent volunteer to accompany them.
C. The activity was not age appropriate for his students.
D. The school budget did not allow for the transportation needed for the activity.

Answer: C. The activity was not age appropriate for his students.

Although the other answers could be factors in scheduling activities within the community, activities need to be appropriate for the age level of the students and include opportunities for interaction with typically developing peers as much as possible.

112. IDEA requires IEP teams to begin to address the transition needs of the individual student in relation to future employment possibilities, independent livings skills, adult services needed, and participation in the community. Transition planning must be addressed by the IEP committee when the student reaches what age? *(Competency 30.0) (Easy)*

A. 16
B. 14
C. 18
D. 21

Answer: B. 14. IDEA stipulates that transition planning must begin at age 14.

TEACHER CERTIFICATION STUDY GUIDE

113. Previous to IDEA 97, what was not accepted? *(Competency 31.0) (Rigorous)*

   A. Using previous assessments to evaluate placement
   B. Parent refusal of IEP team determination (no due process)
   C. Student input on placement and needs
   D. All of the above

Answer: B. Using previous assessments to evaluate placement

Previous to IDEA 97, evaluation of placement always required assessments. No acceptance of previous testing was allowed. This was recognized as creating needless testing for students, as IQs generally do not change, while the student's knowledge base grows.

114. A ruling pertaining to the use of evaluation procedures later consolidated in Public Law 94-142 resulted from which court case listed? *(Competency 31) (Rigorous)*

   A. Diana v. the State Board of Education (1970)
   B. Wyatt v. Stickney
   C. Larry P. v. Riles
   D. PASE v. Hannon

Answer: A. Diana v. the State Board of Education (1970)

Diana v. the State Board of Education resulted in the decision that all children must be evaluated in their native language.

115. Prior to the passage on PL 94-142, which of the following was included in data brought to the attention of Congress regarding the education of students with disabilities? *(Competency 31) (Average Rigor)*

 A. There were a large number of children and youth with disabilities in the United States.
 B. Many children with disabilities were not receiving an appropriate education.
 C. Many parents of children with disabilities were forced to seek services outside of the public realm.
 D. All of the above.

Answer: D. All of the above.

By the time of P.L. 94-142, about half of the estimated 8 million children with disabilities in the United States were either not being appropriately served in school or were excluded from schooling altogether. There were a disproportionate number of minority children placed in special programs. Identification and placement practices and procedures were inconsistent, and parental involvement was generally not encouraged.

116. **The Individuals with Disabilities Education Act (IDEA) was signed into law in and later reauthorized through a second revision in what years?** *(Competency 31) (Rigorous)*

 A. 1975 and 2004
 B. 1980 and 1990
 C. 1990 and 2004
 D. 1995 and 2001

Answer: C. 1990 and 2004

IDEA, Public Law 101-476, is a consolidation and reauthorization of all prior special education mandates, with amendments. It was signed into law by President Bush on October 30, 1990. Revision of IDEA occurred in 2004, when IDEA was re-authorized as the Individuals with Disabilities Education Improvement Act of 2004 (IDEIA 2004). It is commonly referred to as IDEA 2004. IDEA 2004 became effective on July 1, 2005.

117. Guidelines for an Individualized Family Service Plan (IFSP) are described in which legislation? *(Competency 31.0) (Rigorous)*

   A. Education of the Handicapped Act Amendments
   B. IDEA (1990)
   C. IDEA 2004
   D. ADA

Answer: B. IDEA (1990)

Education for All Handicapped Children Act was passed in the Civil Rights era, and its amendment in 1986 provided financial incentive to educate children with disabilities who are three to five years of age. ADA is the Americans with Disabilities Act.

118. The definition of assistive technology devices was amended in the IDEA reauthorization of 2004 to exclude what? *(Competency 31) (Easy Rigor)*

   A. iPods other hand-held devices
   B. Computer enhanced technology
   C. Surgically implanted devices
   D. Braille and/or special learning aids

Answer: C. Surgically implanted devices

The definition of assistive technology devices was amended to exclude devices that are surgically implanted (e.g., cochlear implants) and clarified that students with assistive technology devices shall not be prevented from having special education services. Assistive technology devices may need to be monitored by school personnel, but schools are not responsible for the surgical implantation or replacement of such devices.

TEACHER CERTIFICATION STUDY GUIDE

119. Which is untrue about the Americans with Disabilities Act (ADA)? *(Competency 31) (Rigorous)*

    A. It was signed into law the same year as IDEA by President Bush.
    B. It reauthorized the discretionary programs of EHA.
    C. It gives protection to all people on the basis of race, sex, national origin, and religion.
    D. It guarantees equal opportunities to persons with disabilities in employment, public accommodations, transportation, government services, and telecommunications.

Answer: B. It reauthorized the discretionary programs of EHA

EHA is the precursor of IDEA, the Individuals with Disabilities Education Act. ADA, however, is Public Law 101-336 (Americans with Disabilities Act), which gives civil rights protection to all individuals with disabilities in private sector employment, all public services, public accommodations, transportation, and telecommunications. It was patterned after the Rehabilitation Act of 1973.

120. Requirements for evaluations were changed in IDEA 2004 to reflect that no single assessment or measurement tool can be used to determine special education qualification, with the purpose of ending a disproportionate representation of what types of students? *(Competency 31) (Easy Rigor)*

    A. Disabled
    B. Foreign
    C. Gifted
    D. Minority and bilingual

Answer: D. Minority and bilingual

IDEA 2004 recognized that there existed a disproportionate representation of minorities and bilingual students. It also recognized that pre-service interventions that are *scientifically based on early reading programs, positive behavioral interventions, and support* as well as early intervening services might prevent some of those children from needing special education services.

TEACHER CERTIFICATION STUDY GUIDE

121. What determines whether a person is entitled to protection under Section 504? *(Competency 31)* *(Rigorous)*

    A.   The individual must meet the definition of a person with a disability.
    B.   The person must be able to meet the requirements of a particular program in spite of his or her disability.
    C.   The school, business, or other facility must be the recipient of federal funding assistance.
    D.   All of the above

Answer: D. All of the above.

To be entitled to protection under Section 504, an individual must meet the definition of a person with a disability, which is: any person who (i) has a physical or mental impairment which substantially limits one or more of that person's major life activities, (ii) has a record of such impairment, or (iii) is regarded as having such an impairment. Major life activities are: caring for oneself, performing manual tasks, walking, seeing, hearing, speaking, breathing, learning, and working. The person must also be "otherwise qualified," which means that the person must be able to meet the requirements of a particular program in spite of the disability. The person must also be afforded "reasonable accommodations" by recipients of federal financial assistance.

122. Free and Appropriate Public Education (FAPE) describes special education and related services as? *(Competency 31)* *(Average Rigor)*

    A.   Public expenditure and standard to the state educational agency.
    B.   Provided in conformity with each student's individualized education program, if the program is developed to meet requirements of the law.
    C.   Inclusive of preschool, elementary, and/or secondary education in the state involved.
    D.   All of the above

Answer: D. All of the above.

FAPE states that special education and related services: are provided at public expense; meet the standards of the state educational agency; include preschool, elementary, and/or secondary education in the state involved; and are provided in conformity with each student's IEP in order to meet requirements of the law.

SPECIAL EDU. CROSS-CATEGORY

TEACHER CERTIFICATION STUDY GUIDE

123. **What does the No Child Left Behind Act (NCLB), signed on January 8, 2002, address?** *(Competency 31.0) (Rigorous)*

    A. Accessibility of curriculum to the student
    B. Administrative incentives for school improvements
    C. The funding to provide services required
    D. Accountability of school personnel for student achievement

Answer: D. Accountability of school personnel for student achievement.

NCLB created strong standards in each state for what every child should know and learn in reading and math for grades three through eight. Student progress and achievement are measured for every child annually. Test results are made available in an annual report. Schools are accountable for improving performance of all student groups.

124. **The following words describe an IEP objective EXCEPT:** *(Competency 31.0) (Rigorous)*

    A. Specific
    B. Observable
    C. Measurable
    D. Flexible

Answer: D. Flexible

IEPs are not flexible for interpretation. They are enforceable legal documents that must be followed or modified by the IEP team.

125. Hector is a 10th grader with a severe emotional disturbance. After a classmate taunted him about his mother, Hector threw a desk at the other boy and attacked him. A crisis intervention team tried to break up the fight, and one teacher hurt his knee. The other boy received a concussion. Hector now faces disciplinary measures. How long can he be suspended without the IEP team reviewing a possible "change of placement"? *(Competency 31.0) (Rigorous)*

   A. 5 days
   B. 10 days
   C. 10 + 30 days
   D. 60 days

Answer: B. 10 days.

According to Honig versus Doe (1988), where the student has presented an immediate threat to others, that student may be temporarily suspended for up to 10 school days to give the school and the parents time to review the IEP and discuss possible alternatives to the current placement.

Rigor Table

	Easy %20	Average Rigor %40	Rigorous %40
Question #	8,15,17,19,22,24, 25,28,35,37,62,63, 64,80,86,87,89,91, 92,102,106,107, 112,118,120	5,6,7,9,11,13,18,20,21,23, 26,27,29,30,31,36,40,41, 43,46,47,48,49,51,52,54, 55,57,58,29,60,65,66,67, 71,74,77,78,88,95,96,97, 99,101,104,105,108,109, 115,122	1,2,3,4,10,12,14,16, 32,33,34,38,39,42,44, 45,50,53,56,61,68,69, 70,72,73,75,76,79,81, 82,83,84,85,90,93,94, 98,100,103,109,111, 113,114,116,117,119, 121,123,124,125

DOMAIN I. UNDERSTANDING STUDENTS WITH SPECIAL NEEDS

COMPETENCY 1.0 UNDERSTAND TYPICAL LEARNING PROCESSES AND THE SIGNIFICANCE OF VARIOUS DISABILITIES FOR LEARNING

For example: processes by which learning occurs; applications of learning theories; factors that may affect learning, including socioeconomic, cultural, and language differences; effects of various disabilities on learning; factors that may impede learning (e.g., abuse/neglect, substance abuse, medications, physiological factors); factors that may facilitate learning in students with special needs; and teaching strategies that are responsive to students' needs and take advantage of their strengths.

Similarities and Differences Among Individuals with Disabilities, Including Levels of Severity and Multiple Disabilities

IDEA 2004 §300.8 defines a child with a disability as having mental retardation, a hearing impairment (including deafness), a speech or language impairment, a visual impairment (including blindness), a serious emotional disturbance (referred to in this part as emotional disturbance), an orthopedic impairment, autism, traumatic brain injury, an other health impairment, a specific learning disability, deaf-blindness, or multiple disabilities, and who, by reason thereof, needs special education and related services.

Eligibility for special education services is based on a student having one of the above disabilities (or a combination thereof) and demonstrating educational need through professional evaluation.

Seldom does a student with a disability fall into only one of the characteristics listed in IDEA 2004. For example, a student with a hearing impairment may also have a specific learning disability, or a student on the autism spectrum may also demonstrate a language impairment. In fact, language impairment is inherent in autism. Sometimes the eligibility is defined as multiple disabilities (with one listed as a primary eligibility on the IEP and the others listed as secondary). Sometimes there are overlapping needs that are not necessarily listed as a secondary disability.

Teachers of special education students should be aware of the similarities between areas of disabilities as well as differences.

Students with disabilities (in all areas) may demonstrate difficulties with social skills. For example, a student with hearing impairment may have difficulty with social skills because of not being able to hear social language. The emotionally disturbed student may have difficulty because of a special type of psychological disturbance. An autistic student might be unaware of the social cues given with voice, facial expression, and body language. Each of these students would need social skill instruction in a different way.

Students with disabilities (in all areas) may demonstrate difficulty in academic skills. For example, a student with mental retardation might need special instruction across all areas of academics, while a student with a learning disability may need assistance in only one or two subject areas.

Students with disabilities may demonstrate difficulties with independence or self-help skills. A student with a visual impairment may need specific mobility training, while a student with a specific learning disability may need a checklist to help in managing materials and assignments.

Special education teachers should be aware that although students across disabilities may demonstrate difficulty in similar ways, the causes can be very different. For example, some disabilities are due to specific sensory impairments (hearing or vision), some to cognitive ability (mental retardation), and some to neurological impairment (autism or some learning disabilities). The reason for the difficulty should be a consideration when planning the program of special education intervention.

Additionally, special education teachers should be aware that each area of disability has a range of involvement. Some students may have minimal disability and require no services. Others may need only a few accommodations and have a 504 plan. Some may need an IEP that outlines a specific special education program to be implemented in an inclusion/resource program, in a self-contained program, or in a residential setting.

A student with ADD may be able to participate in the regular education program with a 504 plan that outlines a checklist system to keep the student organized and encourages additional communication between school and home. Other students with ADD may need to be instructed in a smaller group with fewer distractions and served in a resource room.

Special educators should be knowledgeable of the cause and severity of the disability and its manifestations in the specific student when planning an appropriate special education program. Because of the unique needs of the child, such programs are documented in the child's IEP, or Individualized Education Program.

Development Issues that may Affect Individuals with Disabilities

To effectively assess and plan for the developmental needs of individuals with disabilities, special education teachers should first be familiar with the development of the typical child. Developmental areas of speech and language, fine and gross motor skills, cognitive abilities, emotional development, and social skills should be considered.

If a six-year-old child who is missing her front teeth is referred for speech therapy for mispronunciation of words with the /th/ sound, the cause is likely to be her lack of teeth. Without a place to place the tongue, the /th/ cannot be pronounced correctly. Thus, speech therapy would not be warranted. Rather, a typical development stage must be passed.

A second grade student may have difficulty buttoning clothing. Because that is a skill typically mastered around age four, a developmental delay in fine motor skills may be present. It is appropriate for the special educator to request consultation and possibly formal evaluation of the child's needs.

In addition to being aware of the ages of typical developmental milestones, the special education teacher should consider the sequence in which the skills are acquired. While not all children go through every step of development (some children never seem to crawl), most follow a typical sequence. In an example of language development, children name objects with single words long before they form phrases or sentences. In other words, a child cannot understand how to form the sentence *I see a cat on the fence* before he can accurately voice *cat* when he sees a cat or a picture of one.

Sometimes the disability itself will hinder or prevent a child from accomplishing a developmental task. A child with visual-spatial difficulty may not be able to see the components of a certain letter in print. A handwriting program that shows the parts of a letter made with wooden pieces may provide the link to the child mastering that letter formation.

Key to understanding the role of development and the needs of the special education student is being knowledgeable of typical development and seeing such skills in a number of developing students. This is another benefit of the inclusion classroom. Given a foundation of developmental understanding and knowledge of the specific child's disability, the special education teacher can better assess and implement an appropriate education program to meet the unique needs of the child.

Factors that Influence Students with Disabilities and their Families Include Abuse, Neglect, and Substance Abuse

Abuse

Whether it is abuse to the child or to a parent, the effect transcends the immediate situation to interaction with others in the home, school, and community. If the child with a disability is the one who is abused, he or she may be distrustful of others. The child may also continue the cycle of behavior by acting out in abusive ways toward others.

If a parent of the child with a disability is being abused, the child may feel responsible. He or she may actively try to protect the abused parent. The child may carry emotional and possibly psychological effects of living in a home where abuse happens.

A parent who is being abused will be less likely to be able to attend to the needs of the child with a disability. The parent may be secretive about the fact that the abuse even occurs.

Neglect

If a child with a disability is neglected physically or emotionally, he or she may exhibit a number of behaviors. The child will most likely be distrustful of adults in general. He or she may horde classroom materials, snacks, etc., and be unfocused on school work.

In the instances of abuse and neglect (or suspected instances), the special educator (as all educators) is a mandated reporter to the appropriate agency (such as DCFS – Division of Child and Family Services).

Substance Abuse

If a child with a disability or a parent is involved in substance abuse, that abuse will have a negative effect in the areas of finances, health, productivity, and safety. It is important for the special education teacher to be aware of signs of substance abuse. The teacher should be proactive in teaching drug awareness. He or she should also know the appropriate school channels for getting help for the student as well as community agencies that can help parents involved in substance abuse.

Major Theories of Educational Psychology

The teacher of special needs students must have a thorough understanding of the content matter that is taught from kindergarten through 12th grade for two important reasons. First, he or she will be instructing students whose functioning abilities can span all grade levels; second, he or she must be able to use specialized instruction in order to teach content in required subject areas.

The actual content and sequence of concepts that learners with special needs must be taught are the same as those used with the regular student; however, special learning strategies, techniques, and approaches must be utilized. For instance, task sequences must be analyzed and broken down into a hierarchy of subskills for students with learning difficulties. It often helps when the content is made meaningful to learners and when skills are taught in a firsthand, functional manner.

The content areas of reading (such as vocabulary, decoding skills, and comprehension), math-like fact mastery, computational operations, reasoning, verbal problem solving, language arts, and social skills training are broad in scope. They are basic to success in other subject areas and entail a specific instructional sequence that all learners must follow. However, being able to plan, predict, diagnose, and assess the instructional content appropriate for individual learners necessitates a full and complete understanding by the special educator of sequential skills hierarchies.

Jean Piaget recognized the importance of structuring thinking in order to learn. According to his theory, each person approaches the learning task with an existing cognitive structure or schemata. The learner adapts to the environment and structures new knowledge in two complimentary ways: assimilation and accommodation.

Assimilation
In assimilation, learners incorporate new experiences into their already existing cognitive structure. New experiences provide practice and strengthen their existing cognitive structures. For example, a child learns that balls are objects, which can be grasped and thrown.

Accommodation
In accommodation, learners focus on the new gestures of a learning task, thereby changing or modifying their cognitive structures. For example, as the child grasps balls of different sizes, textures, and firmness, he or she learns that balls are different and that some objects that look like balls cannot be thrown.

SPECIAL EDU. CROSS-CATEGORY 59

TEACHER CERTIFICATION STUDY GUIDE

The cognitive stages outlined by Piaget are:

1. <u>Sensorimotor intelligence</u> - birth to 18 months. The child differentiates him or herself from the rest of the world and learns object constancy.
2. <u>Preoperational thought, representational thinking</u> - 18 months to 4-5 years. Private symbols and representations precede language, which begins during this stage. Children are still unable to take another person's view of things.
3. <u>Preoperational thought, intuitional thinking</u> - 5 to 7 years. The child begins to understand conservation of amount, quantity, number, and weight. He or she can attend to more than one aspect of an object at a time and begins to understand the reversibility of some operations. However, he or she cannot explain personal conclusions.
4. <u>Concrete operation</u> - 7 to 11 years. The child organizes perceptions and symbols and becomes able to classify and categorize along several dimensions at the same time.
5. <u>Formal operations</u> - 12 years through adulthood. The learner can deal with abstractions, hypothetical situations, and logical thinking.

Jerome Bruner, like Jean Piaget, believed that knowledge developed in an evolutionary sequence. Bruner suggested that knowledge is represented in three forms: enactive, iconic, and symbolic.

Knowledge is initially acquired at the enactive or concrete action level. It is demonstrated through actions (such as throwing a ball) or by direct manipulation (such as bundling sticks in groups of ten).

The information that is digested and recorded at the enactive stage is recalled in a mental image or seen in a visual representation at the iconic level. Knowledge at this level has a visual or perceptual organization; it is communicated by pictures and forms. An example of iconic knowledge is the mental manipulation of images of concrete objects (such as solving single verbal problems or picturing ones, tens, and hundreds units).

The information reaches the symbolic level through spoken words of written symbols. This type of knowledge represents information about concrete and semi-concrete situations in a symbolic manner. "The use of symbols allows for easy problem-solving actions" (Thornton, Tucker, Dossey, & Bazik, 1983, p. 86). The highest and most formalized level is symbolic knowledge. An example would be the use of symbols in the form of numerals to calculate the answer to a specified mathematical operation. A correspondence between the stages proposed by Piaget and the levels described by Bruner are shown in the figure below.

Developmental Stages and Levels

Piaget	Bruner
Sensorimotor, Concrete Knowledge Stage	Enactive, Concrete Action Level
Perceptually Bound Knowledge	Iconic, Visual, or Perceptual
Preoperational or Concrete Level	Organizational
Formal or Symbolic Stages	Symbolic Level

Both Piaget and Bruner dealt with language as it related to cognitive growth. Bruner theorized that once children begin to acquire language, they use it to further shape their thoughts. Piaget proposed that language is acquired as children take in or assimilate the language in the environment; the children then modify it with their knowledge and ideas. What language is assimilated is directly influenced by each child's reasoning processes. Children's language becomes more sophisticated with age because they are able to understand more complex language, thus modifying it with more complex ideas.

The primary educational implication for the developmental learning movement through theorized stages is its element of predictability. Some students move through developmental stages or levels at a slower or faster pace than others. What students learn depends on their existing cognitive structure, language development, and the experiences and knowledge that they bring to the learning situation. It is important that entry level skills be diagnosed, and that students be able to use the knowledge, experiences, and skills they already possess in learning situations.

Child and Adolescent Psychology

The study of psychology can be broken into four processes of learning: memory, intelligence and mental abilities, motivation, and emotions (Hockenbury and Hockenbury, 2002).

Although learning and intelligence play a significant role in many students with emotional disturbances, the additional and differing components are motivation and emotions.

Nature vs. Nurture

The never-ending question of those who study human behavior is nature vs. nurture. Is the individual born with certain behavioral tendencies, or is the person reacting to the environment and therefore learning behaviors throughout childhood and adulthood?

Founders of psychological theory include:

1. **Freud**, who believed that behaviors stemmed from early experiences in childhood and were often sexual in nature.
2. **Darwin**, who believed that behavior is a functional adaptation to the environment and is passed from generation to generation.
3. **Pavlov**, who believed that behavior can be conditioned through reinforcers. Pavlov is best known for his experiments with dogs.
4. **Leipzig**, who studied sensory and perceptual processes and their impact on behavior.
5. **Watson and Skinner**, who studied behavioralism.

Recognizing the Possible Effects of Medications on Student Learning, Developing, and Functioning (e.g., Cognitive, Physical, Social, Emotional)

Students with disabilities who take medications often experience medication side effects that can affect their behavior and educational development. Teachers may perceive that the child is unmotivated or drowsy, not fully understanding the cognitive effects that medications can have on a child.

Some medications may impair concentration, which can lead to poor processing ability, trigger lower alertness, and cause drowsiness and hyperactivity. Students who take several medications may have an increased risk of behavioral and cognitive side effects.

The student's parents should let the school know when the student is beginning or changing medication, so teachers can look out for possible side effects.

Antidepressants

There are three different classes of antidepressants that students can take. One type is called selective serotonin-reuptake inhibitors (SSRIs). SSRIs block certain receptors from absorbing serotonin. Over time, SSRIs may cause changes in brain chemistry. The side effects of SSRIs include dry mouth, insomnia or restless sleep, increased sweating, and nausea. They can also cause mood swings in people with bipolar disorders.

A second type of antidepressants that may be used are tricyclic anti-depressants. They are considered good for treating depression and obsessive-compulsive behavior. They cause similar side effects to the SSRIs, including sedation, tremors, seizures, dry mouth, light sensitivity, and mood swings in people with bipolar disorders.

A third type of antidepressants are monoamine oxidase inhibitors (MAOIs). They are not as widely used as the other two types because many have unpleasant and life-threatening interactions with other drugs, including common over-the-counter medications. People taking MAOIs must also follow a special diet because these medications interact with many foods. The list of foods to avoid includes chocolate, aged cheeses, and more.

Stimulants are often prescribed to help with attention deficit disorder and attention deficit hyperactivity disorder. These drugs can have many side effects including agitation, restlessness, aggressive behavior, dizziness, insomnia, headache, or tremors.

In severe cases of anxiety, an anti-anxiety medication (tranquilizer) may be prescribed. Most tranquilizers have a potential for addiction and abuse. They tend to be sedating and can cause a variety of unpleasant side effects, including blurred vision, confusion, sleepiness, and tremors.

If educators are aware of the types of medication that their students are taking, along with their myriad of side effects, they will be able to respond more positively when some of the side effects of the medication change their students' behaviors, response rates, and attention spans.

Developing Effective Learning Methods and Strategies for the Student

Communication of Expectations
It is important that the exceptional student has an understanding of the expectations of a lesson. These expectations should include general behavior, participation in the lesson, communication with peers and educators, and the type of learning assessment that will be used (in-class worksheet, homework, project, etc.). These expectations may be listed in some type of checklist for a visual reminder to the student.

Physical Presentation of Learning
While many students enjoy a visually stimulating learning environment, it may not be appropriate for the student with an emotional disturbance who is easily distracted. A classroom divider or study cubicle may help the student(s) stay focused on the task at hand. The materials used should be specific to the lesson. It is important that materials be sturdy, as they may take more than usual wear-and-tear in the special education classroom.

Learning Activities
Activities should address the student's optimum learning mode (e.g., visual, auditory, kinesthetic). The student should also be taught study strategies of preview, consideration of prior knowledge, attention to new information, and review in preparation for assessment (test or other demonstration of knowledge gained).

Feedback
All learners need feedback on their participation in the learning environment. In the case of the emotionally disturbed student, it is crucial that the feedback be consistent and address the expectations initially set forth.

Positive feedback is important for addressing the student's self esteem (often an area of deficit in the student with emotional disturbance). It should be recognized that positive feedback is best if it includes a reward that is recognized by the student (token physical rewards or activities) or falls under the category of socially-accepted feedback (positive comments, grades).

Constructive criticism should also be consistent with the teacher's initial expectations. The educator of an emotionally disturbed student should remember that these children often come from abusive situations and that they (as a result of the specific disturbance) may react inappropriately to typical direction or comment.

Generalization of Material Learned

It is especially important in the classroom with emotionally disturbed students that generalization of learning be given consideration. Because of the isolated learning environment, students may not see the carry-over into other subjects or into daily living and their environments. Activities and outings that address generalization are helpful for learning and participating in the community.

Learning Motivators for Exceptional Students

All students need motivators to stay on task behaviorally and academically. The special educator of the emotionally disturbed may employ a number of motivators or rewards for the students. These may include token rewards of candy or trinkets, or free time for a desired activity (such as time on the computer or for drawing). If the motivators address student interest and reflect the study at hand, two goals have been accomplished. For example, a computer game for studying multiplication can be used as a motivator and also give the student additional practice.

TEACHER CERTIFICATION STUDY GUIDE

COMPETENCY 2.0 UNDERSTAND TYPES AND CHARACTERISTICS OF EMOTIONAL DISABILITIES

For example: major behavioral and social characteristics of students with emotional disabilities; definitions and identifying criteria associated with students with emotional disabilities; and the implications of various types of behavioral, social, and emotional disabilities for students' educational development.

The term **emotional disturbance** covers a range of disorders with varying severity. These are outlined in the Diagnostic and Statistical Manual of Mental Disorders (also referred to as the DSM).

According to IDEA, emotional disturbance means a condition that exhibits one or more of the following characteristics over a long period of time and to a marked degree adversely affects a student's educational performance:

(i) An inability to learn that cannot be explained by intellectual, sensory, or health factors;

(ii) An inability to build or maintain satisfactory interpersonal relationships with peers and teachers;

(iii) Inappropriate types of behavior or feelings under normal circumstances;

(iv) A generally pervasive mood of unhappiness or depression; or

(v) A tendency to develop physical symptoms or fears associated with personal or school problems.

The term emotional disturbance includes schizophrenia. The term does not apply to students who are socially maladjusted, unless it is determined that they have an emotional disturbance.

Children with emotional disabilities or behavioral disorders are not always easy to identify. It is oftentimes easy to identify the acting-out child who is constantly fighting, who cannot stay on task for more than a few minutes, or who shouts obscenities when angry. However, it is not always easy to identify the child who internalizes his or her problems or who may appear to be the "model" student, but suffers from depression, shyness, or fears. Unless the problem becomes severe enough to affect school performance, the internalizing child may go for long periods without being identified or served.

SPECIAL EDU. CROSS-CATEGORY

Studies of children with behavioral and emotional disorders share some general characteristics:

Lower academic performance: While it is true that some emotionally disturbed children have above average IQ scores, the majority are behind their peers in measures of intelligence and school achievement. Most score in the "slow learner" or "mildly mentally retarded" range on IQ tests, averaging about 90. Many have learning problems that exacerbate their acting out or "giving-up" behavior. As the child enters secondary school, the gap between him or her and non-handicapped peers widens until the child may be as many as two to four years behind in reading and/or math skills. Children with severe degrees of impairment may be untestable.

Social skills deficits: Students with deficits may be uncooperative, selfish in dealing with others, unaware of what to do in social situations, or ignorant of the consequences of their actions. This may be a combination of lack of prior training, lack of opportunities to interact, and dysfunctional value systems and beliefs learned from their family.

Classroom behaviors: Students with emotional disturbances often display behaviors that are highly disruptive to the classroom setting. These children are often out of their seat or running around the room; hitting, fighting, or disturbing their classmates; stealing or destroying property; defiant and noncompliant; and/or verbally disruptive. They may not follow directions and often do not complete assignments.

Aggressive behaviors: Aggressive children often fight or instigate their peers to strike back at them. Aggressiveness may also take the form of vandalism or destruction of property. Aggressive children also often engage in verbal abuse.

Delinquency: As emotionally disturbed, acting-out children enter adolescence, they may become involved in socialized aggression (e.g., gang membership) and delinquency. Delinquency is a legal term (rather than a medical one); it describes truancy and actions that would be criminal if they were committed by adults. Of course, not every delinquent is classified as emotionally disturbed, but children with behavioral and emotional disorders are especially at risk for becoming delinquent because of their problems at school (the primary place for socializing with peers), deficits in social skills that may make them unpopular at school, and/or dysfunctional homes.

Withdrawn behaviors: Children who manifest withdrawn behaviors may consistently act in an immature fashion or prefer younger children as playmates. They may cry, cling to the teacher, daydream, complain of being sick in order to "escape" to the clinic, ignore other's attempt to interact, or suffer from fears or depression.

Gender: Many more boys than girls are identified as having emotional and behavioral problems, especially hyperactivity and attention deficit disorder, autism, childhood psychosis, and problems with undercontrol (e.g., aggression, socialized aggression). Girls, on the other hand, have more problems with overcontrol (e.g., withdrawal and phobias). Boys are also more prevalent than girls in problems with mental retardation and language and learning disabilities.

Age Characteristics: When they enter adolescence, girls tend to experience affective or emotional disorders such as anorexia, depression, bulimia, and anxiety at twice the rate of boys, which mirrors the adult prevalence pattern.

Family Characteristics: Having a child with an emotional or behavioral disorder does not automatically mean that the family is dysfunctional. However, there are family factors that create or contribute to the development of behavior disorders and emotional disturbance:
- Abuse and neglect
- Lack of appropriate supervision
- Lax, punitive, and/or lack of discipline
- High rates of negative types of interaction among family members
- Lack of parental concern and interest
- Negative adult role models
- Lack of proper health care and/or nutrition
- Disruption in the family

Emotional Disturbances in the Special Education Classroom

Although some emotional disturbances do not appear until late adolescence or adulthood, others begin in childhood. Severe emotional disturbances are often treated with medication and therapy. These students may receive services from the school social worker and are often receiving educational services in a special education program.

Several emotional disturbances that may be present in the special education classroom are outlined below.

Anxiety Disorders
The National Institute of Mental Health divides this area of mental illness into five kinds: generalized anxiety disorder, obsessive-compulsive disorder, panic disorder, post-traumatic stress disorder, and social phobia. Some individuals with anxiety disorders may also have ADHD.

Bipolar Disorder (Manic Depression)
The National Institute of Mental Health describes children and adolescents with bipolar disorder as having frequent and severe mood swings between mania and depression. Many individuals with bipolar disorder are suicidal.

Bipolar disorder is more common in children of parents who are bipolar, but many bipolar individuals do not have parents who suffer from the illness. This mental illness can also be characterized by aggression and irritability.

Schizophrenia and Psychotic Behaviors
Children with these disorders may have bizarre delusions, hallucinations, incoherent thoughts, and disconnected thinking. Schizophrenia typically manifests itself between the ages of 15 and 45—the younger the onset, the more severe the disorder. These behaviors usually require intensive treatment beyond the scope of the regular classroom setting.

Autism
This behavior appears very early in childhood. It is associated with brain damage and severe language impairment. Six common features of autism are:
- Apparent sensory deficit—The child may appear not to see, hear, or react to a stimulus, followed by reacting in an extreme fashion to a seemingly insignificant stimulus.
- Severe affect isolation—The child does not respond to the usual signs of affection, such as smiles and hugs.
- Self-stimulation—Stereotyped behavior takes the form of repeated or ritualistic actions that make no sense to others, such as hand flapping, rocking, staring at objects, or humming the same sounds for hours at a time.
- Tantrums and self-injurious behavior (SIB)—Autistic children may bite themselves, pull their hair, bang their heads, or hit themselves. They can throw severe tantrums and direct aggression and destructive behavior toward others.
- Echolalia—Also known as "parrot talk," the autistic child may repeat what is played on television or respond to others by repeating what was already said. Alternatively, the child may simply not speak at all.
- Severe deficits in behavior and self-care skills—Autistic children may behave like children much younger than themselves.

TEACHER CERTIFICATION STUDY GUIDE

COMPETENCY 3.0 UNDERSTAND THE EFFECTS OF EMOTIONAL DISABILITIES ON HUMAN DEVELOPMENT AND LEARNING

For example: the influence of emotional disabilities on psychomotor, cognitive, social, emotional, and linguistic development; ways in which emotional disabilities influence personal productivity, interpersonal/intrapersonal effectiveness, communication skills, self-control, and self-monitoring; and the effects of emotional disabilities on adult life roles (e.g., learning, daily living, employment, family life).

Prior to testing a student for an emotional disability, the special educator and parents will see student behaviors that are not typical. While every student is an individual, there is a point when behaviors cross over from an individual personality difference and what is considered socially, behaviorally, and emotionally outside the norm.

Normality in child behavior is influenced by society's attitudes and cultural beliefs about what is normal for children (e.g., the motto for the Victorian era was: "Children should be seen and not heard"). However, criteria for what is "normal" involves consideration of these questions:

- **Is the behavior age appropriate?** An occasional tantrum may be expected for a toddler, but is not typical for a high school student.
- **Is the behavior pathological in itself?** Drug or alcohol use is harmful to children, regardless of how many engage in it.
- **How persistent is the problem?** A kindergarten student may initially be afraid to go to school. However, if the fear persists into first or second grade, then the problem is considered persistent.
- **How severe is the behavior?** Self-injurious, cruel, and extremely destructive behaviors are examples of behaviors that require intervention.
- **How often does the behavior occur?** A brief mood of depression in an adolescent might not be considered problematic. However, if the behaviors occur frequently, that behavior would not be characteristic of normal child development.
- **Do several problem behaviors occur as a group?** Clusters of behaviors, especially severe behaviors that occur together, may be indicative of a serious problem, such as schizophrenia.
- **Is the behavior sex-appropriate?** Cultural and societal attitudes toward gender change over time. While attitudes toward younger boys playing with dolls or girls preferring sports to dolls have relaxed, children are eventually expected as adults to conform to the "normal" behaviors for males and females.

Certain stages of child development have their own sets of problems, and it should be kept in mind that short-term undesirable behaviors can and will occur over these stages. Child development is also a continuum, and children may manifest these problem behaviors somewhat earlier or later than their peers.

About 15-20 percent of the school-aged population between 6 and 17 years old receive special education services. The categories of learning disabilities and emotional disturbance are the most prevalent. Exceptional students are very much like their peers without disabilities. The main difference is that they have an intellectual, emotional, behavioral, or physical deficit that significantly interferes with their ability to benefit from education.

Effects of Emotional Disturbance on Human Development

Behavioral expectations vary from setting to setting—for example, it is acceptable to yell on the football field, but not as the teacher is explaining a lesson to the class. Different cultures have their own standards of behavior, further complicating the question of what constitutes a behavioral problem. People also have their personal opinions and standards for what is tolerable and what is not. Some behavioral problems are openly expressed; others are inwardly directed and not very obvious. As a result of these factors, the terms **behavioral disorders** and **emotional disturbance** have become almost interchangeable. To better serve the child, an educator must know the IDEA definition of emotional disturbance.

The diagnostic categories and definitions used to classify mental disorders come from the American Psychiatric Association's publication *Diagnostic and Statistical Manual of Mental Disorders (DSM-IV)*, the handbook used by psychiatrists and psychologists. The DSM-IV is a multiaxial classification system consisting of dimensions (axes) coded along with the psychiatric diagnosis. The axes are:

- Axis I	Principal psychiatric diagnosis (e.g., overanxious disorder)
- Axis II	Developmental problems (e.g., developmental reading disorder)
- Axis III	Physical disorders (e.g., allergies)
- Axis IV	Psychosocial stressors (e.g., divorce)
- Axis V	Rating of the highest level of adaptive functioning (includes intellectual and social). Rating is called Global Assessment Functioning (GAF) score.

While the DSM-IV diagnosis is one way of diagnosing serious emotional disturbance, there are other ways of classifying the various forms in which behavior disorders manifest themselves. The following tables summarize some of these classifications.

TEACHER CERTIFICATION STUDY GUIDE

Externalizing Behaviors	Internalizing Behaviors
Aggressive behaviors expressed outwardly toward others	Withdrawing behaviors are directed inward to oneself
Manifested as hyperactivity, persistent aggression, and/or irritating behaviors that are impulsive and distractible	Social withdrawal
Examples: hitting, cursing, stealing, arson, cruelty to animals, hyperactivity	Examples: depression, fears, phobias, elective mutism, withdrawal, anorexia and bulimia

Well-known instruments used to assess children's behavior have their own categories (scales) to classify behaviors. The following table illustrates the scales for some of the widely used instruments.

Walker Problem Identification Checklist	Burks' Behavior Rating Scales (BBRS)	Devereux Behavior Rating Scale (Adolescent)	Revised Behavior Problem Checklist (Quay & Peterson)
Acting out	Excessive self-blame	Unethical behavior	Major scales
Withdrawal	Excessive anxiety	Defiant-resistive	Conduct disorder
Distractibility	Excessive withdrawal	Domineering-sadistic	Socialized aggression
Disturbed peer Relations	Excessive dependency	Heterosexual interest	Attention-problems; immaturity
Immaturity	Poor ego strength	Hyperactive expansive	Anxiety; withdrawal
	Poor physical strength	Poor emotional control	
	Poor coordination	Needs approval; dependency	Minor scales
	Poor intellectuality	Emotional disturbance	Psychotic behavior
	Poor academics	Physical inferiority; timidity	Motor excess

SPECIAL EDU. CROSS-CATEGORY

	Poor attention	Schizoid withdrawal	
	Poor impulse control	Bizarre speech and cognition	
	Poor reality contact	Bizarre actions	
	Poor sense of identity		
	Excessive suffering		
	Poor anger control		
	Excessive sense of persecution		
	Excessive aggressiveness		
	Excessive resistance		
	Poor social conformity		

Disturbance may also be categorized in degrees: mild, moderate, or severe. The degree of disturbance will affect the type and degree of interventions and services required by emotionally handicapped students. Degree of disturbance must also be considered when determining the least restrictive environment. An example of a set of criteria for determining the degree of disturbance is the one developed by P.L. Newcomer:

CRITERIA	DEGREE — Mild	OF — Moderate	DISTURBANCE — Severe
Precipitating events	Highly stressful	Moderately stressful	Not stressful
Destructiveness	Not destructive	Occasionally destructive	Usually destructive
Maturational appropriateness	Behavior typical for age	Some behavior untypical for age	Behavior too young or too old
Personal functioning	Cares for own needs	Usually cares for own needs	Unable to care for own needs
Social functioning	Usually able to relate to others	Usually unable to relate to others	Unable to relate to others
Reality index	Usually sees events as they are	Occasionally sees events as they are	Little contact with reality
Insight index	Aware of behavior	Usually aware of behavior	Usually not aware of behavior
Conscious control	Usually can control behavior	Occasionally can control behavior	Little control over behavior
Social responsiveness	Usually acts appropriately	Occasionally acts appropriately	Rarely acts appropriately

Source: Understanding and Teaching Emotionally Disturbed Children and Adolescents, (2nd ed., p. 139), by P.L. Newcomer, 1993, Austin, TX: Pro-De. Copyright 1993. Reprinted with permission.

The Etiology of Emotional Disturbance

Medical Factors

Some emotional disturbances are the result of a chemical imbalance or neurological dysfunction. Schizophrenia, bipolar disorders, and depression fall into this category.

Although medical in nature, these causes are not the result of the student's environment or family life (unless caused by the maternal, prenatal use of a substance such as drugs or alcohol). One example of emotional disturbance that can be caused by maternal, prenatal alcohol consumption is fetal alcohol syndrome. According to the CDC, Centers for Disease Control and Prevention, *children with FASDs are at risk for psychiatric problems, criminal behavior, unemployment, and incomplete education* (2006, http://www.cdc.gov/).

Environmental Factors

- **Shared Psychotic Disorders** are those in which an emotionally disturbed person influences the perceptions and reactions of an otherwise emotionally healthy individual. The previously healthy individual then becomes emotionally disturbed, as well.

- **Abuse**, whether it occurs to the child or to a parent, affects the immediate situation as well as all interaction with others in the home, school, and community. Unfortunately, having a child with a disability puts excessive strain on a marriage, and abusive tendencies may continue to be exaggerated.

- **Neglect** in a child with a disability can be exhibited by a number of behaviors. In the instances of abuse and neglect (or suspected instances), the special educator is mandated to report it to the appropriate agency.

- **Substance Abuse** can occur on many levels. It is important for the special education teacher to be aware of signs of substance abuse and be proactive in teaching drug awareness.

The Implications of Emotional Disturbance Past the Childhood Years

Emotional Disturbance in the Teen Years

Every adolescent progresses at varying rates in developing his or her own abilities. This is especially true in the case of an adolescent with an emotional disturbance. Already atypical responses to self and others are heightened when the student is in the emotionally charged phase of adolescence.

Each adolescent develops his or her own view of the world. Some adolescents may be able to apply logical operations to school work long before they are able to apply them to personal dilemmas. When emotional issues arise, they often interfere with an adolescent's ability to think in more complex ways. A teen's inability to consider possibilities, as well as facts, may influence decision making in negative ways.

Emotional Disturbance in Adulthood

The appearance of those with special needs in media (such as television and movies) are generally those who rise above their "label" as disabled because of an extraordinary skill. Most people in the community are portrayed as accepting of the "disabled" person when that special skill is noted. Those who continue to express revulsion or prejudice toward the person with a disability often feel remorse when the special skill is noted or when peer pressure becomes too intense. This portrayal often ignores those who appear normal by appearance with learning and emotional disabilities, but who often feel and suffer from the prejudices.

The most significant group any individual faces is that of their peers. Pressure to appear normal and not "needy" in any area is still intense from early childhood to adulthood. During teen years, when young people are beginning to express their individuality, the very appearance of walking into a special education classroom often brings feelings of inadequacy and labeling by peers that the student is "special." Being considered normal is the desire of almost all individuals with disabilities, regardless of their age or disability. People with disabilities today, as many years ago, still measure their successes by how their achievements mask or hide their disabilities.

The most difficult cultural and community outlook on those who are disabled comes in the adult work world, where disabilities of persons can become highly evident—often causing those with special needs difficulties in finding work and keeping their jobs. This is a particularly difficult place for those who have not learned to self advocate or accommodate for their area of special needs.

Impact of Emotional Disturbance on Life in Adulthood

Family Life
Family life can be inconsistent, abusive, and at the very least stressful. The emotionally disturbed adult may have difficulty with day-to-day responsibilities of home and parenting. Housekeeping, home maintenance, and following a budget may be overwhelming. Because he or she may have difficulty attaining or keeping a job, family finances can be negatively affected. The cost of needed medications can also present a financial hardship. The effect on children of an emotionally disturbed parent can be extensive. Some children may be neglected or abused verbally or physically.

Self-Advocacy Skills
Self-advocacy involves the ability to effectively communicate one's own rights, needs, and desires and to take responsibility for making decisions that affect one's life.

Students with emotional disabilities need to be taught self-advocacy skills. Learning about one's self involves the identification of learning styles, strengths and weaknesses, interests, and preferences. For students with exceptionalities, developing an awareness of the accommodations they need will help them ask for necessary accommodations on a job and in postsecondary education. Students can also help identify alternative ways they can learn.

Affective and social skills taught throughout the school setting might include: social greetings; eye contact with a speaker; interpretation of facial expression, body language, and personal space; ability to put feelings and questions into words; and using words to acquire additional information.

Career/Vocational Skills

Although counseling and, in some cases, medication can improve the cooperative nature of an emotionally disturbed adult in the workplace, there are many potential difficulties.

Initially, the individual may find it difficult to be hired for a job because of employer prejudice, difficulty with communication, behavioral issues, or environmental challenges.

Students with emotional disturbances should be taught responsibility for actions, a good work ethic, and independence in the academic setting. If students are able to regulate their overall work habits with school tasks, it is likely that the same skills will carry over into the work force. The special education teacher may assess the student's level of career/vocational readiness by using the following list.

- Being prepared by showing responsibility for materials/school tools such as books, assignments, study packets, pencils, pens, and assignment notebooks
- Knowing expectations by keeping an assignment notebook completed
- Asking questions when unsure of the expectations
- Use of additional checklists, as needed
- Use of needed assistive devices
- Completing assignments on time to the best of his or her ability

An additional responsibility of the special educator when teaching career and vocational skills is recognition that a variety of vocations and skills are present in the community. If academics are not an area in which students excel, other exploratory or training opportunities should be provided. Such opportunities might include art, music, culinary arts, childcare, technical trades, or building instruction. These skills can often be included (although not to the exclusion of additional programs) within the academic setting. For example, a student with strong vocational interest in art may be asked to create a poster to show learned information in a science or social studies unit. While addressing career and vocational interests and skills this way, the teacher is also establishing a program of differentiated instruction.

Self-Sufficiency with Students Who Have Emotional Disturbances

Many students with learning and behavior problems are characterized as poor independent workers. Too frequently, these students do not know how to study or work without adult supervision, nor do they view themselves as responsible for their own learning or behavior.

To allow self-sufficiency in the academic arena, the teacher must set the environment and make assurances that the child can function independently. Several concerns must be addressed prior to expecting independent functioning. First, the child must understand the nature of the assignments and the content on which they are based. Next, it must be determined whether the child cannot, rather than will not, do the work. It needs to be determined whether the child is able to ask for help in a positive, appropriate manner. Finally, the task expectations held by the teacher need to be accurately conveyed to the student (e.g., how they should be done and criteria for successful completion).

Modeling is often used as a mechanism for moving the learner from dependence to independence. Modeling refers to the use of significant adults or peers to demonstrate appropriate performance behaviors. Initially, the teacher models the appropriate performance, which is a form of demonstration. The teacher may then encourage the student to copy this behavior; thus, imitation occurs. Next, the teacher might encourage the learner to undertake the task him or herself (with guidance, assistance, and prompting if necessary). Finally, the teacher should provide verbal instruction, without prompting, hopefully leading the student to the point at which he or she can perform the task upon request.

Training in self-instruction can be combined with modeling. The underlying purpose of this approach is to encourage the learner to develop verbal control of behavior. Meichenbaum (1975) advocates the use of the following components:

1. **Cognitive modeling**, in which the adult model performs a task while narrating (talking through) how the task should be performed.
2. **Overt, self-guidance**, in which the child performs the same task, imitating instructions spoken by the model.
3. **Faded, overt, self-guidance**, in which the child softly repeats the instructions while repeating the task.
4. **Covert self-instruction**, in which the child performs the task while silently instructing him or herself.

Self-monitoring refers to procedures by which the learner records whether he or she is engaging in certain behaviors, particularly those that would lead to increased academic achievement and/or social behavior.

Self-reinforcement is important to the success of self-monitoring; it may be administered as verbal self-acknowledgment or as tangible rewards. Checklists or other means of keeping a record may be faded upon evidence of progress. This system encourages self-responsibility and independence.

TEACHER CERTIFICATION STUDY GUIDE

COMPETENCY 4.0 UNDERSTAND TYPES AND CHARACTERISTICS OF SPECIFIC LEARNING DISABILITIES

For example: types (e.g., oral or written expression, basic reading skills, reading or listening comprehension, mathematics calculation or reasoning) and characteristics (e.g., perception and memory disorders; difficulties with concept formation, processing, and problem solving) of specific learning disabilities; and differences between specific learning disabilities and other types of impairments.

Specific learning disability means a disorder in one of more of the basic psychological processes involved in understanding or using language—spoken or written—which may manifest itself in an imperfect ability to listen, think, speak, read, write, spell, or do mathematical calculations. The term includes such conditions as perceptual handicaps, brain injury, minimal brain dysfunction, dyslexia, and developmental aphasia. The term does not include children who have learning problems that are primarily the result of visual, hearing, or motor handicaps; mental retardation; emotional disturbance; or environmental, cultural, or economic disadvantage.

Characteristics of Students with Learning Disabilities

The individual with a specific learning disability exhibits a discrepancy between achievement and potential. Deficiencies can occur within a spectrum of skill areas. The youngster typically shows a low level of performance in one of several skill areas; rarely is a uniform pattern of academic development demonstrated. The cause of delayed academic performance is not due to limited cognitive ability, sensory and physical impairments, emotional disturbances, or environmental deprivation. The child or youth with a disability may be characterized by:

1. **Hyperactivity:** a rate of motor activity higher than normal
2. **Perceptual difficulties:** visual, auditory, and haptic perceptual problems
3. **Perceptual-motor impairments:** poor integration of visual and motor systems, often affecting fine motor coordination
4. **General coordination deficits:** clumsiness in physical activities
5. **Disorders of memory and thinking:** memory deficits; trouble with problem solving, concept formation, and association; poor awareness of own metacognitive skills (learning strategies)
6. **Disorders of attention:** short attention span, distractibility, lack of selective attention, perseveration.
7. **Emotional ability:** frequent changes in mood, low tolerance for frustration, sensitivity to others
8. **Impulsiveness:** takes action before considering consequences; poor impulse control, often followed by remorsefulness

SPECIAL EDU. CROSS-CATEGORY

9. **Academic problems in reading, math, writing, or spelling:** significant discrepancies in ability levels
10. **Disorders in speech, hearing, and sight:** high proportion of auditory and visual perceptual difficulties
11. **Equivocal neurological signs and electroencephalogram (EEG) irregularities:** neurological abnormalities (soft signs), which may or may not be due to brain injury
12. **Social adjustment:** poor social adjustment; low self-esteem; social isolation or reckless and uninhibited, learned helplessness; poor motivation; external focus of control; poor reaction to environmental changes
13. **Interpersonal problems:** over-excitable in a group, better relations with limited number of peers, frequent poor judgment exhibited, often overly affectionate and clinging
14. **Problems in achievement:** academic disability, poor graphics (wiring), disorganization, slow in finishing work

Characteristics of Perceptual and Memory Disorders Typically Seen with Those Who Have Learning Disabilities

Perceptual disorders refer to visual processing problems that occur when an individual has problems making sense of information that is seen through the eyes. (This is not to be confused with problems that result from sight or sharpness of vision. People who have perceptual disorders have problems processing visual information, not problems seeing it.)

Students with perceptual disorders have problems identifying the position of objects in space. They cannot precisely view objects in space when placed next to other objects.

The problems of spatial relationships are significant in reading and math. Both subjects require the use of symbols, letters, numbers, punctuation, and signs. Some examples of problems associated with perception include not being able to view words and numbers as separate entities, confusion with letters that resemble each other (such as b, d, and p), and having problems with directions in reading and math.
The significance of having perceptual acuity is especially present throughout math. In order to fully master mathematical concepts, individuals have to be able to ascertain that certain digits go together to create a single number (such as 25), and that other digits are single digit numbers. They must also know that addition, subtraction, and multiplication signs are separate from the numbers but show a relationship between the numbers.

There are three different types of memories significant in the learning process:

- **Working memory** is the ability to hold on to parts of information until the pieces come together to formulate a complete thought or concept. An example of this is when you read a sentence and, at the end of it, are able to comprehend the full context.
- **Short-term memory** is the active process of storing and retaining information for a brief period of time. The information is available for a short while and is not yet stored for long-term memorization.
- **Long-term memory** is information that has been stored and is available for use over a long period of time.

Some people may have problems with auditory or visual memory. Auditory memory is the ability to store and recall information that is received verbally. Visual memory is the ability to store and recall information that is received visually.

Sequencing problems stem from people with problems learning information in the correct sequence. For example, a student can have problems memorizing the order of the alphabet or the months of the year.

Abstraction problems occur when an individual has problems deducing the meaning of words or concepts. Someone with abstraction problems may have difficulty understanding jokes, sarcasm, idioms, or words with different meanings.

Organization problems occur when an individual has problems keeping things organized. These students may constantly lose, forget, or misplace homework, school assignments, and papers. They also have problems keeping their work environment organized and have difficulty with projects that may be due on a particular date.

Knowledge of Characteristics of Thinking Disorders Typically Seen with Those Who Have Learning Disabilities

Thinking disorders associated with learning disabilities include problems forming concepts and solving problems. Problem solving is the systematic use of a step-by-step system to respond to hard questions. Concept formation is the process of combining a series of features that group together to create a class of ideas or objects.

Without the formation of concepts, people would have to learn and recall the word that stands for every unique thing in the world. For example, each type of chair, flower, or truck would require its own name in order to learn and communicate about it in any significant manner.

Difficulties with higher order thinking skills are problematic for students studying mathematics, because these skills are needed for many problems in upper level math classes. Students must determine the solution to questions that are asked indirectly, and some have difficulties correctly identifying the problem and the steps necessary to go about finding the solution. Students may also have difficulties with problems that contain many steps. Students with disabilities sometimes cannot determine how to begin working on the problem. They may also be unable to finish the problem once they have completed some of the steps, therefore leaving an incomplete resolution.

Students' underdeveloped processing skills may also lead to problems deducing important information from insignificant information when resolving word problems. Numerous problems that the students are faced with entail too much or too little information, which then requires the student to deduce what information is required to solve the problem. This makes it even harder for students who have problems with multi-step problem solving and higher order thinking skills.

The Differences Between Learning Disabled and Other Disabilities

Student with a disability means a student with a disability who has not attained the age of 21 prior to September 1st; who is entitled to attend public schools; who, because of mental, physical or emotional reasons, has been identified as having a disability; and who requires special services and programs approved by the department. The terms used in this definition are defined as follows:

> (1) *Autism* means a developmental disability significantly affecting verbal and nonverbal communication and social interaction, generally evident before age three, which adversely affects a student's educational performance. Other characteristics often associated with autism are engagement in repetitive activities and stereotyped movements, resistance to environmental change or change in daily routines, and unusual responses to sensory experiences. The term does not apply if a student's educational performance is adversely affected primarily because the student has an emotional disturbance. A student who manifests the characteristics of autism after age three could be diagnosed as having autism if the criteria in this paragraph are otherwise satisfied.

> (2) *Deafness* means a hearing impairment that is so severe that the student is impaired in processing linguistic information through hearing, with or without amplification, which adversely affects a student's educational performance.

(3) *Deaf-blindness* means concomitant hearing and visual impairments, the combination of which causes such severe communication and other developmental and educational needs that the student cannot be accommodated in special education programs solely for students with deafness or students with blindness.

(4) *Emotional Disturbance* means a condition exhibiting one or more of the following characteristics over a long period of time and to a marked degree, which adversely affects a student's educational performance:

(i) an inability to learn that cannot be explained by intellectual, sensory, or health factors;

(ii) an inability to build or maintain satisfactory interpersonal relationships with peers and teachers;

(iii) inappropriate types of behavior or feelings under normal circumstances;

(iv) a generally pervasive mood of unhappiness or depression; or

(v) a tendency to develop physical symptoms or fears associated with personal or school problems.

The term emotional disturbance includes schizophrenia. The term does not apply to students who are socially maladjusted, unless it is determined that they have an emotional disturbance.

(5) *Hearing Impairment* means an impairment in hearing, whether permanent or fluctuating, which adversely affects the child's educational performance but which is not included under the definition of *deafness* in this section.

(6) *Learning Disability* means a disorder in one or more of the basic psychological processes involved in understanding or in using language—spoken or written—which manifests itself in an imperfect ability to listen, think, speak, read, write, spell, or do mathematical calculations. The term includes such conditions as perceptual disabilities, brain injury, minimal brain dysfunction, dyslexia, and developmental aphasia. The term does not include learning problems that are primarily the result of: visual, hearing, or motor disabilities; mental retardation; emotional disturbance; or environmental, cultural, or economic disadvantage.

(7) *Mental Retardation* means significantly sub-average general intellectual functioning existing concurrently with deficits in adaptive behavior, manifested during the developmental period, and adversely affecting a student's educational performance.

(8) *Multiple Disabilities* means concomitant impairments (such as mental retardation-blindness, mental retardation-orthopedic impairment, etc.), the combination of which cause such severe educational needs that the student cannot be accommodated in a special education program solely for one of the impairments. The term does not include deaf-blindness.

(9) *Orthopedic Impairment* means a severe orthopedic impairment that adversely affects a student's educational performance. The term includes impairments caused by congenital anomaly (e.g., clubfoot, absence of some member, etc.), impairments caused by disease (e.g., poliomyelitis, bone tuberculosis, etc.), and impairments from other causes (e.g., cerebral palsy, amputation, fractures or burns that cause contractures, etc.).

(10) *Other Health-Impairment* means having limited strength, vitality, or alertness—including a heightened alertness to environmental stimuli—which results in limited alertness with respect to the educational environment and adversely affects a student's educational performance. It may be due to chronic or acute health problems, including but not limited to a heart condition, tuberculosis, rheumatic fever, nephritis, asthma, sickle cell anemia, hemophilia, epilepsy, lead poisoning, leukemia, diabetes, attention deficit disorder, attention deficit hyperactivity disorder, or Tourette's syndrome.

(11) *Speech or Language Impairment* means a communication disorder (such as stuttering, impaired articulation, a language impairment, or a voice impairment) that adversely affects a student's educational performance.

(12) *Traumatic Brain Injury* means an acquired injury to the brain caused by an external physical force or certain medical conditions (such as stroke, encephalitis, aneurysm, anoxia, or brain tumors), with resulting impairments that adversely affect educational performance. The term includes open or closed head injuries or brain injuries from certain medical conditions resulting in mild, moderate, or severe impairments in one or more areas, including cognition, language, memory, attention, reasoning, abstract thinking, judgment, problem solving, sensory, perceptual and motor abilities, psychosocial behavior, physical functions, information processing, and speech. The term does not include injuries that are congenital or caused by birth trauma.

(13) *Visual Impairment including blindness* means an impairment in vision that, even with correction, adversely affects a student's educational performance. The term includes both partial sight and blindness.

COMPETENCY 5.0   UNDERSTAND THE EFFECTS OF SPECIFIC LEARNING DISABILITIES ON HUMAN DEVELOPMENT AND LEARNING

For example: the influence of specific learning disabilities on psychomotor, cognitive, social, emotional, and language development; and the implications of various types of specific learning disabilities on students' educational development.

- *Please refer to Competency 4.0*

COMPETENCY 6.0 UNDERSTAND TYPES AND CHARACTERISTICS OF MILD, MODERATE, AND SEVERE MENTAL RETARDATION

For example: major cognitive, behavioral, and social characteristics of individuals with mental retardation; the concepts of intellectual functioning and adaptive behavior; known causes of, contributing factors related to, and prevention of mental retardation; and definitions and criteria associated with types and levels of mental retardation.

Mental retardation, called intellectual disabilities in some states, refers to significantly sub-average general intellectual functioning existing concurrently with impairments in adaptive behavior. Sub-average intellectual functioning is determined by scores of two or more standard deviations below the mean on a standardized test of intelligence. Students exhibiting mental handicaps typically show a flat profile in academic areas.

Adaptive behavior differs according to age and situation. For example, during infancy and early childhood, sensory motor, self-help, communication, and socialization skills are considered important. During middle childhood and early adolescence, abilities involving learning processes and interpersonal social skills are essential. During late adolescence and adulthood, vocational skills, vocational abilities, and social responsibilities are important.

The general characteristics of individuals with intellectual disabilities are as follows:

1. IQ of 70 or below
2. Limited cognitive ability; delayed academic achievement, particularly in language-related subjects
3. Deficits in memory, which often relate to poor initial perception; inability to apply stored information to relevant situations
4. Impaired formulation of learning strategies
5. Delayed language development with frequent speech defects
6. Difficulty in attending to relevant aspects of stimuli; slowness in reaction time or in employing alternative strategies
7. Short attention span in which student is easily distracted.
8. Delayed academic readiness; slower rate of learning
9. Delayed social skills
10. Poor motivation; dependency; reliance on external focus of control

Characteristics with regard to the degree of retardation fall into four categories.

1. Mild (IQ of 55 to 70)
   a. Delays in most areas (e.g., communication, motor, academics)
   b. Often not distinguished from "normal" children until school age
   c. Can acquire both academic and vocational skills; can become self-supporting.
2. Moderate (IQ of 35-40 to 50-55)
   a. Only fair motor development; clumsy
   b. Poor social awareness
   c. Can be taught to communicate
   d. Can profit from training in social and vocational skills; needs supervision, but can perform semiskilled labor as an adult
3. Severe (IQ of 20-25 to 35-40)
   a. Poor motor development
   b. Minimal speech and communication
   c. Minimal ability to profit from training in health and self-help skills; may contribute to self-maintenance under constant supervision as an adult
4. Profound (IQ below 20-25)
   a. Gross retardation, both mental and sensory-motor
   b. Little or no development of basic communication skills
   c. Dependency on others to maintain basic life functions
   d. Lifetime of complete supervision (e.g., institution, home, nursing home)

Possible Causes of Mental Retardation

Problems in Fetal Brain Development
During pregnancy things can go wrong in the development of the brain, which alters how the neurons form or interconnect. Throughout pregnancy, brain development is vulnerable to disruptions. If the disruption occurs early, the fetus may die, or the infant may be born with widespread disabilities and possibly mental retardation. If the disruption occurs later, when the cells are becoming specialized and moving into place, it may leave errors in the cell makeup, location, or connections. Some scientists believe that these errors may later show up as learning disorders.

Tobacco, Alcohol, and Other Drug Use

Many drugs taken by the mother pass directly to the fetus during pregnancy. Research shows that a mother's usage of cigarettes, alcohol, or other drugs during pregnancy may have damaging effects on the unborn child. Mothers who smoke during pregnancy are more likely to have smaller birth weight babies. Newborns who weigh less than five pounds are more at risk for learning disorders.

Heavy alcohol use during pregnancy has been linked to fetal alcohol syndrome, a condition resulting in low birth weight, intellectual impairment, hyperactivity, and certain physical defects.

More Possible Causes of Mild Disabilities

Experts in the field have reported that about 6 to 12 percent of special education students are identified as having severe to profound disabilities, an estimated 12 to 25 percent have moderate disabilities, while approximately 75 to 87 percent have mild disabilities (Henly, Ramsey, and Algozzine, 1993). Because of the larger number in the latter group, it can be difficult to trace the disability's origins. Mild learning and behavior difficulties usually remain undetected until children enter school.

Causes for disabilities can primarily be subdivided into two major categories: organic (biological) and environmental. The figure below presents common causes of mild disabilities.

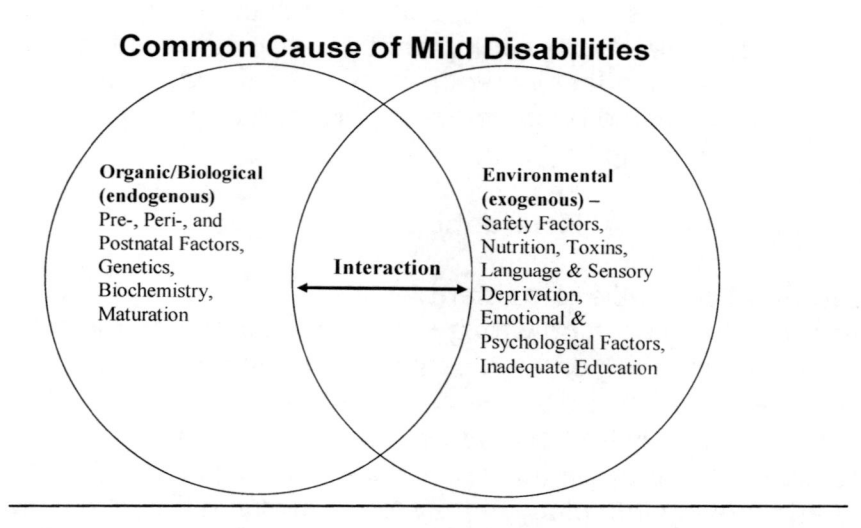

Common Cause of Mild Disabilities

- **Organic/Biological (endogenous)**
  Pre-, Peri-, and Postnatal Factors, Genetics, Biochemistry, Maturation

- **Interaction** ↔

- **Environmental (exogenous)** –
  Safety Factors, Nutrition, Toxins, Language & Sensory Deprivation, Emotional & Psychological Factors, Inadequate Education

Adapted from: M. Henley, R.S. Ramsey and R. Algozzine, Characteristics of and Strategies for Teaching Students with Mild Disabilities, 1993, Allyn and Bacon p. 43.

Under the organic category, pre-, peri-, and postnatal factors; genetic factors; biochemical factors; and maturational lag are listed. These contributors originate within the body (i.e., endogenous). Included under environmental reasons for mild learning and behavior disabilities are factors relating to poverty, nutrition, toxins, language differences, sensory deprivation, emotional problems, and inadequate education. Although some environmental factors (e.g., toxins) cause organic dysfunction, the point of origin is outside the body (i.e., exogenous).

COMPETENCY 7.0   UNDERSTAND THE EFFECTS OF MILD, MODERATE, AND SEVERE MENTAL RETARDATION ON HUMAN DEVELOPMENT AND LEARNING

For example: the influence of mental retardation on orthopedic (physical), sensory, motor, adaptive, cognitive, language, social, and emotional development; learning characteristics of students with mental retardation and ways to address these characteristics; and the implications of mental retardation on students' educational opportunities and adult life roles (i.e., domestic, recreation/leisure, community, and employment).

- o   *The current information available about the topic at this moment is inconclusive.*

TEACHER CERTIFICATION STUDY GUIDE

COMPETENCY 8.0   **UNDERSTAND TYPES AND CHARACTERISTICS OF ORTHOPEDIC (PHYSICAL) AND OTHER HEALTH IMPAIRMENTS**

For example: types of orthopedic (physical) disabilities and health impairments and their characteristics; terms related to orthopedic (physical) disabilities and health impairments; the educational implications for students with orthopedic (physical) or other health impairments; and prenatal, perinatal, and postnatal causes of orthopedic (physical) disabilities and health impairments.

Children with physical impairments possess a variety of disabling conditions. Although there are significant differences among these conditions, similarities also exist. Each condition usually affects one particular system of the body: the cardiopulmonary system (i.e., blood vessels, heart, and lungs), the musculoskeletal system (i.e., bones and muscles), and or the nervous system (i.e., spinal cord and brain nerves). Some conditions develop during pregnancy, birth, or infancy because of conditions that affect the fetus or newborn infant. Other conditions occur later due to injury (trauma), disease, or factors not fully understood.

In addition to motor disorders, individuals with physical disabilities may have multi-disabling conditions such as concomitant hearing impairments, visual impairments, perceptual disorders, speech defects, behavior disorders, mental handicaps, lowered performance, and poor emotional responsiveness.

Some characteristics that may occur in individuals with physical disabilities and other health impairments are:

1. Lack of physical stamina; fatigue
2. Chronic illness; poor endurance
3. Deficient motor skills; normal movement may be prevented
4. Physical limitations or impeded motor development; a prosthesis or orthotics may be required
5. Mobility and exploration of one's environment may be limited
6. Limited self-care abilities
7. Progressive weakening and degeneration of muscles
8. Frequent speech and language defects; communication may be prevented; echolatia orthosis may be present
9. Pain and discomfort throughout the body
10. Emotional (psychological) problems, which require treatment
11. Social adjustments may be needed; maladaptive social behavior
12. Requirement of long-term medical treatment
13. Embarrassing side effects from certain diseases or treatment methods
14. Erratic or poor attendance patterns

SPECIAL EDU. CROSS-CATEGORY

In 1981, the condition of autism was moved from the exceptionality category to the seriously emotionally disturbed category and then to that of other health impaired by virtue of a change in language in the original definitions under Public Law 94-142 ("Education of Handicapped Children." Federal Register, 1977). With IDEA in 1990, autism was made into a separate exceptionality category.

COMPETENCY 9.0 UNDERSTAND THE EFFECTS OF ORTHOPEDIC (PHYSICAL) AND OTHER HEALTH IMPAIRMENTS ON HUMAN DEVELOPMENT AND LEARNING

For example: the effects of orthopedic (physical) disabilities and health impairments on psychomotor, cognitive, social, emotional, and language development; the implications of various types of orthopedic (physical) and health impairments on students' educational development; and the effects of orthopedic (physical) and health impairments on adult life roles (e.g., learning, daily living, employment, family life).

- *The current information available about the topic at this moment is inconclusive.*

TEACHER CERTIFICATION STUDY GUIDE

DOMAIN II.	ASSESSING STUDENTS AND DEVELOPING INDIVIDUALIZED EDUCATION PROGRAMS (IEPs)

COMPETENCY 10.0 UNDERSTAND TYPES AND CHARACTERISTICS OF ASSESSMENT INSTRUMENTS AND METHODS

For example: basic terminology used in assessment; types, characteristics, and methods of formal and informal assessment; principles of and procedures for creating, selecting, and evaluating educational assessment instruments and methods, including those used in prereferral situations; and advantages, disadvantages, and limitations of various assessment instruments and methods.

Knowledge of Tests and Interpretation of the Results

The following terms are frequently used in behavioral as well as academic testing and assessment. They represent basic terminology and not more advanced statistical concepts.

Baseline - also known as establishing a baseline. This procedure means collecting data about a target behavior or performance of a skill before certain interventions or teaching procedures are implemented. Establishing a baseline will enable a person to determine if the interventions are effective.

Criterion-Referenced Test - a test in which the individual's performance is measured against mastery of curriculum criteria rather than comparison to the performance of other students. Criterion-referenced tests may be commercially prepared or teacher made. Since these tests measure what a student can or cannot do, results are especially useful for identifying goals and objectives for IEPs and lesson plans.

Curriculum-Based Assessment - assessment of an individual's performance of objectives of a curriculum, such as a reading or math program. The individual's performance is measured in terms of what objectives were mastered.

Duration Recording - measuring the length of time a behavior lasts (e.g., tantrums, time out of class, crying).

Error Analysis - the mistakes on an individual's test are noted and categorized by type. For example, an error analysis in a reading test could categorize mistakes by miscues, substituted words, omitted words or phrases, and miscues that are self corrected.

Event Recording - the number of times a target behavior occurs during an observation period.

SPECIAL EDU. CROSS-CATEGORY

Formal Assessment - standardized tests that have specific procedures for administration, norming, scoring, and interpretation. These include intelligence and achievement tests.

Frequency - the number of times a behavior (such as out-of-seat behavior, hitting, and temper tantrums) occurs in a time interval.

Frequency Distribution - plotting the scores received on a test and tallying how many individuals received those scores. A frequency distribution is used to visually determine how the group of individuals performed on a test, illustrate extreme scores, and compare the distribution to the mean or other criterion.

Informal Assessment - non-standardized tests such as criterion-referenced tests and teacher-prepared tests. There are no rigid rules or procedures for administration or scoring.

Intensity - the degree of a behavior as measured by its frequency and duration.

Interval Recording - this technique involves breaking the observation into an equal number of time intervals (such as 10-second intervals during a 5-minute period). At the end of each interval, the observer notes the presence or absence of the target behavior. The observer can then calculate a percentage by dividing the number of intervals in which the target behavior occurred by the total number of intervals in the observation period. This type of recording works well for behaviors (such as on- or off-task behavior, pencil tapping, or stereotyped behaviors) that occur with high frequency or for long periods of time. The observer does not have to constantly monitor the student, yet can gather enough data to get an accurate idea of the extent of the behavior.

Latency - the length of time that elapses between the presentation of a stimulus (e.g., a question) and the response (e.g., the student's answer).

Mean - the arithmetic average of a set of scores, which are calculated by adding the set of scores and dividing the sum by the number of scores. For example, if the sum of a set of 35 scores is 2935, dividing that sum by 35 (the number of scores) yields a mean of 83.9.

Median - the middle score: 50 percent of the scores are above this number and 50 percent of the scores are below this number. In the example above, if the middle score were 72, 17 students would have scored less than 72, and 17 students would have scored more than 72.

Mode - the score most frequently tallied in a frequency distribution. In the example above, the most frequently tallied score might be 78. It is possible for a set of scores to have more than one mode.

Momentary Time Sampling - this is a technique used for measuring behaviors of a group of individuals or several behaviors from the same individual. Time samples are usually brief, and may be conducted at fixed or variable intervals. The advantage of using variable intervals is increased reliability, as the students will not be able to predict when the time sample will be taken.

Multiple Baseline Design - this may be used to test the effectiveness of an intervention in a skill performance or to determine if the intervention accounted for the observed changes in a target behavior. First, the initial baseline data is collected, followed by the data during the intervention period. To get the second baseline, the intervention is removed for a period of time and data is collected again. The intervention is then reapplied, and data collected on the target behavior. An example of a multiple baseline design might be ignoring a child who calls out in class without raising his hand. Initially, the baseline could involve counting the number of times the child calls out before applying interventions. During the time the teacher ignores the child's call-outs, data is collected. For the second baseline, the teacher would resume the response to the child's call-outs in the way she did before ignoring. The child's call-outs would probably increase again if ignoring actually accounted for the decrease. If the teacher reapplies the ignoring strategy, the child's call-outs would probably decrease again.

Multiple baseline designs may also be used with single-subject experiments where:

- The same behavior is measured for several students at the same time. An example would be observing off-task or out-of-seat behavior among three students in a classroom.
- Several behaviors may be measured for one student. The teacher may be observing call-outs, off-task, and out-of-seat behavior for a particular child during an observation period.
- Several settings are observed to see if the same behaviors are occurring across settings. A student's aggressive behavior toward his or her classmates may be observed at recess, in class, going to or from class, or in the cafeteria.

Norm-Referenced Test - an individual's performance is compared to the group that was used to calculate the performance standards in this standardized test. Some examples are the CTBS, WISC-R, and Stanford-Binet.

Operational Definition - the description of a behavior and its measurable components. In behavioral observations, the description must be specific and measurable so that the observer will know exactly what constitutes instances and non-instances of the target behavior. Otherwise, reliability may be inaccurate.

Pinpoint - specifying and describing the target behavior for change in measurable and precise terms. "On time for class" may be interpreted as arriving physically in the classroom when the tardy bell has finished ringing, it may mean being at the pencil sharpener, or it may mean being in one's in seat and ready to begin work when the bell has finished ringing. Pinpointing the behavior makes it possible to accurately measure the behavior.

Profile - plotting an individual's behavioral data on a graph.

Rate - the frequency of a behavior over a specified time period, such as five talk-outs during a 30-minute period, or typing 85 words per minute.

Raw Score - the number of correct responses on a test before they have been converted to standard scores. Raw scores are not meaningful because they have no basis of comparison to the performance of other individuals.

Reliability - the consistency (stability) of a test over time to measure what it is supposed to measure. Reliability is commonly measured in four ways:

- Test-retest method: the test is administered to the same group or individual after a short period of time, and the results are compared.
- Alternate form (equivalent form): measures reliability by using alternative forms to measure the same skills. If both forms are administered to the same group within a relatively short period of time, there should be a high correlation between the two sets of scores if the test has a high degree of reliability.
- Interrater: this refers to the degree of agreement between two or more individuals observing the same behaviors or observing the same tests.
- Internal reliability: this is determined by statistical procedures or by correlating one-half of the test with the other half of the test.

Standard Deviation - a statistical measure of the variability of the scores. The more closely the scores are clustered around the mean, the smaller the standard deviation will be.

Standard Error of Measurement - measures the amount of possible error in a score. If the standard error of measurement for a test is + or -3, and the individual's score is 35, then the actual score may be anywhere between 32 and 35.

Standard Score - a derived score with a set mean (usually 100) and a standard deviation. Examples are T-scores (mean of 50 and a standard deviation of 10), Z-scores (mean of 0 and standard deviation of 1), and scaled scores. Scaled scores may be given for age groups or grade levels. IQ scores, for instance, use a mean of 100 and a standard deviation of 15.

Task Analysis - breaking an academic or behavioral task down into its sequence of steps. Task analysis is necessary when preparing criterion-referenced tests and performing error analysis. A task analysis for a student learning to do laundry might include:

1. Sort the clothes by type (white, permanent press, delicate)
2. Choose a type and select the correct water temperature and setting
3. If doing a partial load, adjust the water level
4. Measure the detergent
5. Turn on the machine
6. Load the clothes
7. Add bleach, fabric softener at the correct time
8. Wait for the machine to stop spinning completely before opening it
9. Remove the clothes from the machine and place in a dryer (a task analysis could be done for drying and folding as well)

Validity - the degree to which a test measures what it claims to measure (such as reading readiness, self-concept, or math achievement). A test may be highly reliable, but it will be useless if it is not valid. There are several types of validity to examine when selecting or constructing an assessment instrument:

- Content: this type of validity examines the question of whether the types of tasks in the test measure the skill or construct the test claims to measure. That is, a test that claims to measure mastery in algebra would probably not be valid if the majority of the items involved basic operations with fractions and decimals.
- Criterion-referenced validity: involves comparing the test results with a valid criterion. For example, a doctoral student preparing a test to measure reading and spelling skills may check the test against an established test (such as the WRAT-T) or another valid criterion (such as school grades).
- Predictive validity: refers to how well a test will relate to a future criterion level, such as the ability of a reading test administered to a first grader to predict that student's performance at third or fifth grade.
- Concurrent validity: refers to how well the test relates to a criterion measure given at the same time. For example, a new test that measures reading achievement may be given to a group that also takes the WRAR-R (which has already established validity). The test results are then compared using statistical measures. The recommended coefficient is 80 or better.
- Construct validity: refers to the ability of the test to measure a theoretical construct, such as intelligence, self-concept, and other non-observable behaviors. Ways to determine construct validity include factor analysis and correlation studies with other instruments that measure the same construct.

Identify Types, Characteristics, and Methods of Formal and Informal Assessment

Formal assessments include standardized-criterion, norm-referenced instruments, and commercially-prepared inventories, which are developmentally appropriate for students across the spectrum of disabilities. Criterion-referenced tests compare a student's performance to a previously established criterion rather than to other students from a normative sample. Norm-referenced tests use normative data for scoring, including performance norms for age, gender, and ethnic group.

Informal assessment strategies include non-standardized instruments such as checklists, developmental rating scales, observations, error analysis, interviews, teacher reports, and performance-based assessments, which are all developmentally appropriate for students across disabilities. Informal evaluation strategies rely on the knowledge and judgment of the professional and are an integral part of the evaluation. An advantage of using informal assessments is the ease of design and administration, as well as the usefulness of information the teacher can gain about the student's strength and weaknesses.

Some instruments can be both formal and informal. For example, observation may incorporate structured observation instruments as well as other informal observation procedures, including professional judgment. When evaluating a child's developmental level, a professional may use a formal adaptive rating scale while simultaneously using professional judgment to assess the child's motivation and behavior during the evaluation process.

IDEA requires that a variety of assessment tools and strategies be utilized when conducting assessments. Before utilizing a formal or informal tool, the practitioner should make sure that the tool is the most appropriate one that can be used for that particular population group. Many assessment tools can be used across disabilities. Depending on the disability in question (such as blindness, autism, or hearing impaired), some assessment tools will give more information than others.

Some of the informal and formal assessments that can be used across disabilities are curriculum-based assessments, multiple baseline design, norm-referenced test, and momentary time sampling.

Types of Assessment

It is useful to consider the types of assessment procedures that are available to the classroom teacher. The types of assessment discussed here represent many of the more common types, but the list is not comprehensive.

Anecdotal Records
These are notes recorded by the teacher concerning an area of interest or concern with a particular student. These records should focus on observable behaviors and be descriptive in nature. They should not include assumptions or speculations regarding effective areas like motivation or interest. These records are usually compiled over a period of several days or several weeks.

Rating Scales and Checklists
These assessments are generally self-appraisal instruments completed by the students or observation-based instruments completed by the teacher. The focus is frequently on behavior or effective areas such as interest and motivation.

Portfolio Assessment
The use of student portfolios for some aspect of assessment has become quite common. The purpose, nature, and policies of portfolio assessment vary greatly from one setting to another. In general, a student's portfolio contains samples of work collected over an extended period of time. The nature of the subject, age of the student, and scope of the portfolio all contribute to the specific mechanics of analyzing, synthesizing, and otherwise evaluating the portfolio contents.

In most cases, the student and teacher make joint decisions as to which work samples go into the student's portfolio. A collection of work compiled over an extended time period allows teacher, student, and parents to view the student's progress from a unique perspective. Qualitative changes over time can be readily apparent from work samples. Such changes are difficult to establish with strictly quantitative records typical of the scores recorded in the teacher's grade book.

Questioning
One of the most frequently occurring forms of assessment in the classroom is oral questioning by the teacher. As the teacher questions the students, he or she collects a great deal of information about the degree of student learning and potential sources of confusion for the students. While questioning is often viewed as a component of instructional methodology, it is also a powerful assessment tool.

Additional Types of Tests

Tests and similar direct assessment methods represent the most easily identified types of assessment. Thorndike (1997) identifies three types of assessment instruments:

1. Standardized achievement tests
2. Assessment material packaged with curricular materials
3. Teacher-made assessment instruments
    Pencil and paper test
    Oral tests
    Performance tests
    Effective measures, rubrics (p.199)

Kellough and Roberts (1991) take a slightly different perspective. They describe "three avenues for assessing student achievement:

a) What the learner says,
b) What the learner does, and
c) What the learner writes..." (p.343)

Purposes for Assessment

There are a number of different classification systems used to identify the various purposes for assessment. A compilation of several lists identifies some common purposes:

1. Diagnostic assessments are used to determine individual weakness and strengths in specific areas.
2. Readiness assessments measure prerequisite knowledge and skills.
3. Interest and attitude assessments attempt to identify topics of high interest or areas in which students may need extra motivational activities.
4. Evaluation assessments are generally programmed or teacher focused.
5. Placement assessments are used for purposes of grouping students or determining appropriate beginning levels in leveled materials.
6. Formative assessments provide ongoing feedback of student progress and of the success of instructional methods and materials.
7. Summative assessments define student accomplishment with the intent to determine the degree of student mastery or learning that has taken place.

TEACHER CERTIFICATION STUDY GUIDE

For most teachers, assessment purposes vary according to the situation. It may be helpful to consult several sources to help formulate an overall assessment plan. Kellough and Roberts (1991) identify six purposes for assessment. These are:

1. To evaluate and improve student learning
2. To identify student strengths and weaknesses
3. To assess the effectiveness of a particular instructional strategy
4. To evaluate and improve program effectiveness
5. To evaluate and improve teacher effectiveness
6. To communicate to parents their children's progress (p.341)

Limitations of Various Types of Assessment
The existence of various types of assessments stems from the unique needs of children with disabilities and the environments in which the disabilities are most troublesome. A student who demonstrates difficulty interacting with peers and acts impulsively may not be effectively evaluated with a portfolio. Anecdotal records, questioning, and certain checklists may give a better picture of the extent to which such peer interactions are detrimental to the student's (and others') well-being and success. Conversely, a student who displays academic difficulty is better assessed with samples of work (portfolio) and carefully chosen formal tests. In short, assessments are as valuable as the appropriate choice and use thereof.

Demonstrating Knowledge of Alternative Assessments (e.g., authentic assessment, portfolio assessment)

Test taking is not a pleasant experience for many students with behavioral and/or learning problems. They may lack study skills, experience anxiety before or during a test, or have problems understanding and differentiating the task requirements for different tests.

The skills necessary to be successful vary with type of test. Certain students have difficulty with writing answers, but may be able to express their knowledge of subject matter verbally. Therefore, modifications of content area material may be extended to methods and modifications for evaluation and assessment of student progress.

Information about the student's achievement is gathered in a variety of ways, including assessments (such as intelligence tests and various achievement tests). In addition to those assessments, other information is gathered through alternate assessments, including observations, performance-based assessments, portfolios, and interviews.

Observations
Observations are the recording of information about the student as the behavior occurs.

SPECIAL EDU. CROSS-CATEGORY

Performance-Based Assessments

Performance assessment is a form of testing that requires students to perform a task rather than select an answer from a ready-made list. The teacher then judges the quality of the student's work based on a predetermined set of criteria.

Portfolios

Portfolios are selected collections of a variety of the students' work. They include work samples that are demonstrative of the students' strengths and weaknesses.

Interviews

Formal or informal interviews are often conducted of persons who have a close relationship to the student and can offer valuable information about the student's progress socially and academically.

Demonstrating Familiarity with Strategies for Collaboration with Families and Other Professionals in the Assessment Process

The assessment process is an essential part of developing an individualized program for students. The needs of the whole child must be considered in order to address all of his or her needs. Therefore, information should be gathered by using various sources of information.

Besides the general education teacher, a vital person or persons in the assessment process should be the parent. The parent can provide needed background information on the child, such as a brief medical, physical, and developmental history. Paraprofessionals, doctors, and other professionals are also very helpful in providing necessary information about the child.

Ways of gathering information:

Interview: Interviews can be in person or on paper. The related parties can be invited to a meeting to conduct the interview; if the parent does not respond after several attempts, the paper interview may be sent or mailed home.

Questionnaires: Questionnaires are also a good way of gathering information. Some questionnaires may include open-ended questions, and some may contain several questions to be answered using a rating scale. In this form, the answerer circles ratings ranging from 1 to 5 or 1 to 7 (from Strongly Disagree to Strongly Agree).

Conference/ Meeting: With parents' permission, it may be useful to conduct a meeting, one-on-one or in a group setting, to gather information about the child. Everyone involved with the child who may be able to offer information about the child's academic progress, physical development, social skills, behavior, medical history, and/or needs should be invited to attend.

COMPETENCY 11.0 UNDERSTAND ASSESSMENT PROCEDURES OF THE MULTIDISCIPLINARY EVALUATION TEAM FOR EVALUATING INDIVIDUAL DIFFERENCES AND MAKING PLACEMENT AND PROGRAMMING DECISIONS FOR STUDENTS WITH DISABILITIES

For example: roles and functions of members of the multidisciplinary evaluation team; components of a full and individual evaluation used to determine eligibility for and placement within special education and related services; ethical practices and legal provisions regarding unbiased assessment; procedural requirements for conducting an evaluation; interpretation and use of assessment data to plan a student's educational program and placement; awareness of students' behavior, communication, and assistive technology needs; the impact of cultural diversity and linguistic differences on evaluation and placement decisions in special education; and appropriate application and interpretation of scores.

Demonstrating an Understanding of Legal Provisions, Regulations, Guidelines, and Ethical Concerns Related to Assessment, Including Preserving Confidentiality

If instructional modifications in the regular classroom have not proven successful, a student may be referred for multidisciplinary evaluation. The evaluation is comprehensive and includes norm and criterion-referenced tests (e.g., IQ and diagnostic tests), curriculum-based assessment, systematic teacher observation (e.g., behavior frequency checklist), samples of student work, and parent interviews. The results of the evaluation are twofold: to determine eligibility for special education services and to identify a student's strengths and weaknesses in order to plan an individual education program.

The wording in federal law is very explicit about the manner in which evaluations must be conducted and about the existence of due process procedures that protect against bias and discrimination. Provisions in the law include the following:

1. The testing of children in their native or primary language unless it is clearly not feasible to do so
2. The use of evaluation procedures selected and administered to prevent cultural or ethnic discrimination
3. The use of assessment tools validated for the purpose for which they are being used (e.g., achievement levels, IQ scores, adaptive skills)
4. Assessment by a multidisciplinary team utilizing several pieces of information to formulate a placement decision

Furthermore, parental involvement must occur in the development of the child's educational program. According to the law, parents must:

1. Be notified before initial evaluation or any change in placement by a written notice in their primary language, which will describe the proposed school action, the reasons for it, and the available educational opportunities

2. Consent, in writing, before the child is initially evaluated

Parents may:

1. Request an independent educational evaluation if they feel the school's evaluation is inappropriate

2. Request an evaluation at public expense if a due process hearing decision is that the public agency's evaluation was inappropriate

3. Participate on the committee that considers the evaluation, placement, and programming of the student

All students referred for evaluation for special education should have the results of a relatively current vision and hearing screening on file. This will determine the adequacy of sensory acuity and ensure that learning problems are not due to a vision and/or hearing problem.

All portions of the special education process—from assessment to placement—are strictly confidential to parties outside of those who directly service the student. Under no circumstances should information be shared with those other than parents/guardians and those providing related services without the consent of the parent/guardian.

Understanding the Implications of Limited English Proficiency in the Assessment of Students with Disabilities

The No Child Left Behind legislation includes students with limited English proficiency, as well as students with disabilities in the accountability system. It judges them by the same standard used for all other students. In the past, students with limited English proficiency (LEP) were often excluded from high-stake, large-scale assessments because educators believed it was not in the best interest of these students to take the tests. Students who have LEP and a disability have an even greater chance of their educational needs not being met. In many cases educators will have to assess whether their problem in the classroom can be attributed to their language difficulties, to their disability, or to a combination of both.

SPECIAL EDU. CROSS-CATEGORY 103

The NCLB legislation was designed to make sure that students in subgroups with low percentages of students meeting standards receive attention in schools. Educators are concerned that excluding students from testing may be detrimental to students, because it allows their needs to remain unknown. Students who are not tested may not get the services they need to improve their academic achievement. Many educational researchers now believe that LEP students and students with disabilities should be included in the assessments, when practical, to ensure that the needs of these students are not ignored.

The policies for LEP students and students with disabilities under the No Child Left Behind legislation was changed in February 2004. One change was that schools were no longer required to give students with limited English proficiency their state's reading test if the students were enrolled in a U.S. school for less than a year. Schools are still required to give those students the state's math test, but they may substitute an English-proficiency test for the reading test during the first year of enrollment.

As was the case before this change, states have a one-year grace period before they must include the scores of students with limited English proficiency in the calculations for adequate yearly progress. The second rule change permits states to count students who have become proficient in English within the past two years in their calculations of adequate yearly progress.

Interpreting and Applying Formal and Informal Assessment Data (e.g., standard scores, percentile ranks, stanines, grade equivalent scores, age equivalent scores, environmental inventories, rubrics) to Develop an Individualized Instructional Program

Knowing how to interpret and apply formal and informal assessment data is very important in the development of IEPs. An individualized educational instructional program is designed around the child's strengths and weaknesses. An educator must know how to interpret formal and informal assessment data to assist him or her in determining some of those strengths and weaknesses.

Results of formal assessments are given in derived scores, which compare the student's raw score to the performance of a specified group of subjects. Criteria for the selection of the group may be based on characteristics such as age, sex, or geographic area. The test results of formal assessments must always be interpreted in light of what type of tasks the individual was required to perform. The most commonly used derived scores follow.

TEACHER CERTIFICATION STUDY GUIDE

Age and Grade Equivalents
These scores are considered developmental scores because they attempt to convert the student's raw score into an average performance of a particular age or grade group.

- **Age equivalents** are expressed in years and months (e.g., 7-3). In the standardization procedure, a mean is calculated for all individuals of the particular age who took the test. If the mean or median number of correct responses for children 7 years and 3 months was 80, then an individual whose raw score was 80 would be assigned an age-equivalent of 7 years and 3 months.

- **Grade equivalents** are written as years and tenths of years (e.g., 6.2 would read sixth grade, second month). Grade equivalents are calculated on the average performance of the group, and have been criticized for their use to measure gains in academic achievement and to identify exceptional students.

- **Quartiles, deciles, and percentiles** indicate the percentage of scores that fall below the individual's raw score. Quartiles divide the score into four equal parts; the first quartile is the point at which 25 percent of the scores fall below the full score. Deciles divide the distribution into 10 equal parts; the seventh decile would mark the point below which 70 percent of the scores fall. Percentiles are the most frequently used. A percentile rank of 45 would indicate that the person's raw score was at the point below which 45 percent of the other scores fell.

Standard Scores
These are raw scores with the same mean (average) and standard deviation (variability of asset of scores). In the standardization of a test, about 68 percent of the scores fall above or below one standard deviation of the mean of 100. About 96 percent of the scores fall within the range of two standard deviations above or below the mean. A standard deviation of 20, for example, means that 68 percent of the scores fall between 80 and 120, with 100 as the mean. The most common are T-scores, Z-scores, stanines, and scaled scores. Standard scores are useful because they allow for direct comparison of raw scores from different individuals. In interpreting scores, it is important to note what type of standard score is being used.

Criterion-Referenced Tests and Curriculum-Based Assessments
These are interpreted on the basis of the individual's performance on the objectives being measured. Such assessments may be commercially prepared or teacher-made, and can be designed for a particular curriculum or a scope and sequence. These assessments are made by selecting objectives, task analyzing those objectives, and selecting measures to test the skills necessary to meet those tasks.

Results for these tests are calculated for each objective. For example, an educator might find that Cindy was able to divide 2-digit numbers by 1-digit numbers 85 percent of the time and was able to divide 2-digit numbers by 2-digit numbers 45 percent of the time. These tests are useful for gaining insight into the types of error patterns the student makes. Because the student's performance is not compared to others in a group, results are useful for writing IEPs as well as deciding what to teach.

Ability to Interpret Test Results into Layman's Terms

The special educator must be able to communicate assessment results in an understandable language for a variety of individuals. These individuals may include parents or guardians, paraprofessionals, professionals in general education or administration, and (in the case of older students) even the student.

A review of assessment and evaluation results may be done during an IEP meeting in which the formal test lingo is used but paired with an interpretation in layman's terms. Results may also be presented in the form of a written report.

Ability to Represent Test Results and Educational Implications in Written Format

Although the school psychologist often completes student evaluations and writes a report, this may be the task of the special educator when assessment is done in the classroom in preparation for the student's annual review. In this case, the special education teacher is asked to write a report summarizing assessment findings and educational implications. The teacher should be able to organize the data in a concise, readable format. Some components of such a report include:

- Identifying information (student name, age, date of birth, address, gender)
- Reason for assessment
- Test administration information (date, time, duration of test, response of student)
- Test results
- Summary of educational recommendations

Knowledge of the Level of Functioning of the Student's Typically Developing Peers

Standardized test results without comparison to what typically developing students of the same age are doing are of little value. IEP programming and implementation depend on the areas where the student shows significant delay. For example, a student may show progress in the area of reading and still be several grade levels behind his or her peers. In this case, goals and objectives for reading are warranted.

Oftentimes, students with disabilities show peaks and valleys in their abilities. A student may be progressing at a similar rate and at a similar level as his or her peers in language arts, but may have delays in math. Again, IEP goals and objectives in the area of delay (in this case math) are needed.

Sometimes, students demonstrate splinter skills. For example, a young deaf child may be able to rote count by tens to five hundred. This does not mean that that student has comparable math skills to those of a first grader. Knowledge of typical range and sequence of developmental skills is needed and should be communicated to those involved in IEP meetings.

Knowledge of the Various Program Options within the School District and Probable Appropriate Placement

An overall picture of the student with a disability (including his or her assessment results) and knowledge of the cascade of services provided must be communicated to the CSE team.

Options for placement of special education students are given on what is called a "cascade of services," the term coined by Deno (1970). The multidisciplinary team must be able to match the needs of the student with an appropriate placement in the cascade system of services.

Cascade System of Special Education Services

Level 1	Regular classroom, including students with disabilities able to learn with regular class accommodations, with or without medical and counseling services
Level 2	Regular classroom with supportive services (e.g., consultation, inclusion)
Level 3	Regular class with part-time special class (e.g., itinerant services, resource room)
Level 4	Full-time special class (e.g., self-contained)
Level 5	Special stations (e.g., special schools)
Level 6	Homebound
Level 7	Residential (e.g., hospital, institution)

Adapted from 1. Deno, "Special Education as Developmental Capital." Exceptional Children 1970, 37, 239, 237 Copyright 1970 by The Council for Exceptional Children Reprinted with permission from The Council for Exceptional Children.

Methods for Evaluating and Documenting Student Progress in Acquiring, Generalizing, and Maintaining Skills Related to Interpersonal Interactions and Participation in Activities Across Settings (e.g., school, home, community)

Special education teachers must be associated with the various methods of alternative assessments in order to properly evaluate the goals and objectives of their students. This is especially true for students who are not able to be assessed by standardized tests that utilize "paper and pencil methods."

Naturalistic Assessments
These (both informal and authentic) address the functional skills that enhance a person's independence and social interactions in a variety of settings (e.g., school, home, community, etc.). Functional skills best addressed by this method are vocational skills, including following directions, socially acceptable behavior, and measurable work ethics. Naturalistic assessments require planning for instruction to occur in various settings. The advantages of this method include creating a "real world setting" that still allows for culturally appropriate materials. The disadvantages of this method include the requirements for long-range planning and reduced efficiency in both teaching and assessing the skill that is to be measured.

Performance-Based Assessments
These use a form of evaluation that examines a skill necessary to complete a project. An example of this method is evaluating the math skill of "order of operations" by evaluating how an algebraic expression was solved. Another example is observing how the skill of buttoning a shirt is progressing when having a student complete the task of putting on a shirt.

Portfolio Assessments
These are a mode of evaluation that provides a good way to document the beginning, middle, and end of a student's yearly progress. This method utilizes compiling samples of work throughout a given period of time. Portfolio assessment is a tool often used to track academic growth/progress in writing within regular education classrooms. The portfolio assessment also provides the teacher with a way to explain a student's present levels to parents.

Dynamic Assessments

These are tailor-made evaluation tools that look at how a student learns as well as possible impediments to a student's successful completion of a goal. Dynamic assessments look first at what must be taught and how it is taught to the student. Next, possible impediments to the student's success in this goal are examined to provide insight as to his or her success/failure to meet a goal. When the impediments have been examined, it is possible to look at the goal and distinguish between performance and ability. For this reason, it is an ideal method to use when evaluating student progress that may have been inhibited by a cultural norm. Identifying impediments allows for the evaluator to assess if a different teaching strategy may be more effective for students to attain objectives and goals on their IEPs.

Recommended Reading: Alternative Approaches to Assessing Young Children by Angela Losardo, Ph.D., & Angela Notari-Syverson, Ph.D. © 2001 Paul H. Brookes Publishing Co.

TEACHER CERTIFICATION STUDY GUIDE

COMPETENCY 12.0 UNDERSTAND PROCEDURES AND CRITERIA FOR EVALUATING AND IDENTIFYING THE EDUCATIONAL STRENGTHS AND NEEDS OF STUDENTS WITH EMOTIONAL DISABILITIES

For example: principles and procedures for screening, assessing, evaluating, and diagnosing students with emotional disabilities.
- *For information about this skill, please refer to the Arizona Department of Education website at www.ade.state.az.us/*

COMPETENCY 13.0 UNDERSTAND PROCEDURES AND CRITERIA FOR EVALUATING AND IDENTIFYING THE EDUCATIONAL STRENGTHS AND NEEDS OF STUDENTS WITH SPECIFIC LEARNING DISABILITIES

For example: principles and procedures for screening, assessing, evaluating, and diagnosing students with specific learning disabilities.
- *For information about this skill, please refer to the Arizona Department of Education website at www.ade.state.az.us/*

COMPETENCY 14.0 UNDERSTAND PROCEDURES AND CRITERIA FOR EVALUATING AND IDENTIFYING THE EDUCATIONAL STRENGTHS AND NEEDS OF STUDENTS WITH MENTAL RETARDATION

For example: principles and procedures for screening, assessing, evaluating, and diagnosing students with mental retardation.
- *For information about this skill, please refer to the Arizona Department of Education website at www.ade.state.az.us/*

COMPETENCY 15.0 UNDERSTAND PROCEDURES AND CRITERIA FOR EVALUATING AND IDENTIFYING THE EDUCATIONAL STRENGTHS AND NEEDS OF STUDENTS WITH ORTHOPEDIC (PHYSICAL) OR OTHER HEALTH IMPAIRMENTS

For example: principles and procedures for screening, assessing, evaluating, and diagnosing the strengths and needs of students with orthopedic (physical) or other health impairments.
- *For information about this skill, please refer to the Arizona Department of Education website at www.ade.state.az.us/*

TEACHER CERTIFICATION STUDY GUIDE

COMPETENCY 16.0 UNDERSTAND THE USES OF ONGOING ASSESSMENT IN THE EDUCATION OF STUDENTS WITH SPECIAL NEEDS

For example: procedures for using and maintaining ongoing classroom assessment; methods for determining learning styles and strengths; application of assessment data to modify a student's educational program; and the interpretation of assessment data to evaluate students' academic progress, determine students' needs, revise IEPs, and modify programming.

Use Ongoing Assessment to Evaluate and Modify Instruction

Assessment skills should be an integral part of teacher training, where teachers are able to monitor student learning using pre- and post-assessments of content areas; analyze assessment data in terms of individualized support for students and instructional practice for teachers; and design lesson plans that have measurable outcomes and definitive learning standards. Assessment information should be used to provide performance-based criteria and academic expectations for all students in evaluating whether students have learned the expected skills and content of the subject area.

For example, in an Algebra I class, teachers can use assessments to determine whether students have learned the prior knowledge to engage in the subject area. If the teacher provides students with a pre-assessment on algebraic expression and ascertains that the lesson plan should be modified to include a pre-algebraic expression lesson refresher unit, the teacher can create quantifiable data. This data will support the need of additional resources to support student learning. Once the teacher has taught the unit on algebraic expression, a post assessment test can be used to test student learning, and a mastery exam can be used to test how well students understand and can apply the knowledge to the next unit of math content learning.

Teachers can use assessment data to inform and impact instructional practices by making inferences on teaching methods and gathering clues for student performance. By analyzing the various types of assessments, teachers can gather more definitive information on projected student academic performance. Instructional strategies for teachers provide learning targets for student behavior, cognitive thinking skills, and processing skills that can be employed to diversify student learning opportunities.

Learning styles refer to the ways in which individuals learn best. Physical settings, instructional arrangements, available materials, techniques, and individual preferences are all factors in the teacher's choice of instructional strategies and materials. Information about the student's preference can be done through a direct interview or by utilizing a Likert-style checklist where the student rates his or her preferences.

SPECIAL EDU. CROSS-CATEGORY 111

The assessment information gathered from various sources is key in identifying the strengths and the weaknesses of the student. Each test and each person has something to offer about the child; therefore, increasing the opportunity to create a well-developed plan is important to assist in the success of the student. The special education and general education teacher, along with other professionals, use the assessment data to make appropriate instructional decisions and to modify the learning environment so it is conducive to learning.

The information gathered can be used to make some of the following instructional decisions:

I **Classroom Organization:** The teacher can vary grouping arrangements (e.g., large group, small group, peer tutoring, or learning centers) and methods of instruction (e.g., teacher directed, student directed)

II **Classroom Management:** The teacher can vary grading systems, vary reinforcement systems, and vary the rules (differentiate for some students)

III **Methods of Presentation:**
   A. Content: amount to be learned, time to learn, and concept level
   B. General Structure: advance organizers, immediate feedback, memory devices, and active involvement of students.
   C. Type of Presentation: verbal or written, transparencies, audiovisual

IV **Methods of Practice:**
   A. General Structure: amount to be practiced; time to finish; group, individual, or teacher-directed; and varied level of difficulty
   B. Level of Response: copying, recognition, or recall with and without cues
   C. Types of Materials: worksheets, audiovisual, texts

V **Methods of Testing:**
   A. Type: verbal, written, or demonstration
   B. General Structure: time to complete, amount to complete, group or individual testing
   C. Level of Response: multiple choice, essay, recall of facts

TEACHER CERTIFICATION STUDY GUIDE

Instructional Decisions

Presentation of Subject Matter
Subject matter should be presented in a fashion that helps students <u>organize</u>, <u>understand</u>, and <u>remember</u> important information. Advance organizers and other instructional devices can help students to:

- Connect information to what is already known
- Make abstract ideas more concrete
- Gain interest in the material
- Organize the information and visualize the relationships.

Organizers can be visual aids (such as diagrams, tables, charts, and guides) or verbal cues that alert students to the nature and content of the lesson. Organizers may be used:

- **Before the lesson** to alert the student to the main point of the lesson, establish a rationale for learning, and activate background information
- **During the lesson** to help students organize information, keep focused on important points, and aid comprehension
- **At the close of the lesson** to summarize and remember important points

Examples of organizers include:

- Question- and graphic-oriented study guide
- Concept diagramming: students brainstorm a concept and organize information into three lists (always present, sometimes present, and never present)
- Semantic feature analysis: students construct a table with examples of the concept in one column and important features or characteristics in the other column
- Semantic webbing: the concept is placed in the middle of the chart or chalkboard, relevant information is placed around it, and lines are used to show the relationships
- Memory (mnemonic) devices such as diagrams, charts, and tables

Instructional modifications are typically tried in an attempt to accommodate the student in the regular classroom. Through them, effective instruction is geared toward individual needs and recognizes differences in how students learn. Modifications are tailored to individual student needs. Some strategies for modifying regular classroom instruction are shown in the table below. They are effective with at-risk students with disabilities as well as students without learning or behavior problems.

SPECIAL EDU. CROSS-CATEGORY 113

Strategies for Modifying Classroom Instruction

Strategy 1 Provide active learning experiences to teach concepts. Student motivation is increased when students can manipulate, weigh, measure, read, or write using materials and skills that relate to their daily lives.

Strategy 2 Provide ample opportunities for guided practice of new skills. Frequent feedback on performance is essential to overcome student feelings of inadequacy. Peer tutoring and cooperative projects provide non-threatening practice opportunities. Individual student conferences, curriculum-based tests, and small group discussions are three useful methods for checking progress.

Strategy 3 Provide multisensory learning experiences. Students with learning problems sometimes have sensory processing difficulties; for instance, an auditory discrimination problem may cause misunderstanding about teacher expectations. Lessons and directions that include visual, auditory, tactile, and kinesthetic modes are preferable to a single sensory approach.

Strategy 4 Present information in a manner that is relevant to the student. Particular attention to this strategy is needed when there is a cultural or economic gap between the lives of teachers and students. Relate instruction to a youngster's daily experience and interests.

Strategy 5 Provide students with concrete illustrations of their progress. Students with learning problems need frequent reinforcement for their efforts. Charts, graphs, and check sheets provide tangible markers of student achievement.

COMPETENCY 17.0 UNDERSTAND PROCEDURES FOR DEVELOPING AND IMPLEMENTING INDIVIDUALIZED EDUCATION PROGRAMS (IEPS) FOR STUDENTS WITH SPECIAL NEEDS

For example: roles and functions of IEP team members; factors and procedures in gathering information, creating and maintaining records, determining appropriate placements, and developing IEPs for students with special needs; components of an IEP; and evaluation of students' progress with respect to IEP goals.

Effective Strategies for Involving the Individual and Family in Setting Instructional Goals and Charting Progress

Involving the special education student (when appropriate) and his or her family in setting instructional goals is necessary to develop a well-rounded IEP. When families help set goals for things that are important to the special education student, subsequent increased family cooperation and involvement are usually evident. It is understood that the parents of any child will be closest to him or her, and the meshing of school goals and those of the family will provide a program that is most thorough in meeting the student's needs.

Progress on these mutually accepted goals (as well as those initiated by the school) can be charted or measured in a variety of ways. The method used to track the goals should be those indicated in the goals and objectives section of the IEP.

Charting is a formal tracking method of student behavior and progress. Often based on a functional behavioral assessment portion of the IEP, the chart includes behaviors (positive or negative), time covered, and frequency of the behavior, which is often shown with tally marks.

Anecdotal records are a journaling of behaviors observed in the home or classroom. Such records may be notes kept by the classroom teacher or therapist or notes from the parent (often literally in the form of paper notes, passbook entries, or emails) regarding student success and challenges.

Observations are a more focused form of anecdotal records, wherein a specific activity, class, or time period is observed and the behaviors and skills of the individual student are recorded. Oftentimes, a comparison of student behavior in various settings gives information needed to write appropriate IEP goals.

Rating scales are frequently used to assess a student's behavior or level of functioning in a particular environment (e.g., home, classroom, or playground). These scales are often given to more than one person (e.g., parent, teacher, and therapist) to complete, so that a more comprehensive picture of the student is obtained.

Commonly used rating scales with a component for professionals and parents include the Conners' Rating Scale, the Vineland Adaptive Behavior Scale, and the Child Development Inventory.

Informal tests are ways of tracking a student's behaviors through the use of classroom tests and assignments in various subject areas.

Formal tests may include standardized tests that are administered to all students at the local and state levels, alternative assessment as indicated on the child's IEP, and tests used by a psychologist or therapist to assess skills and deficiencies. Formal testing results give measurable data, which can be used in school-parent discussions for planning IEP goals and objectives.

At present, the following elements are required of an IEP:

1. The student's present level of academic performance and functional performance, which is determined by various formal and informal assessments. Some assessments may include, but are not limited to, IQ tests, achievement tests, work samples, observations, interviews, etc.

2. A statement of how the disability affects the student's involvement and progress in the general education curriculum. Preschool children must have a statement explaining how the disability affects the child's participation in appropriate activities.

3. A statement of annual goals or anticipated attainments.

4. Short-term objectives are no longer required on every IEP. Students with severe disabilities or those taking an alternate assessment may need short-term objectives, which lead to the obtainment of annual goals.

5. A statement of when the parents will be notified of their child's progress, which must be at least as often as the regular education student.

6. Modifications or accommodations for participation in state-wide or city-wide assessments; or, if it is determined that the child cannot participate, why the assessment is inappropriate for the child and how the child will be assessed.

7. Specific educational services, assistive technology, and related services to be provided, as well as those who will provide them.

8. Evaluative criteria and timelines for determining whether instructional objectives have been achieved.

9. Projected dates for initiating services with their anticipated frequency, location, and duration.

10. The extent to which the child will not participate in the regular education program.

11. Transition plan:

    a) Beginning when a student is 14, and annually thereafter, the student's IEP must contain a statement of his or her transition service needs under the various components of the IEP that focus on the student's courses of study (e.g., vocational education or advanced placement); and, when appropriate, interagency responsibilities and links for possible future assistance.

    b) Beginning at least one year before the student reaches the age of majority under state law, the IEP must contain a statement that the student has been informed of the rights under the law that will transfer to him or her upon reaching the age of majority.

Role and Responsibilities of IEP Team Members

School Psychologist
The school psychologist participates in the referral, identification, and program planning processes. He or she contributes to the multidisciplinary team by adding important observations, data, and inferences about the student's performance. As the psychologist conducts an evaluation, he or she observes the student in the classroom environment, takes a case history, and administers a battery of formal and informal individual tests. The psychologist is involved as a member of a professional team throughout the stages of referral, assessment, placement, and program planning.

Physical Therapist
This person works with disorders of bones, joints, muscles, and nerves following medical assessment. Under the prescription of a physician, the therapist applies treatment to the students in the form of heat, light, massage, and exercise to prevent further disability or deformity. Physical therapy includes the use of adaptive equipment and prosthetic and orthotic devices to facilitate independent movement. This type of therapy helps individuals with disabilities to develop or recover their physical strength and endurance.

Occupational Therapist
This specialist is trained in helping students develop self-help skills (e.g., self-care, motor, perceptual, and vocational skills). The students are actively involved in the treatment process to quicken recovery and rehabilitation.

Speech and Language Pathologist
This specialist assists in the identification and diagnosis of children with speech or language disorders. In addition, he or she makes referrals for medical or habilitation needs, counsels family members and teachers, and works with the prevention of communicative disorders. The speech and language therapist concentrates on rehabilitative service delivery and continuing diagnosis.

Administrators
Building principals and special education directors (or coordinators) provide logistical as well as emotional support. Principals implement building policy procedures and control designation of facilities, equipment, and materials. Their support is crucial to the success of the program within the parameters of the base school. Special education directors provide information about federal, state, and local policy, which is vital to the operation of a special education unit. In some districts, the special education director may actually control certain services and materials. Role clarification, preferably in writing, should be accomplished to ensure effectiveness of program services.

Guidance Counselors, Psychometrists, and Diagnosticians
These persons often lead individual and group counseling sessions. They are trained in assessment, diagnostic, and observation skills, as well as personality development and functioning abilities. They can apply knowledge and skills to multidisciplinary teams and assist in the assessment, diagnosis, placement, and program planning process.

Social Worker
The social worker is trained in interviewing and counseling skills. This person possesses knowledge of available community and school services, and makes these known to parents. He or she often visits homes of students, conducts intake and assessment interviews, counsels individuals and small groups, and assists in district enforcement policies.

School Nurse

This person offers valuable information about diagnostic and treatment services. He or she is knowledgeable about diets, medications, therapeutic services, health-related services, and care needed for specific medical conditions. Reports of communicable diseases are filed with the health department, to which a health professional has access. A medical professional can sometimes obtain cooperation with the families of children with disabilities in ways that are difficult for the special education teacher.

Regular Teachers and Subject Matter Specialists

These professionals are trained in general and specific instructional areas, teaching techniques, and overall child growth and development. They serve as a vital component in the referral process, as well as the subsequent treatment program if the student is determined eligible. They work with the students with special needs for the majority of the school day and function as a link to the children's special education and medical programs.

Paraprofessional

This staff member assists the special educator and often works in the classroom with the special needs students. He or she helps prepare specialized materials, tutor individual students, lead small groups, and provide feedback to students about their work.

Procedures for Safeguarding Confidentiality with Regard to Students with Disabilities (e.g., by maintaining the confidentiality of electronic correspondence and records, ensuring the confidentiality of conversations) and Recognition of the Importance of Respecting Students' Privacy

One of the most important professional practices a teacher must maintain is student confidentiality. This extends far beyond paper records and goes into the realm of oral discussions. Teachers are expected not to mention the names of students (and often the specifics of their characters) in conversations with those who are not directly involved with them, inside and outside of school.

In the school environment, teacher recordkeeping comes in three main formats with specific confidentiality rules. All of the records stated below should be kept in a locked place within the classroom or an office within the school:

1) *Teacher's personal notes on a student*
   When a teacher takes notes on a student's actions (including behaviors and/or grade performance) that are not intended to be placed in a school recorded format, such as a report card, the teacher may keep this information private and confidential to his or her own files. Teachers may elect to share this information or not.

2) *Teacher daily recorded grades and attendance of the student*
Teacher's grade books and attendance records are to be open to the parent/guardian of that child. Only that child's information may be shared—not that of others.

3) *Teacher- recorded notations on records that appear in the student cumulative file*
There are specific rules regarding the sharing of the cumulative records of students.

   a) Cumulative files will follow a student who transfers from school to school within the district.
   b) All information placed in a cumulative file may be examined by a parent at any time it is requested. If a parent shows up to review his or her child's cumulative file, the file should be shown as it is in its current state (this includes IEPs).
   c) When information from a cumulative file is requested by a person/entity other than the parent/guardian, the information may not be released without the express written consent of the parent/guardian. The parental consent must specify which records may be shared with the other interested party.

A school in which a student may intend to enroll can receive the student's educational record without parental consent. However, the school sending that information must make a reasonable attempt to notify the parent/guardian of the request (FERPA).

In today's digital environment, teachers often communicate via e-mail and keep records in digital formats. Teachers should keep in mind that e-mail and other electronic formats can be forwarded and are as "indelible" as permanent ink. They should maintain a professional decorum just as when they are writing their own records that will be seen outside of their personal notations.

TEACHER CERTIFICATION STUDY GUIDE

DOMAIN III.   **PROMOTING STUDENT DEVELOPMENT AND LEARNING**

COMPETENCY 18.0   **UNDERSTAND HOW TO ESTABLISH A POSITIVE AND PRODUCTIVE LEARNING ENVIRONMENT FOR ALL STUDENTS**

For example: ways that disabilities may affect students' progress in the general education curriculum; factors in the learning environment that affect students' self-esteem and attitudes toward learning; strategies for modifying learning environments to address diverse student needs; and individual and group management strategies and intervention techniques for achieving instructional management goals (e.g., maintaining standards of behavior, maximizing time spent in learning).

Physical Environment (Spatial Arrangements)

The physical setting of the classroom contributes a great deal to the propensity for students to learn. An adequate, well-built, and well-equipped classroom invites students to learn. This has been called "invitational learning." Among the important factors to consider in the physical setting of the classroom:

    a)   Adequate physical space
    b)   Repair status
    c)   Lighting adequacy
    d)   Adequate entry/exit access (including handicap accessibility)
    e)   Ventilation/climate control
    f)   Coloration

A classroom must have adequate physical space so students can conduct themselves comfortably. Some students are distracted by windows, pencil sharpeners, doors, etc. Some students prefer the front, middle, or back rows.

The teacher has the responsibility to report any items of classroom disrepair to maintenance staff. Broken windows, falling plaster, exposed sharp surfaces, leaks in ceiling or walls, and other items of disrepair present hazards to students.

Another factor that must be considered is adequate lighting. Report any inadequacies in classroom illumination. Florescent lights placed at acute angles often burn out faster. A healthy supply of spare tubes is a sound investment.

Local fire and safety codes dictate entry and exit standards. In addition, all corridors and classrooms should be wheelchair accessible for students and others who use them. Older schools may not have this accessibility.

SPECIAL EDU. CROSS-CATEGORY

Another consideration is adequate ventilation and climate control. Some classrooms use air conditioning extensively, which can make the rooms so cold as to be considered a distraction. Specialty classes (such as science) require specialized hoods for ventilation. Physical education classes have the added responsibility for shower areas and specialized environments that must be heated (such as pools).

Classrooms with warmer, subdued colors contribute to students' concentration on task items. Neutral hues for coloration of walls, ceiling, and carpet or tile are generally used in classrooms, so that distraction due to classroom coloration may be minimized.

In the modern classroom, there is a great deal of furniture, equipment, supplies, appliances, and learning aids to help the teacher teach and students learn. The classroom should be provided with furnishings that fit the purpose of the classroom. For example, the kindergarten classroom may have a reading center, a playhouse, a puzzle table, student work desks/tables, a sandbox, and any other relevant learning/interest areas.

Whatever the arrangement of furniture and equipment may be, the teacher must provide for adequate traffic flow. Rows of desks must have adequate space between them for students to move and for the teacher to circulate. All areas must be open to line-of-sight supervision by the teacher.

In all cases, proper care must be taken to ensure student safety. Furniture and equipment should be situated safely at all times. No equipment, materials, or boxes should be placed where there is danger of falling over. Doors must have entry and exit accessibility at all times.

Noise levels should also be considered as part of the physical environment. Students vary in the degree of quiet that they need and the amount of background noise or talking that they can tolerate without getting distracted or frustrated. Therefore, a teacher must maintain an environment that is conducive to the learning of each child.

Major emergency responses include two categories for student movement: tornado warning response and building evacuation; which includes most other emergencies (fire, bomb threat, etc.). For tornadoes, the prescribed response is to evacuate all students and personnel to the first floor of multi-story buildings, and to place students along walls away from windows. All persons, including the teacher, should then crouch on the floor and cover their heads with their hands. These are standard procedures for severe weather.

Most other emergency situations require evacuation of the school building. Teachers should be thoroughly familiar with evacuation routes established for each classroom in which they teach. Teachers should accompany and supervise students throughout the evacuation procedure, and check to see that all students under their supervision are accounted for. Teachers should then continue to supervise students until the building may be reoccupied (upon proper school or community authority), or until other procedures are followed for students to officially leave the school area and cease to be the supervisory responsibility of the school. Elementary students evacuated to another school can wear nametags, and parents or guardians should sign them out at a central location.

Scheduling and Grouping Considerations

Instructional Arrangements
Some students work well in large groups; others prefer small groups or one-to-one instruction with the teacher, aide, or volunteer. Instructional arrangements also involve peer-tutoring situations with the student as tutor or tutee. The teacher also needs to consider how well the student works independently with seatwork.

Five basic types of grouping arrangements are typically used in the classroom.

1. Large Group with Teacher
Examples of appropriate activities include show and tell, discussions, watching plays or movies, brainstorming ideas, and playing games. Science, social studies, and most other subjects (with the exception of reading and math) are taught in large groups.

The advantage of large-group instruction is that it is time-efficient and prepares students for higher levels of secondary and post-secondary education settings. However, with large groups, instruction cannot be as easily tailored to high or low levels of students, who may become bored or frustrated. Mercer and Mercer recommend guidelines for effective large-group instruction:

- Keep instruction short, ranging from 5 to 15 minutes for first grade to seventh grade; and 5 to 40 minutes for eighth to 12th grade..
- Use questions to involve all students, use lecture-pause routines, and encourage active participation among the lower-performing students.
- Incorporate visual aids to promote understanding and maintain a lively pace.
- Break up the presentation by using different rates of speaking, giving students a "stretch" break", varying voice volume, etc.
- Establish rules of conduct for large groups and praise students who follow the rules.

2. Small Group Instruction

Small group instruction usually includes five to seven students, and is recommended for teaching basic academic skills such as math facts or reading. This model is especially effective for students with learning problems. Composition of the groups should be flexible to accommodate different rates of progress through instruction. The advantages of teaching in small groups is that the teacher is better able to provide feedback, monitor student progress, and give more instruction, praise, and feedback. With small groups, the teacher will need to make sure to provide a steady pace for the lesson, provide questions and activities that allow all to participate, and include plenty of positive praise.

3. One Student with Teacher

One-to-one tutorial teaching can be used to provide extra assistance to individual students. Such tutoring may be scheduled at set times during the day or provided as the need arises. The tutoring model is typically found more in elementary and resource classrooms than secondary settings.

4. Peer Tutoring

In an effective peer tutoring arrangement, the teacher trains the peer tutors and matches them with students who need extra practice and assistance. In addition to academic skills, the arrangement can help both students work on social skills such as cooperation and self-esteem. Both students may be working on the same material, or the tutee may be working to strengthen areas of weakness. The teacher determines the target goals, selects the material, sets up the guidelines, trains the student tutors in the rules and methods of the sessions, and monitors and evaluates the sessions.

5. Cooperative Learning

Cooperative learning differs from peer tutoring in that students are grouped in teams or small groups. The methods are based on teamwork, individual accountability, and team reward. Individual students are responsible for their own learning and share of the work, as well as the group's success. As with peer tutoring, the goals, target skills, materials, and guidelines are developed by the teacher. Teamwork skills may need to be taught, as well. By focusing on team goals, all members of the team are encouraged to help each other and improve their individual performances.

Curriculum Design

Effective curriculum design assists in a wide range of activities, from teacher demonstration to independent practice. Components of curriculum design include:

- Quizzes or reviews of the previous lesson
- Step-by-step presentations with multiple examples
- Guided practice and feedback
- Independent practice that requires the student to produce faster responses

The chosen curriculum should introduce information in a cumulative sequence and not introduce too much new information at a time. Teachers should review difficult material and practice to aid retention. New vocabulary and symbols should be introduced one at a time, and the relationships of components to the whole should be stressed. Students' background information should be recalled to connect new information to the old. In addition, it is recommended to teach strategies or algorithms first and then move on to tasks that are more difficult.

Course objectives may be obtained from the department head at the local school. The ESE coordinator may have copies of objectives for functional courses or applied ESE courses. District program specialists also have lists of objectives for each course provided in the local school system. Additionally, publishers of textbooks have scope and sequence lists in the teacher's manual.

Modification of Materials

Modifying materials is a great accommodation to use in order to include students in the general education classroom. Materials, usually textbooks, are often modified because of reading level. The goal of modification is to present the material in manner that the student can understand while preserving the basic ideas and content. Modifications of course material may take the form of:

Simplifying Texts
a) Use a highlighter to mark key terms, main ideas, and concepts. In some cases, a marker may be used to delete nonessential content.
b) Cut and paste. The main ideas and specific content are cut and pasted on separate sheets of paper. Additional headings or other graphic aids can be inserted to help the student understand and organize material.
c) Supplement with graphic aids or tables.
d) Supplement with study guides, questions, and directed preview.
e) Use self-correcting materials.
f) Allow additional time or break content material into smaller, more manageable units.

Taped Textbooks
Textbooks can be taped by the teacher or aide for students to follow along. In some cases, the students may qualify for recordings of textbooks from agencies such as Recordings for the Blind.

Parallel Curriculum
Projects such as Parallel Alternative Curriculum (PAC) or Parallel Alternative Strategies for Students (PASS), which present the content at a lower grade reading level, come with tests, study guides, vocabulary activities, and tests.

Supplementary Texts
Book publishers such as Steck-Vaughn publish series of content-area texts that have been modified for reading level, amount of content presented on pages, highlighted key items, and visual aids.

Variance of Material Format
Students with disabilities often experience insufficient access to and a lack of success in the general education curriculum. To promote improved access to the general curriculum for all learners, information should be presented in various formats using a variety of media forms; students should be given numerous methods to express and demonstrate what they have learned, and they should be provided with multiple entry points to engage their interest and motivate their learning.

Printed reading materials can be challenging to individuals with disabilities. Technology can help alleviate some of these difficulties by providing a change from printed text to electronic text that can be modified, enhanced, programmed, linked, and searched.

Text styles and font sizes can be changed as required by readers with visual disabilities. Text can be read aloud with computer-based text-to-speech translators and combined with illustrations, videos, and audio. Electronic text provides alternative formats for reading materials that can be tailored to match learner needs. It can also be structured in ways that enhance the learning process and expand both physical and cognitive access.

Addressing Students' Needs in Curricula Planning

There are a number of procedures teachers can use to address the varying needs of their students. Here are some of the more common procedures:

Vary Assignments
A variety of assignments on the same content allows students to match learning styles and preferences with the assignment. If all assignments are writing assignments, for example, students who are hands-on or visual learners are at a disadvantage unrelated to the content base itself.

Cooperative Learning
Cooperative learning activities allow students to share ideas, expertise, and insight within a non-threatening setting. The focus tends to remain on positive learning rather than competition.

Structure Environment
Some students need and benefit from clear structure that defines the expectations and goals of the teacher. The student knows what is expected and can work and plan accordingly.

Clearly Stated Assignments
Assignments should be clearly stated along with the expectation and criteria for completion. Reinforcement and practice activities should not be a guessing game for the students. The exception to this is, of course, those situations in which a discovery method is used.

Independent Practice
Independent practice involving application and repetition is necessary for thorough learning. Students become independent learners by practicing independent learning. These activities should always be within the student's abilities to perform successfully without assistance.

Repetition
Very little learning is successful with a single exposure. Learners generally require multiple exposures to the same information for learning to take place. However, this repetition does not have to be dull and monotonous. As stated above, varied assignments can provide repetition of content or skill practice without repetition of specific activities. This helps keep learning fresh and exciting for the student.

Overlearning
As a principle of effective learning, overlearning recommends that students continue to study and review after they have achieved initial mastery. The use of repetition in the context of varied assignments offers the means to help students pursue and achieve overlearning.

Differentiated Instruction

The effective teacher will seek to connect all students to the subject matter through multiple techniques, with the goal that all students, through their own abilities, will relate to one or more techniques and excel in the learning process. Differentiated instruction encompasses several areas:

Content: What is the teacher going to teach? Or, perhaps better put, what does the teacher want the students to learn? Differentiating content means that students will have access to content that piques their interest about a topic, with a complexity that provides an appropriate challenge to their intellectual development.

Process: This is a classroom management technique wherein instructional organization and delivery is maximized for the diverse student group. These techniques should include dynamic, flexible grouping activities, where instruction and learning occurs both as whole-class, teacher-led activities, as well peer learning and teaching (while teacher observes and coaches) within small groups or pairs.

Product: The product is the expectations and requirements placed on students to demonstrate their knowledge or understanding. The type of product expected from each student should reflect each student's own capabilities.

Specific Learning Strategies and Study Skills

Preview

Previewing material before a lesson is presented is helpful for the student with emotional disturbances (as with all students). Previewing a lesson might include examining pictures and captions, graphs and charts, headings, bold-faced words, and key points or questions included by the author.

The purpose of previewing material is to get the mind thinking about the topic ahead of time. When the student goes into the lesson, he or she is not introduced to the information for the first time.

In general, previewing of material takes only a few minutes. The special educator, however, will need to model this skill and give students guided practice at first. Such a lesson may be a full class period's instruction and may need to be repeated or reviewed throughout the course of the year.

Consideration of Previous Knowledge

As the student previews the lesson, he or she will automatically think of things that he already knows about the topic. This is considered the student's previous knowledge. Because concepts are presented in a spiral fashion over the course of a student's education, and because students do not live in a bubble (especially given the information sources of television and the internet), it is almost certain that the student will have some previous knowledge on the topic.

Questions

As the student previews the material and considers what he or she already knows, the student will most likely have questions about the topic. These can be written for later use in the actual lesson. Again, this preview technique creates a student mindset before the actual lesson begins.

Use of Peer Note Taker

Oftentimes, the student with emotional disturbance may find attending during a lesson to be challenging. Taking notes, in addition to listening and answering questions, may be overwhelming. Enlisting another student to take notes is an effective strategy to assist an emotionally disturbed student in maintaining self-control and success in the classroom.

Peer note takers may use a pressure sensitive paper that will automatically make a copy, or they may simply write the notes on regular paper to be photocopied later.

When choosing a note taker, consideration should be given to neatness of handwriting and clarity of information that is written. The best students in the class are not necessarily the best note takers. Indeed, those students may take minimal notes.

Use of Audio Books

Some students with emotional disturbances who also have a learning disability may qualify for audio books. Audio books are available from a number of government sources as well as commercial companies.

Audio books provide a stress-free way to "read" the material. They can be used as a motivator for emotionally disturbed students who may already struggle with academics. Once the student has been instructed on how to follow the text while listening to the tape (operating the equipment), this can be another way to foster student independence in study strategies.

Division of Study Time

Emotionally disturbed students are often impulsive. Their use of study time is often poorly planned or nonexistent. In addition, emotionally disturbed students do not always plan to study until there is an imminent test or project (and possibly not even then). These students may believe that "to study" means to take everything home every evening.

These students benefit from instruction in prioritizing their work and spreading out test practice (such as practicing spelling words nightly or dividing test information into sections) and larger assignments over a number of nights.

Review

1) *Review of the Day's Lesson*

    This is similar to the preview technique, except that the student has now heard the lesson. When the student reviews, he or she will be focusing on the information for the third time (preview, lesson, and review). It is helpful during the review to answer the questions that are included at the end of the lesson text.

2) *Study Cards*

    Many students find study cards to be an effective way to review material. Each card should contain a single question on one side and answer on the other, or they may have a vocabulary word on one side and a definition on the other. As the student masters certain cards, they can be placed in separate pile for less frequent review. The unfamiliar material can then be reviewed more frequently.

3) *Textbook Chapter Reviews*

    Most textbooks have review questions at the end of each lesson and/or chapter. Some books also have a practice test section that can serve as a valuable study aid.

Accommodations in Test-Taking Situations

Test taking is not a pleasant experience for many students with behavioral and/or learning problems. They may lack study skills, may experience anxiety before or during a test, and may have problems understanding and differentiating the task requirements for different tests. The skills necessary to be successful vary with type of test. Certain students have difficulty with writing answers, but may be able to express their knowledge of subject matter verbally. Therefore, modifications of content area material may be extended to methods and modifications for evaluation and assessment of student progress.

Some of the ways that teachers can modify assessment for individual needs include:

- Help students to get used to timed tests with timed practice tests
- Provide study guides before tests
- Make tests easier to read by leaving ample space between the questions
- Modify multiple choice tests by reducing the number of choices, reforming questions to yes-no, or using matching items
- Modify short-answer tests with cloze (fill-in) statements, or provide a list of facts or choices from which the student can choose
- Essay tests can be modified by using partial outlines for the student to complete, allowing additional time, or using test items that do not require extensive writing

Alternative Assessments

Alternative assessments are assessments wherein students create an answer or a response to a question or task, as opposed to traditional, inflexible assessments wherein students choose a prepared response from among a selection of responses (such as matching, multiple choice, or true/false).

When implemented effectively, an alternative assessment approach exhibits these characteristics, among others:

- Requires higher-order thinking and problem-solving
- Provides opportunities for student self-reflection and self-assessment
- Uses real world applications to connect students to the subject
- Provides opportunities for students to learn and examine subjects on their own, as well as to collaborate with their peers.
- Encourages students to continuing learning beyond the requirements of the assignment
- Clearly defines objective and performance goals

Effective teachers know the value of giving assignments that meet the individual abilities and needs of students. After instruction, discussion, questioning, and practice should be provided, rather than assigning one task to all students. Teachers must ask students to generate tasks that will show their knowledge of the information presented. Students should be given choices, thereby affording them the opportunity to demonstrate more effectively the skills, concepts, or topics that they have learned. In this way, student choice increases student originality, intrinsic motivation, and higher mental processes.

TEACHER CERTIFICATION STUDY GUIDE

COMPETENCY 19.0 UNDERSTAND APPROACHES AND TECHNIQUES USED TO IMPROVE STUDENTS' READING SKILLS

For example: types and characteristics of reading difficulties associated with various disabilities; principles of and methods for teaching prereading skills, phonological awareness, decoding, word recognition, reading comprehension, and print integration skills; various approaches to reading instruction (e.g., skills-based, whole-language, combined approaches); and promoting appreciation of reading.

Three Categories of the Reading Process

Most reading programs conceptually separate the reading process into three major categories: sight word vocabulary, word attack skills, and comprehension. These three areas constitute the basic questions that should be asked by a teacher when assessing a student's current level of functioning. The pertinent questions are:

1. How large is the student's sight word vocabulary?
2. What kinds of word attack skills does the student employ?
3. How well developed are the student's comprehension skills?

Sight words are printed words that are easily identified by the learner. The selection of words to be learned rely to some extent on the age and abilities of the student. Primary age students use word lists composed of high-frequency words like basal readers and the Dolch Word List.

Word attack skills are those techniques that enable a student to decode an unknown word so he or she can pronounce and understand it in the right context. Word attack skills are included in the areas of phonics, structural analysis, contextual and configuration clues, and decoding.

SPECIAL EDU. CROSS-CATEGORY 133

Comprehension skills are categorized into levels of difficulty. The teacher should consider the following factors when analyzing a student's reading comprehension level (Schloss & Sedlak, 1986):

1. The past experience of the reader
2. The content of the written passage
3. The syntax of the written passage
4. The vocabulary used in the written passage
5. The oral language comprehension of the student
6. The questions being asked to assess comprehension

Teachers must also consider the major categories of reading skills, basic reading skills within these categories, and strategies for the development of each skill..

Comprehension involves understanding what is read regardless of purpose or thinking skills employed. Comprehension can be delineated into categories of differentiated skills. Benjamin Bloom's taxonomy includes knowledge, comprehension, application, analysis, synthesis, and evaluation. Thomas Barrett suggests that comprehension categories be classified as literal meaning, reorganization, inference, evaluation, and appreciation.

Strategies that might prove beneficial in strengthening a student's comprehension are:

1. Asking questions of the student before he or she reads a passage. This type of directed reading activity assists the student in focusing attention on the information in the text that will help to answer the questions.
2. Using teacher questions to assist the student in developing self-questioning skills covering all levels of comprehension.

Silent reading refers to the inaudible reading of words or passages. Since the act of reading is done on a covert basis, the accuracy of the reading process can only be inferred through questions or activities required of the student following his or her reading. What may be observed is attention given to the printed material, eye movements indicative of relative pace, and body language signifying frustration or ease of reading.

Strategies that might assist the child in reading silently are:

1. Preparing activities or questions pertaining to the printed passage. Vary the activities so that some are asking specific comprehension questions and other are geared toward creative expressions like art or written composition.
2. Allowing time for pleasurable reading.

Understand Evaluation, Selection, and Adaptation of Instructional Strategies, Materials, Resources, and Technologies to Individualize Instruction and Facilitate Student Achievement in Reading/Language Arts

A teacher's responsibility to students extends beyond the four walls of the school building. In addition to offering well-planned and articulately delivered lessons, the teacher must consider the effects of both body language and spoken language on students' learning. Further, today's educator must address the needs of diverse learners within a single classroom.

Teachers must attain materials necessary for the majority of the regular education students and some of the special needs children and, more and more frequently, of one individual student. The effective teacher knows that there are currently hundreds of adaptive materials that could be used to help these students increase achievement and develop skills.

Student-centered classrooms contain not only textbooks, workbooks, and literature materials but also rely heavily on a variety of audio-visual equipment and computers. There are tape recorders, language masters, filmstrip projectors, and CD players to help meet the learning styles of the students.

Although most school centers cannot supply all the materials that special needs students require, many districts have resource centers where teachers can check out special equipment. Most communities support agencies that offer assistance in providing the necessities of special needs individuals, including students. Teachers must know how to obtain a wide range of materials, including school supplies, medical care, clothing, food, adaptive computers and books (such as Braille), eye glasses, hearing aids, wheelchairs, counseling, and transportation.

A teacher's job would be relatively easy if simply instructing students in current curriculum objectives was his or her only responsibility. However, today's educator must also ensure that the students are able to come to school, are able to attend to the curriculum, have individual learning styles met, and are motivated to work to their fullest capacity.

In addition, the challenges of meeting the needs of all students in the classroom require that the teacher is a lifelong learner. Ongoing participation in professional staff development; attendance at local, state, and national conferences; and continuing education classes help teachers grow in many ways.

Most special needs students have an Individual Educational Plan or a 504 Plan. These documents clearly state the students' educational objectives and learning needs, as well as persons responsible for meeting these objectives. A well-written Individual Educational Plan contains evidence that the student is receiving resources from the school and the community to assist in meeting the physical, social, and academic needs of the student.

Understand Curriculum Scope and Sequence in Reading/Language Arts; General Strategies for Promoting Learning, Fostering Critical Thinking, and Problem Solving in Relation to Reading/Language Arts

Beginning Reading Approaches

Methods of teaching beginning reading skills may be divided into two major approaches: code emphasis and meaning emphasis. Both approaches have their supporters and their critics. Advocates of code emphasis instruction point out that reading fluency depends on accurate and automatic decoding skills, while advocates of meaning emphasis favor this approach for reading comprehension. Teachers may decide to blend aspects of both approaches to meet the individual needs of their students.

Bottom-Up or Code-Emphasis Approach
- Letter-sound regularity is stressed.
- Reading instruction begins with words that consist of letter or letter combinations that have the same sound in different words. Component letter-sound relationships are taught and mastered before introducing new words.

Examples: phonics, linguistic, modified alphabet, and programmed reading series such as the Merrill Linguistic Reading Program and DISTAR Reading

Top-Down or Meaning Emphasis Model
- Reading for meaning is emphasized from the first stages of instruction.
- Programs begin with words that appear frequently, which are assumed to be familiar and easy to learn. Words are identified by examining meaning and position in context; they are decoded by techniques such as context, pictures, initial letters, and word configurations. Thus, a letter may not necessarily have the same sound in different words throughout the passage.

Examples: whole language, language experience, and individualized reading programs.

Other approaches that follow beginning reading instruction are available to help teachers design reading programs. Choice of approach will depend on the student's strengths and weaknesses. No matter what approach or combination of approaches is used, the teacher should encourage independent reading and build activities into the reading program that stimulate students to practice their skills through independent reading.

TEACHER CERTIFICATION STUDY GUIDE

Developmental Reading Approaches

Developmental reading programs emphasize daily, sequential instruction. Instructional materials usually feature a series of books, often basal readers, as the core of the program.

Basal Reading

Basal reader series form the core of many widely used reading programs, from pre-primers to eighth grade. Depending on the series, basal readers may be meaning-emphasis or code-emphasis. Teacher manuals provide a highly structured and comprehensive scope and sequence, lesson plans, and objectives. Vocabulary is controlled from level to level, and reading skills cover word recognition, word attack, and comprehension.

Advantages of basal readers are the structured, sequential manner in which reading is taught. The teacher manuals have teaching strategies, controlled vocabulary, assessment materials, and objectives. Reading instruction is in a systematic, sequential, and comprehension-oriented manner.

Many basal reading programs recommend the directed reading activity procedure for lesson presentation. Students proceed through the steps of: preparing for the new concepts and vocabulary, guided reading, answering questions that give a purpose or goal for the reading, developing strengths through drills or workbook, applying skills, and being evaluated.

A variation of the directed reading method is direct reading-thinking, where the student must generate the purposes for reading the selection, form questions, and read the selection. After reading, the teacher asks questions designed to get the group to think of and justify answers.

Disadvantages of basal readers are the emphasis on teaching to a group rather than the individual. Critics of basal readers claim that the structure may limit creativity and not provide enough instruction on organizational skills and reading for secondary content levels. Basal readers, however, offer the advantage of a prepared comprehensive program, and may be supplemented with other materials to meet individual needs.

Phonics Approach

In phonics, word recognition is taught through grapheme-phoneme associations, with the goal of teaching the student to independently apply these skills to new words. Phonics instruction may be synthetic or analytic. In the synthetic method, letter sounds are learned before the student goes on to blend the sounds to form words. The analytic method teaches letter sounds as integral parts of words.

SPECIAL EDU. CROSS-CATEGORY 137

The sounds are usually taught in sequence: vowels, consonants, consonant blends at the beginning of words (e.g., bl and dr), consonant blends at the end of words (e.g., ld and mp), consonant and vowel digraphs (e.g., ch and sh), and diphthongs (e.g., au and oy).

Critics of the phonics approach point out that the emphasis on pronunciation may lead to the student focusing more on decoding than comprehension. Some students may have trouble blending sounds to form words, and others may become confused with words that do not conform to the phonetic "rules."

However, advocates of phonics say that the programs are useful with remedial reading and developmental reading. Examples of phonics series include *Science Research Associates, Merrill Phonics,* and DML's *Cove School Reading Program.*

Linguistics Approach
In many programs, the whole-word approach is used. This means that words are taught in families as a whole (e.g., cat, hat, pat, and rat). The focus is on words instead of isolated sounds. Words are chosen on the basis of similar spelling patterns, and irregular spelling words are taught as sight words. Examples of programs using this approach are *SRA Basic Reading Series* and *Miami Linguistic Readers* by D.C. Heath.

Some advantages of this approach are that the student learns that reading is basically talk written down, and it develops a sense of sentence structure. The consistent visual patterns of the lessons guide students from familiar words to less familiar words to irregular words. Reading is taught by associating with the student's natural knowledge of his or her own language. Disadvantages are the extremely controlled vocabulary, in which word-by-word reading is encouraged. Others criticize the programs for their emphasis on auditory memory skills and the use of nonsense words in the practice exercises.

Whole Language Approach
In the whole language approach, reading is taught as a holistic, meaning-oriented activity and is not broken down into a collection of skills. This approach relies heavily on literature or printed matter selected for a particular purpose. Reading is taught as part of a total language arts program, and the curriculum seeks to develop instruction in real problems and ideas. Two examples of whole language programs are *Learning through Literature* (Dodds and Goodfellow) and *Victory!* (Brigance). Phonics is not taught in a structured, systematic way.

Students are assumed to develop their phonetic awareness through exposure to print. Writing is taught as a complement to reading. Writing centers are often part of this program, as students learn to write their own stories and read them back, or follow along with an audiotape of a book while reading.

While the integration of reading with writing is an advantage of the whole language approach, the approach has been criticized for the lack of direct instruction in specific skill strategies. When working with students with learning problems, instruction that is more direct may be needed to learn the word-recognition skills necessary for achieving comprehension of the text.

Language Experience Approach
The language experience approach is similar to the whole language approach in that reading is considered as a personal act, literature is emphasized, and students are encouraged to write about their own life experiences. The major difference is that written language is considered a secondary system to oral language (whole language treats the two as parts of the same structure). The language experience approach is used primarily with beginner readers, but can also be used with older elementary students and with other older students for corrective instruction. Reading skills are developed along with listening, speaking, and writing skills. The materials consist, for the most part, of the student's skills. The philosophy of language experience includes:

- What students think about, they can talk about.
- What students say, they can write, or have someone write.
- What students write or have someone write for them, they can read.

In this approach, students dictate a story to a teacher as a group activity. Ideas for stories can originate from student artwork, news items, personal experiences, or they may be creative. Topic lists, word cards, or idea lists can also be used to generate topics or ideas for a class story. The teacher writes down the story in a first draft, and the students read them back. The language patterns come from the students as they read their own written thoughts. The teacher provides guidance on word choice, sentence structure, and the sounds of the letters and words. The students edit and revise the story on an experience chart. The teacher provides specific instruction in grammar, sentence structure, and spelling, if the need arises, rather than using a specified schedule.

As the students progress, they create their individual storybooks, adding illustrations if they wish. The storybooks are placed in folders to share with others. Progress is evaluated in terms of the changes in the oral and written expression as well as in mechanics. There is no set method of evaluating student progress, which is one disadvantage of the language experience approach. However, the emphasis on student experience and creativity stimulates interest and motivates the students.

Individualized Reading Approach

According to this approach, students select their own reading materials from a variety, according to interest and ability, which enables them to progress at their own individual rates. Word recognition and comprehension are taught as the student needs them. The teacher's role is to diagnose errors and prescribe materials, although the final choice is made by the students. Individual work may be supplemented by group activities with basal readers and workbooks for specific reading skills. The lack of systematic check of developmental skills and emphasis on self-learning may be a disadvantage for students with learning problems.

Students' Enjoyment and Independent Involvement in Reading

When students are able to independently use reading skills for enjoyment, a key goal of literacy development has been attained. Initially, special education teachers should choose books with a high correlation between text that has been already read aloud in class and pictures. These may be displayed in a classroom reading area for students to read independently. (Note that the emergent reader may, at first, be paraphrasing the story or reciting the words from memory instead of actually reading the words.) Special education teachers may also select a set of books from which to choose during library time.

As students progress in reading skills, the special educator changes the materials that are available for the students to read. Typically, material read for enjoyment is at a reading level that is easy for the student, so that he or she maintains interest and effort. Materials such as hi/lo (high interest/low reading level) books are often good choices for the student with significant reading delays.

After a certain level of reading is reached, special education students may enjoy participating in reading reward programs such as Accelerated Reader, Reading Counts, Book It, or others through which the child can acquire prizes, fast food coupons, or tickets for theme parks and sporting events. It is the role of the special educator to evaluate if the amount of required reading is realistic for the student with disabilities, or if it should be modified per individual needs.

Students with disabilities who also come from diverse cultural or linguistic backgrounds will need materials that are even more specific to their needs. Many publishers now print books specifically for bilingual children.

In addition to traditional print books, students may be motivated to read classroom magazines or graphic novels independently because of the engaging illustrations and topics. Students with disabilities often enjoy reading text or directions for games and activities on the computer. The typically shortened text, graphics, audio components, and interactive features of computer materials appeal to many students with disabilities. Other considerations are box or board games that incorporate reading skills, such Scrabble Jr. and Boggle, Jr.

Schloss, Marriman, and Pfiefer (cited in Schloss & Sedlack, 1986) describe a procedure that systematically and sequentially reduces teacher involvement in written production by students. The procedure calls for these actions by the teacher during the instruction:

1. Present a topic or elicit one from the student.
2. Say each sentence before writing it.
3. Inform the student that spelling assistance will be given if needed.
4. Give the student at least 20 seconds to self-initiate a sentence.
5. Provide a motivational prompt if, after 20 seconds, a sentence has not been vocalized (for example, "Just try to do your best").
6. Provide a content prompt if, after another 20 seconds, a sentence has not been vocalized (for example, "Write about what the cat did to the dog").
7. Provide a literal prompt if, after a third 20-second interval, a sentence has not been produced (for example, "Write 'the dog chased the cat up the tree'").
8. After the student writes a sentence, return to step four and repeat the sequence as needed while the student is writing the composition.
9. Upon completion of the activity, discuss with the student the number of sentences that were produced at each level.
10. Reinforce the student for producing larger numbers of sentences at levels indicative of greater student independence.

Strategies for Integrating Language Arts Skills across the Content Areas

Traditionally, language arts are considered to cover the skills of reading, writing, speaking, listening, and the study of literature. Although the language arts areas of reading (literature), speech, and English are subjects in their own rights, language arts skills may be incorporated into every content area subject.

Reading
Students read a variety of materials for enjoyment and to gain new information. In the content areas of science and social studies, students may read a textbook or read information from other print and electronic sources.

In particular, the reading strategies of summarization, question answering, question generating, use of graphic organizers, use of text structure and marking, comprehension monitoring, and discussion are useful in science, mathematics, and social studies.

Writing
Students may be asked to answer questions with short or extended responses, take notes during teaching, or write reports to demonstrate understanding of the material being taught.

Speaking
Students use the language arts skills of speaking when they give oral presentations or participate in discussions.

Listening
Students use listening skills when attending to the oral presentations of other students, their teachers, or guest speakers. Listening is also important during classroom discussions.

The Study of Literature
Literature study transcends basic reading skills to act as a source for gathering information about a time in history, a culture, a geographic area, a vocation or career.

Integrating Language Arts Skills across Content Areas for the Student with Special Needs

When the special education or inclusion classroom has students with a variety of ability levels, different assignments (appropriate for the individual student) may need to be given. Oral presentations or verbally answers to the questions on a test may offer a more appropriate way of demonstrated learning for some learning disabled students. Special education students who have significant delays in reading skills may be able to listen to a literature selection to gain information about something such as a certain weather type. (An example of this would be Betsy Byars' book *Tornado*.)

Additionally, as special education students use knowledge of text structures, they are better able to approach text that may be at a difficult reading level for them and to find needed answers for class assignments.

Special education students may use a graphic organizer to show learned information or to set up information from research (which may later be used in report writing). Using a combination of language arts activities across content areas in this way can provide differentiated instruction for students with special needs.

TEACHER CERTIFICATION STUDY GUIDE

COMPETENCY 20.0   UNDERSTAND STRATEGIES AND TECHNIQUES USED TO PROMOTE STUDENTS' WRITTEN EXPRESSION

For example: types and characteristics of written language difficulties associated with various disabilities; principles and methods for improving students' spelling, grammar, mechanics, word usage, and syntax; principles and methods for teaching students how to convey ideas logically; and how to communicate to different audiences.

Applying Knowledge of Prewriting Strategies (e.g., brainstorming, prioritizing, and selecting topics including clustering and other graphic organizers)

Students gather ideas before writing. Prewriting may include clustering, listing, brainstorming, mapping, free writing, and charting. Providing many ways for a student to develop ideas on a topic will increase his or her chances for success.

Remind students that as they prewrite, they need to consider their audience. Prewriting strategies assist students in a variety of ways. Listed below are the most common prewriting strategies students can use to explore, plan, and write on a topic. It is important to remember when teaching these strategies that not all prewriting must eventually produce a finished piece of writing. In fact, in the initial lesson of teaching prewriting strategies, it might be more effective to have students practice prewriting strategies without the pressure of having to write a finished product.

- Keep an idea book so that students can jot down ideas that come to mind.
- Write in a daily journal.
- Write down whatever comes to mind (i.e., free writing). Students do not stop to make corrections or interrupt the flow of ideas. A variation of this technique is focused free writing (writing on a specific topic) to prepare for an essay.
- Make a list of all ideas connected with their topic (i.e., brainstorming). Make sure students know that this technique works best when they let their minds work freely. After completing the list, students should analyze it to see if a pattern or a way to group the ideas emerges.
- Ask the questions who, what, when, where, when, and how. Help the writer approach a topic from several perspectives.
- Create a visual map on paper to gather ideas. Cluster circles and lines to show connections between ideas. Students should try to identify the relationship that exists between their ideas. If they cannot see the relationships, have them pair up, exchange papers, and have their partners look for some related ideas.
- Observe details of sight, hearing, taste, touch, and taste.
- Visualize by making mental images of something and write down the details in a list.

SPECIAL EDU. CROSS-CATEGORY 143

After they have practiced with each of these prewriting strategies, ask the students to pick out the ones they prefer and discuss how they might use the techniques to help them with future writing assignments. It is important to remember that students can use more than one prewriting strategy at a time. Students may also find that different writing situations may suggest certain techniques.

Identifying Effective Techniques of Note Taking, Outlining, and Drafting

Being effective note takers require consistent technique, whether the mode of note taking is on 5X7 note cards, lined notebook paper, or on a computer. Organizing all collected information according to a research outline allows the user to take notes on each section and begin the writing process. If the computer is used, then the actual format of the report can be word-processed and information put in to speed up the writing process of the final research report. Creating a title page and the bibliography page will allow each downloaded report to have its resources cited immediately in that section.

Note taking involves identification of specific resources that include the author's or organization's name, year of publication, title, publisher location, and publisher. When taking notes, whether on the computer or using note cards, use the author's last name and page number on cited information. In citing information for major categories and subcategories on the computer, create a file for notes that includes summaries of information and direct quotes. When direct quotes are put into a word file, the cut and paste process for incorporation into the report is quick and easy.

In outline information, it is crucial to identify the headings and subheadings for the topic being researched. When researching information, it is easier to cut and paste information under the indicated headings in creating a visual flow of information for the report. In the actual drafting of the report, the writer is able to lift direct quotations and citations from the posted information to incorporate in the writing.

Revising Written Texts to Improve Unity and Logical Organization (e.g., formulating topic sentences, reordering paragraphs or sentences, adding transition words and phrases, eliminating distracting sentences)

Revision is probably the most important step for the writer in the writing process. Here, students examine their work and make changes in wording, details, and ideas. So many times, students write a draft and then feel they're done; however, effective teachers know students must be encouraged to develop, change, and enhance their writing as they go as well as once they've completed a draft.

Revision and editing go hand-in-hand. Students must often move back and forth between these stages during the course of one written work. These stages can be practiced in small groups, pairs, and/or individually. Students must learn to analyze and improve their own work as well as the works of their peers. Some methods to use include:

- Students working in pairs to analyze sentences for variety.
- Students working in pairs or groups to ask questions about unclear areas in the writing or to help others add details, information, etc.
- Students performing the final edit.

Many teachers introduce Writer's Workshop to their students to maximize learning about the writing process. Writer's Workshops vary across classrooms, but the main idea is for students to become comfortable with the process necessary to produce written work. A basic Writer's Workshop includes a block of classroom time committed to writing various projects (e.g., narratives, memoirs, book summaries, fiction, book reports, etc). Students use this time to write, meet with others to review/edit writing, make comments on writing, revise their own work, proofread, meet with the teacher, and publish their work.

Teachers who facilitate effective Writer's Workshops are able to meet with students one at a time and can guide that student in his or her individual writing needs. This approach allows the teacher to differentiate instruction for each students' writing level.

Students need to be trained to become effective at proofreading, revising, and editing strategies. Begin by training them using both desk-side and scheduled conferences. Listed below are some strategies to use to guide students through the final stages of the writing process (and these can easily be incorporated into Writer's Workshop).

- Provide some guide sheets or forms for students to use during peer responses.
- Allow students to work in pairs and limit the agenda.
- Model the use of the guide sheet or form for the entire class.
- Give students a time limit or number of written pieces to be completed in a specific amount of time.
- Have the students read their partners' papers and ask at least three who, what, when, why, how questions. The students answer the questions and use them as a place to begin discussing the piece.
- At this point in the writing process, a mini-lesson that focuses on some of the problems students are having would be appropriate.

To help students revise, provide them with a series of questions that will assist them in revising their writing:

- Do the details give a clear picture? Add details that appeal to more than just the sense of sight.
- How effectively are the details organized? Reorder the details, if needed.
- Are the thoughts and feelings of the writer included? Add personal thoughts and feelings about the subject.

As the teacher discusses revision, he or she should begin with discussing the definition of revise. Also, it is important to state that all writing must be revised to improve it. After students have revised their writing, it is time for the final editing and proofreading.

Writing Introductions

It is important to remember that in the writing process, the introduction should be written last. Until the body of the paper has been determined (e.g., thesis, development), it is difficult to make strategic decisions regarding the introduction. The Greek rhetoricians called this part of a discourse *exordium*, a "leading into." The basic purpose of the introduction, then, is to lead the audience into the discourse. It can let the reader know what the purpose of the discourse is, and it can condition the audience to be receptive to what the writer wants to say. It can be very brief or take up a large percentage of the total word count. Aristotle said that the introduction could be compared to the flourishes that flute players make before their performance—an overture in which the musicians display what they can play best in order to gain the favor and attention of the audience for the main performance.

In order to do this, the writer must first of all know what he or she is going to say; who the readership is likely to be; what the social, political, and economic climate is; what preconceived notions the audience is likely to have regarding the subject; and how long the discourse is going to be. This can be done if the writer can:

- Show that the subject is important.
- Show that although the points being presented may seem improbable, they are true.
- Show that the subject has been neglected, misunderstood, or misrepresented in the past.
- Explain an unusual mode of development.
- Forestall any misconception of the purpose.
- Apologize for a deficiency.
- Arouse interest in the subject with an anecdotal lead-in.
- Ingratiate oneself with the readership.
- Establish one's own credibility.

The introduction often ends with the thesis: the point or purpose of the paper. However, this is not set in stone. The thesis may open the body of the discussion, or it may conclude the discourse. The most important thing to remember is that the purpose and structure of the introduction should be deliberate if it is to serve the purpose of "leading the reader into the discussion."

Writing Conclusions

It's easier to write a conclusion after the decisions regarding the introduction have been made. Aristotle taught that the conclusion should strive to do five things:

1. Inspire the reader with a favorable opinion of the writer.
2. Amplify the force of the points made in the body of the paper.
3. Reinforce the points made in the body.
4. Rouse appropriate emotions in the reader.
5. Restate in a summary way what has been said.

The conclusion may be short or it may be long depending on its purpose in the paper. Recapitulation, a brief restatement of the main points (or certainly of the thesis), is the most common form of effective conclusion writing. A good example is the closing argument in a court trial.

Text Organization

In studies of professional writers and how they produce their successful works, it has been revealed that writing is a process that can be clearly defined (although, in practice, it must have enough flexibility to allow for creativity). The teacher must be able to define the various stages that a successful writer goes through in order to make a statement that has value. There must be a discovery stage when ideas, materials, and supporting details are deliberately collected. These may come from many possible sources: the writer's own experience and observations, deliberate research of written sources, interviews of live persons, television presentations, or the internet.

The next stage is organization, where the purpose, thesis, and supporting points are determined. Most writers will put forth more than one possible thesis—in the next stage, the writing of the paper, they will settle on one as the result of trial and error. Once the paper is written, the editing stage is probably the most important stage. This is not just the polishing stage. At this point, decisions must be made regarding whether the reasoning is cohesive: Does it hold together? Is the arrangement the best possible one, or should the points be rearranged? Are there holes that need to be filled in? What form will the introduction take? Does the conclusion lead the reader out of the discourse? Is it inadequate? Too abrupt?

It is important to remember that the best writers engage in all of these stages recursively. They may go back to discovery at any point in the process. They may go back and rethink the organization. To help students become effective writers, the teacher needs to give them adequate practice in the various stages and encourage them to engage deliberately in the creative thinking that makes writers successful.

Editing Written Work to Ensure Conformity to Conventions of Standard English Usage (e.g., eliminating misplaced or dangling modifiers, eliminating sentence fragments, correcting errors in subject-verb agreement and pronoun-antecedent agreement)

Revise Misplaced or Dangling Modifiers
Particular phrases that are not placed near the one word they modify often result in misplaced modifiers. Phrases that do not relate to the subject being modified result in dangling modifiers.

> Error: Weighing the options carefully, a decision was made regarding the punishment of the convicted murderer.

> Problem: Who is weighing the options? No one capable of weighing is named in the sentence; thus, the participle phrase weighing the options carefully dangles. This problem can be corrected by adding a subject of the sentence capable of doing the action.

> Correction: Weighing the options carefully, the judge made a decision regarding the punishment of the convicted murderer.

Sentence Completeness
Avoid fragments and run-on sentences. Recognition of sentence elements necessary to make a complete thought, proper use of independent and dependent clauses, and proper punctuation will correct such errors.

Recognize simple, compound, complex, and compound-complex sentences. Use dependent (subordinate) and independent clauses correctly to create these sentence structures.

Simple	Joyce wrote a letter.
Compound	Joyce wrote a letter, and Dot drew a picture.
Complex	While Joyce wrote a letter, Dot drew a picture.
Compound/Complex	When Mother asked the girls to demonstrate their new-found skills, Joyce wrote a letter, and Dot drew a picture.

Note: Do not confuse compound sentence elements with compound sentences.

Simple sentence with compound subject

Joyce and Dot wrote letters.

The girl in row three and the boy next to her were passing notes across the aisle.

Simple sentence with compound predicate

Joyce wrote letters and drew pictures.

The captain of the high school debate team graduated with honors and studied broadcast journalism in college.

Subject-Verb Agreement
A verb agrees in number with its subject. Making them agree relies on the ability to properly identify the subject.

One of the boys was playing too rough.

No one in the class, not the teacher nor the students, was listening to the message from the intercom.

The candidates, including a grandmother and a teenager, are debating some controversial issues.

If two singular subjects are connected by *and*, the verb must be plural.

A man and his dog were jogging on the beach.

If two singular subjects are connected by *or* or *nor,* a singular verb is required.

Neither Dot nor Joyce has missed a day of school this year.

Either Fran or Paul is missing.

If one singular subject and one plural subject are connected by *or* or *nor,* the verb agrees with the subject nearest to the verb.

> Neither the coach nor the players were able to sleep on the bus.

If the subject is a collective noun, its sense of number in the sentence determines the verb: singular if the noun represents a group or unit and plural if the noun represents individuals.

> The House of Representatives has adjourned for the holidays.

> The House of Representatives have failed to reach agreement on the subject of adjournment.

COMPETENCY 21.0 UNDERSTAND STRATEGIES AND TECHNIQUES USED TO PROMOTE STUDENTS' MATH SKILLS

For example: types and characteristics of mathematical reasoning and calculation difficulties associated with various disabilities; principles and methods for improving students' computation, reasoning, and problem-solving; and measurement skills and application of math skills

Reid (1985) describes four processes directly related to understanding numbers. Children typically begin learning these processes in early childhood through the opportunities provided by their caretakers. Children who do not get these opportunities have difficulties when they enter school.

- Describing: characterizing objects, sets, or events in terms of their attributes (such as calling all cats "kitties" whether they are tigers or house cats).
- Classifying: sorting objects, sets, or events in terms of one or more criterion such as color, size or shape (black cats versus white cats versus tabby cats).
- Comparing: determining whether two objects, sets, or events are similar or different on the basis of a specified attribute (such as differentiating quadrilaterals from triangles on the basis of the number of sides).
- Ordering: comparing two or more objects, sets, or events (such as ordering children in a family on the basis of age or height).

Children usually begin learning these concepts during early childhood:

- Equalizing: making two or more objects or sets alike on an attribute (such as putting more milk into a glass so that it matches the amount of milk in another glass).
- Joining: putting together two or more sets with a common attribute to make one set (such as buying packets of X-Men trading cards to create a complete series).
- Separating: dividing an object or set into two or more sets (such as passing out cookies from a bag to a group of children so that each child gets three cookies).
- Measuring: attaching a number to an attribute (such as three cups of flour or ten gallons of gas).
- Patterns: recognizing, developing, and repeating patterns (such as secret code messages or designs in a carpet or tile floor).

However, most children are not developmentally ready to understand these concepts before they enter school:

- <u>Understanding and working with numbers larger than 10;</u> children may be able to recite larger numbers, but are not able to compare or add them.
- <u>Part-whole concept</u>: the idea of one number as being a part of another number.
- <u>Numerical notation</u>: place value, additive system, and zero symbol.

Children with learning problems often have difficulty with these concepts after they enter public school either because they have had not had many experiences with developing these concepts, or they are not developmentally ready to understand them.

Sequence of Mathematics Understanding

The understanding of mathematical concepts proceeds in a developmental context from concrete to semi-concrete to abstract. Children with learning difficulties may still be at the semi-concrete level when their peers are ready to work at the abstract level. This developmental sequence has implications for instruction because the teacher will need to incorporate concrete and/or semi-concrete into lessons for students who did not master these stages of development in their mathematics background. These levels may be explained as follows:

- <u>Concrete:</u> an example of this would be demonstrating 3 + 4 = 7 by counting out three buttons and four buttons to equal seven buttons.
- <u>Semi-concrete</u>: an example would be using pictures of three buttons and four buttons to illustrate 3 + 4 = 7.
- <u>Abstract</u>: the student solves 3 + 4 = 7 without using manipulatives or pictures.

In summary, the levels of mathematics content involve:

- Concepts such as the understanding of numbers and terms
- Development of mathematical relationships
- Development of mathematical skills such as computation and measuring
- Development of problem-solving ability not only in books, but also in the environment

TEACHER CERTIFICATION STUDY GUIDE

Understand General Strategies for Promoting Learning and Fostering Critical Thinking and Problem Solving in Relation to Mathematics

Problem Solving

The skills of analysis and interpretation are necessary for problem solving. Students with learning disabilities find problem solving difficult, with the result that they avoid many of these types of activities. Skills necessary for problem solving include:

1) *Identifying the main idea:* what is the problem about?
2) *Ascertaining the question of the problem:* what is the problem asking for?
3) *Identifying important facts:* what information is necessary to solve the problem?
4) *Choosing a strategy and an operation:* how will the student solve the problem and with what operation?
5) *Solving the problem:* perform the computation
6) *Checking accuracy of computation and comparing the answer to the main question:* does it sound reasonable?
7) *If solution is correct, repeating the steps.*

Identify Effective Teaching Methods for Developing the Use of Math Skills in Problem Solving

One of the main reasons for studying mathematics is to acquire the ability to perform problem-solving skills. Problem solving is the process of applying previously acquired knowledge to new and novel situations. Mathematical problem solving is generally thought of as solving word problems; however, there are more skills involved in problem solving than merely reading word problems, deciding on correct conceptual procedures, and performing the computations.

Problem-solving skills involve posing questions; analyzing situations; hypothesizing, translating, and illustrating results; drawing diagrams; and using trial and error. When solving mathematical problems, students need to be able to apply logic, thereby determining which facts are relevant.

SPECIAL EDU. CROSS-CATEGORY

Problem solving has proven to be the primary area of mathematical difficulty for students. The following methods for developing problem-solving skills have been recommended.

1. Allot time for the development of successful problem-solving skills. It is complex process and needs to be taught in a systematic way.
2. Be sure prerequisite skills have been adequately developed. The ability to perform the operations of addition, subtraction, multiplication, and division are necessary sub-skills.
3. Use error analysis to diagnose areas of difficulty. An error in procedure or choice of mathematical operation, once corrected, will eliminate subsequent mistakes following the initial error like the domino effect. Look for patterns of similar mistakes to prevent a series of identical errors. Instruct children on the usage of error analysis to perform self-appraisal of their own work.
4. Teach students appropriate terminology. Many words have a different meaning when used in a mathematical context than in every day life. For example "set" in mathematics refers to a grouping of objects, but it may be used differently on a daily basis, such as in "set the table." (Other words that should be defined include "order," "base," "power," and "root.")
5. Have students estimate answers. Teach them how to check their computed answer to determine how reasonable it is. For example, imagine Teddy is asked how many hours he spent doing his homework. If he worked on it two hours before dinner and one hour after dinner, and his answer came out to be 21, Teddy should be able to conclude that 21 hours is the greater part of a day, and is far too large to be reasonable.
6. Remember that development of math readiness skills enables students to acquire prerequisite concepts and to build cognitive structures. These prerequisite skills appear to be related to problem-solving performance.

SPECIAL EDU. CROSS-CATEGORY 154

Understand Evaluation, Selection, and Adaptation of Instructional Strategies, Materials, Resources, and Technologies to Individualize Instruction and Facilitate Student Achievement in Mathematics

Etiologies of the learning challenges some students face can be diverse, as can their outcomes. Teachers of students with special needs are skilled at assessing, observing, implementing, reassessing, and making changes to the educational environment, tools, and approaches they use with students.

To accomplish this with math instruction, teachers must begin by identifying the nature of math as a curricular area, using that information to task-analyze the concepts, skills, and strategies they want to teach. The teachers then focus on each student's observed and documented strengths and challenges, as well as the relevant information from in his or her formal assessments and individualized education plan (IEP). Such analysis may constitute an initial assessment.

In the NCTM journal article "Planning Strategies for Students with Special Needs" (*Teaching Children Mathematics*, 2004), Brodesky et al. suggest that the next step in deciding on strategies, materials, and resources is to identify the "barriers" that students' documented and observed challenges present as they work to meet the goals and objectives of the math curriculum and their IEPs. Data-based assessments are an alternative or adjunct to such observational and recorded review. This information can help direct teachers' thinking about proactive solutions, including the selection and/or adaptation of the best strategies, materials, and resources.

Once teachers have thus developed a clear picture of the goals and needs of their math students with learning differences, they can seek resources for best practices, including school district-based support, the federal and state departments of education, teacher training programs, and education literature. Ultimately, skilled teachers will layer creativity and keen observation with their professional skills to decide how best to individualize instruction and facilitate student achievement. Examples include:
- Varying learning modalities (visual, kinesthetic, tactile, aural)
- Integrating technology (calculators, computers, game consoles)
- Providing tools and manipulatives (Cuisinart rods, beans, protractors)
- Developing a range of engaging activities (games, music, storytelling)
- Using real world problem solving (fundraising, school-wide projects, shopping, cooking, budgeting)
- Adopting a cross-curricular approach (studying historical events strongly influenced by math or music theory)
- Developing basic skills (guided practice, pencil-and-paper computation, journaling and discussing problem-solving strategies)
- Adaptations (extended wait time, recorded lessons, concept videos, ergonomic work areas, mixed-ability learning groups)

TEACHER CERTIFICATION STUDY GUIDE

COMPETENCY 22.0 UNDERSTAND STRATEGIES AND TECHNIQUES USED TO PROMOTE STUDENTS' ACQUISITION OF ACADEMIC SKILLS

For example: ways the presence of disabilities may affect students' progress in the general curriculum; various approaches for content-area instruction; strategies for integrating reading, writing, and mathematics instruction into daily routines; and strategies for developing students' academic study skills.

In order to promote learning, an educator must be knowledgeable of the "whole" child, along with educational strategies to teach every child. An educator must have knowledge of the child's disability and the characteristics related to the disability (See Competency 1.0), know how to interpret assessment results and adjust teaching strategies according to the child's strengths and weaknesses, and be knowledgeable of the child's culture, as it may somehow affect the child's education.

Teachers should have a toolkit of instructional strategies, materials, and technologies to encourage and teach students how to problem solve and think critically about subject content. With each curriculum chosen by a district for school implementation comes an expectation that students must master benchmarks and standards of learning skills.

There is an established level of academic performance and proficiency in public schools that students are required to master in today's classrooms. Research of national and state standards indicate that there additional benchmarks and learning objectives in the subject areas of science, foreign language, english language arts, history, art, health, civics, economics, geography, physical education, mathematics, and social studies that students are required to master in state assessments (Marzano & Kendall, 1996).

A critical thinking skill is a skill target that teachers help students to develop. It sustains learning in specific subject areas that can be applied within other subject areas. For example, when learning to understand algebraic concepts in solving a math word problem, imagine this problem: How much fencing material is needed to build a fence around a backyard area that is of 8' x 12" size? For solving algebraic expressions such as this, a math student must understand the order of numerical expression. Teachers can provide instructional strategies that show students how to group the fencing measurements into an algebraic word problem that, with minor addition, subtraction, and multiplication, can produce a simple number equal to the amount of fencing materials needed.

SPECIAL EDU. CROSS-CATEGORY

Students use basic skills to understand things that are read (such as a reading passage, a math word problem, or directions for a project). However, students apply additional thinking skills to fully comprehend how what was read could be applied to their own lives or how to make comparatives or choices based on the factual information given. These higher-order thinking skills are called critical thinking skills, as students *think* about thinking. Teachers are instrumental in helping students use these skills in everyday activities:

- Analyzing bills for overcharges
- Comparing shopping ads or catalogue deals
- Finding the main idea from readings
- Applying what's been learned to new situations
- Gathering information/data from a diversity of sources to plan a project
- Following a sequence of directions
- Looking for cause and effect relationships
- Comparing and contrasting information in synthesizing information

Attention to learner needs during planning is foremost. It includes identifying that which the students already know or need to know; matching learner needs with instructional elements such as content, materials, activities, and goals; and determining whether or not students have performed at an acceptable level, following instruction.

Since most teachers want their educational objectives to use higher-level thinking skills, teachers need to direct students to these higher levels on the taxonomy. Questioning is an effective tool to build up students to these higher levels.

Low-order questions are useful to begin the process. They ensure the student is focused on the required information and understands what needs to be included in the thinking process. For example, if the objective is for students to be able to read and understand the story "Goldilocks and the Three Bears," the teacher may wish to start with low-order questions such as "What are some things Goldilocks did while in the bears' home?" (knowledge) or "Why didn't Goldilocks like the Papa Bear's chair?" (analysis).

Through a series of questions, the teacher can move the students up the taxonomy. In this same example, the teacher could ask "If Goldilocks had come to your house, what are some things she may have used?" (application), "How might the story be different if Goldilocks had visited the three fishes?" (synthesis), or "Do you think Goldilocks was good or bad? Why?" (evaluation).

Through questioning, the teacher can control the thinking process of the class. As students become more involved in the discussion, they are systematically being lead to higher-level thinking.

SPECIAL EDU. CROSS-CATEGORY 157

Personal and professional charting of student's academic and emotional growth within the performance-based assessment of individualized portfolios is a toolkit for both students and teachers. Teachers can use semester portfolios to gauge student academic progress and personal growth of students who are constantly changing their self-images and worldviews. When a student is studying to master a math concept and is able to create a visual of what he or she has learned, it may transcend beyond the initial concept to create a bridge connecting a higher level of thinking and application of knowledge. The teacher can then share a moment of enjoyable math comprehension with the student.

The idea of using art concepts as visual imagery in helping students process conceptual learning of reading, math, and science skills creates a mental mind mapping of learning for students processing new information. One instructional strategy teachers can use to guide students into further inquiry of subject matter is using graphic organizers and concept web guides that center around a concept and the applications of the concept. Imagine the research of the German chemist Fredrich August Kekule when he looked into a fire one night and solved the molecular structure of benzene, and you can imagine fostering that same creativity in students. Helping students understand the art of "visualization" and the creativity of discovery may impart a student visualizing the cure for AIDS, the cure for cancer, or knowledge of how to create reading programs for the next generation of readers.

It is important to help students become effective note takers and stimulate a diversity of perspectives for spatial techniques that can be applied to learning. These are proactive teacher strategies for creating a visual learning environment where art and visualization become natural art forms for learning. In today's computer environment, students must understand that computers cannot replace the creative thinking and skill application that comes from the greatest computer on record: the human mind.

COMPETENCY 23.0 UNDERSTAND STRATEGIES AND TECHNIQUES USED TO PROMOTE STUDENTS' ACQUISITION OF FUNCTIONAL SKILLS

For example: components of a functional curriculum; techniques for designing and implementing functional skills instruction (e.g., observation, task analysis, establishing behavioral outcomes, teaching in context, community-based instruction); strategies for teaching functional skills in the major domains (e.g., self-help skills, daily living skills); and techniques for promoting skill transfer and generalization.

Understand the Need for a Functional Curriculum

A functional curriculum approach focuses on what students need to learn that will be useful to them and prepare them for functioning in society as adults. With this approach, concepts and skills needed for personal-social, daily living, and occupational readiness are taught to students. The specific curriculum contents need to be identified in a student's individualized educational program (IEP), and be considered appropriate for his or her chronological age and current intellectual, academic, or behavioral performance levels (Clark, 1994).

The need for a functional curriculum has been heightened by the current focus on transition and movement from one level to another until the individual is prepared to live a life in a self-sufficient manner. The simplest form of this includes movement from school to the world of work. However, like career education, life preparation includes not only occupational readiness, but also personal-social and daily living skills.

Halpern (1992) contends that special education curriculum tends to focus too much on remedial academics and not enough on functional skills.

A functional curriculum includes like skills and teaches them in the classroom and community. When using this approach, basic academic skills are reinforced in an applied manner. For instance, math skills may be taught in budgeting, balancing checkbooks, and/or computing interest payments for major purchases.

The Adult Performance Level (APL) has been adapted for secondary level students in special education in a number of school districts in Texas and Louisiana. The APL serves as a core curriculum blending practical academic development with applications to the various demands of community living in adulthood.

Functional competence, as addressed in APL, is conceptualized as two-dimensional. Major skill areas are integrated into general content and knowledge domains. The major skills that have been identified by this curriculum model as requisite for success are reading, writing, speaking, listening, viewing, problem solving, interpersonal relations, and computation.

Recognizing that Cultural, Linguistic, and Gender Differences Need to be Taken into Account when Developing Instructional Content, Materials, Resources, and Strategies for Promoting Students' Functional Living Skills

Writing functional living skills curriculum for a student requires understanding that it is not just IQ that defines the label and diagnosis of mental retardation. The American Association on Mental Retardation reminds us of the impact culture has on everyone's development by adding two assumptions to the validating of the diagnosis of mental retardation:

1) Limitations in present functioning must be considered within the context of community environments typical of the individual's age peers and *culture*.
2) Valid assessment considers *cultural and linguistic* diversity as well as differences in communication, sensory, motor, and behavioral factors.

Teachers must recognize these facts in relation to everyday life for their students. Interviewing parents is one way of including them on your development of a functional skills program; this allows you to learn what is considered a cultural norm in your student's home life. The planned method of instruction may be considered culturally insensitive and must be examined for this possibility.

Materials and resources must also be considered as a potential offense to some cultures. Checking before implementing a functional living skills program can negate this issue.

Instructional methods of functional skills can best avoid cultural conflict when utilizing the following methods:
1. Using the think-aloud process: When demonstrating a specific skill, teachers should state simple questions and answer them as part of the thought process. Teachers should also allow for group discussions and questions on the specific skill being addressed.
2. Creating opportunities for students to ask open-ended questions regarding the skill to be completed.
3. Providing multiple examples of how to attain a skill.
4. Including the use of student-designed art to show how a skill must be completed.
5. Scaffolding allows for a skill to be taught through small steps. It is important to reach a small objective and build upon each one to reach a selected skill.

Transfer of Learning

Transfer of learning occurs when experience with one task influences performance on another task. Positive transfer occurs when the required responses and the stimuli are similar (such as moving from baseball or handball to racquetball, or field hockey to soccer). Negative transfer occurs when the stimuli remain similar, but the required responses change (such as shifting from soccer to football, tennis to racquetball, or boxing to karate).

Instructional procedures should stress the similar features between the activities and the dimensions that are transferable. Specific information should emphasize when stimuli in the old and new situations are the same as well as when responses used in the old situation apply to the new one.

To facilitate learning, instructional objectives should be arranged in order according to their patterns of similarity. Objectives involving similar responses should be closely sequenced; thus, the possibility for positive transfer is stressed. Likewise, learning objectives that involve different responses should be programmed within instructional procedures in the most appropriate way possible. For example, students should have little difficulty transferring handwriting instruction to writing in other areas; however, there might be some negative transfer when moving from manuscript to cursive writing. By using transitional methods and focusing on the similarities between manuscript and cursive writing, negative transfer can be reduced.

Generalization

Generalization is the occurrence of a learned behavior in the presence of a stimulus other than the one that produced the initial response (e.g., novel stimulus). It is the expansion of a student's performance beyond conditions initially anticipated. Students must be able to generalize what is learned to other settings (e.g., reading to math word problems; resource room to regular classroom).

Generalization training is a procedure in which a behavior is reinforced in each of a series of situations until it generalizes to other members of the same stimulus class. Stimulus generalization occurs when responses that have been reinforced in the presence of a specific stimulus, also known as the discriminative stimulus (SD), occur in the presence of related stimuli (e.g., bathrooms labeled women, ladies, dames). In fact, the more similar the stimuli, the more likely it is that stimulus generalization will occur.

This concept applies to inter-task similarity in that the more one task resembles another, the greater the probability the student will be able to master it. For example, if Johnny has learned the initial consonant sounds of "b" and "d," and he has been taught to read the word "dad," it is likely that when he is shown the word "bad," he will be able to pronounce this formerly unknown word.

Generalization may be enhanced if teachers do the following:

- Use many examples in teaching to deepen application of learned skills.
- Use consistency in initial teaching situations, and later introduce variety in format, procedure, and use of examples.
- Have the same information presented by different teachers, in different settings, and under varying conditions.
- Include a continuous reinforcement schedule at first, later changing to delayed and intermittent schedules as instruction progresses.
- Teach students to record instances of generalization and to reward themselves at that time.
- Associate naturally occurring stimuli, when possible.

TEACHER CERTIFICATION STUDY GUIDE

COMPETENCY 24.0 UNDERSTAND STRATEGIES AND TECHNIQUES USED TO IMPROVE STUDENTS' INDEPENDENT LEARNING SKILLS

For example: principles and techniques for promoting students' self-confidence, independence, decision making, responsibility, and personal ownership of tasks and goals; ways to help students apply self-management strategies; techniques for responding to the motivational characteristics of individual students; and strategies and activities for helping students to organize and manage time, develop productive routines, seek help when needed, follow instructions, work independently, choose and use technology, persevere at tasks, manage frustration and change, manage leisure time, and participate in problem-solving, decision-making, and conflict resolution processes.

Demonstrate an Understanding of the Influence of the School-Home Relationship on the Development of Adaptive Life Skills

Adaptive life skills refer to the skills that people need to function independently at home, school, and in the community. Adaptive behavior skills include communication and social skills (intermingling and communicating with other people); independent living skills (shopping, budgeting, and cleaning); personal care skills (eating, dressing, and grooming); employment/work skills (following directions, completing assignments, and being punctual for work); and functional academics (reading, solving math problems, and telling time).

Teaching adaptive behavior skills is part of the special education program for students with disabilities. Parent input is a critical part of the adaptive behavior assessment process, as there are many daily living skills observed primarily at home that are not prevalent in the educational setting.

The measurement of adaptive behavior should consist of surveys of the child's behavior and skills in a diverse number of settings, including his or her class, school, home, neighborhood, and community. Since it is not possible for one person to observe a child in all of the primary environments, measurement of adaptive behavior depends on the feedback from a number of people. Because parents have many opportunities to observe their child in an assortment of settings, they are normally the best source of information about adaptive behavior.

The most prevalent method for collecting information about a child's adaptive behavior skills in the home environment is to have a school social worker, school psychologist, or guidance counselor interview the parents using a formal adaptive behavior assessment rating scale. These individuals may interview the parents at home or hold a meeting at the school to talk with the parent about their child's behavior. Adaptive behavior information, necessary to understand how the child functions in the school environment, can be procured from school personnel who work with the student.

SPECIAL EDU. CROSS-CATEGORY 163

There are a variety of strategies for teaching adaptive life skills, including incorporating choice, which entails allowing students to select the assignment and the order in which they complete tasks. In addition, priming or pre-practice is an effective classroom intervention for students with disabilities. Priming entails previewing information or activities that a student is likely to have problems with before they begin working on that activity. Partial participation or multilevel instruction is another strategy. It entails allowing a student with a disability to take part in the same projects as the rest of the class with specific adaptations so that it suits his or her specific abilities and requirements. Additional instructional practices include self-management, which entails teaching the student to function independently without relying on a teacher or a one-on-one aid. This strategy allows the student to become more involved in the intervention process, thereby improving autonomy.

Cooperative groups are an effective instructional technique for teaching social skills. They have been known to result in increased frequency, duration, and quality of social interactions. Peer tutoring entails two students working together on an activity, with one student giving assistance, instruction, and feedback to the other.

Creating Opportunities for Individual and Group Decision Making

Decision making is a key factor in life success. The special educator plays a significant role in the student's development of sound decision making.

When working with a young emotionally disturbed student, writing a behavior contract together allows the student to take part in the process of decision making. For example, consider what reward will the student work toward. While the choice may not be open-ended, the educator may offer two appropriate choices, and the student can then choose which one he or she wants most.

Decision making also bears consequences. These may be positive (as in the reward offered for fulfilling an agreement), or they may be disciplines that result from poor behavior choices. For example, if a student bumps another student into a row of lockers, the consequence may be losing a recess or visiting the principal.

Opportunities to learn sound decision making continue throughout school. At the high school level, the student receives an outline of class expectations that include assignments to be completed. The student either chooses to complete the assignments and therefore receive the associated credit, or the student chooses to disregard the responsibility and possibly fails the class.

Students practice group decision making (a precursor to our democratic government) when they vote on a movie that will be shown for a class reward or vote for a preferred class activity (math games on the computer vs. math flashcards with a buddy).

Creating Opportunities for Problem Solving

Problem solving is another skill necessary for life success. The following steps are key for individual and group conflict resolution:.

1. Awareness of the problem. (This may also include empathy toward another individual or a group.)
2. Brainstorming possible solutions.
3. Implementation of a chosen plan.
4. Evaluation of the effectiveness of the plan.
5. Continuation of the successful plan or implementation of a new plan.

Consider the situation of a school in which too many students want to play on the basketball court at lunch recess. Students decide that Group A will use the court on odd days, and Group B will use the court on even days. After two weeks, the situation is again discussed to evaluate the effectiveness of their plan.

TEACHER CERTIFICATION STUDY GUIDE

COMPETENCY 25.0 UNDERSTAND THE DEVELOPMENT AND IMPLEMENTATION OF BEHAVIOR INTERVENTIONS

For example: types, characteristics, strengths, and limitations of various behavior intervention approaches; conducting functional behavior assessments to determine the purposes of given behaviors; strategies and techniques for developing and implementing supports and systematic behavior intervention plans for students with special needs (e.g., using behavioral contracts, teaching new behaviors to replace problem behaviors); appropriate ways of involving family members in behavior intervention plans; strategies for recognizing when plans are not working and making changes; and the importance of coordinating behavior intervention approaches among persons involved in the implementation of IEPs.

Classroom Management Techniques

Classroom management plans should be in place when the school year begins. Developing a management plan takes a proactive approach—that is, it is important to decide what behaviors will be expected of the class as a whole, anticipate possible problems, and teach the behaviors early in the school year.

Behavior management techniques should focus on positive procedures that can be used at home as well as at school. Involving the students in the development of classroom rules lets the students know the rationale for the rules and allows them to assume responsibility in the rules. When students get involved in helping establish the rules, they are more likely to assume responsibility for following them. Once the rules are established, enforcement and reinforcement for following them should begin right away.

Consequences should be introduced when the rules are introduced, clearly stated, and understood by all of the students. The severity of the consequence should match the severity of the offense; it must also be enforceable. The teacher must apply the consequence consistently and fairly, so the students will know what to expect when they choose to break a rule.

Like consequences, students should understand what rewards to expect for following the rules. The teacher should never promise a reward that cannot be delivered, and they should follow through with the reward as soon as possible. Consistency and fairness are also necessary for rewards to be effective. Students are likely to become frustrated and give up if they see that rewards and consequences are not delivered timely and fairly.

About four to six classroom rules should be posted where students can easily see and read them. These rules should be stated positively and describe specific behaviors so they are easy to understand. Certain rules may also be tailored to meet target goals and IEP requirements of individual students. (For example, a new student who has had problems with leaving the classroom may need an individual behavior contract to assist him or her with adjusting to the class rule about remaining in the assigned area.) As the students demonstrate the behaviors, the teacher should provide reinforcement and corrective feedback. Periodic "refresher" practice can be done as needed; for example, it may be appropriate after a long holiday or if students begin to "slack off." A copy of the classroom plan should be readily available for substitute use, and the classroom aide should also be familiar with the plan and procedures.

The teacher should clarify and model the expected behavior for the students. In addition to the classroom management plan, a management plan should be developed for special situations (e.g., fire drills) and transitions (e.g., going to and from the cafeteria). Periodic review of the rules, as well as modeling and practice, may be conducted as needed.

Procedures that use social humiliation, withholding of basic needs, pain, or extreme discomfort should never be used in a behavior management plan. Emergency intervention procedures used when the student is a danger to him or herself or others are not considered behavior management procedures.

Throughout the year, the teacher should periodically review the types of interventions being used, assess the effectiveness of the interventions used in the management plan, and make revisions as needed for the best interests of the child.

Motivation

Before the teacher begins instruction, he or she should choose activities that are meaningful, relevant, and at the appropriate level of student difficulty. Teacher behaviors that motivate students include:

- Maintain success expectations through teaching, goal setting, establishing connections between effort and outcome, and self-appraisal and reinforcement.
- Have a supply of intrinsic incentives such as rewards, appropriate competition between students, and value for academic activities.
- Focus on students' intrinsic motivation by adapting the tasks to students' interests, providing opportunities for active response, including a variety of tasks, providing rapid feedback, incorporating games into the lesson, and allowing students the opportunity to make choices, create, and interact with peers.
- Stimulate students' learning by modeling positive expectations and attributions. Teachers should project enthusiasm and personalize abstract concepts. Students will be better motivated if they know what they will be learning. The teacher should also model problem solving and task-related thinking so students can see how the process is done.

For adolescents, motivation strategies are usually aimed at getting the student actively involved in the learning process. Since the adolescent has the opportunity to get involved in a wider range of activities outside the classroom (things like a job, car, or being with friends), stimulating motivation may be the focus even more than academics.

Motivation may be achieved through extrinsic reinforcers or intrinsic reinforcers. This is accomplished by allowing the student a degree of choice in what is being taught or how it will be taught. The teacher should, if possible, obtain a commitment either through a verbal or written contract between the student and the teacher. Adolescents often respond to regular feedback, especially when that feedback shows that they are making progress.

Rewards for adolescents often include free time for recreation, games, or listening to music. They may like extra time for a break or exemption from a homework assignment. They may receive rewards at home for satisfactory performance at school. Other rewards include self-charting progress, and tangible reinforcers. Motivational activities may be used for goal setting, self-recording of academic progress, self-evaluation, and self-reinforcement.

Classroom Interventions

Classroom interventions anticipate student disruptions and nullify potential discipline problems. Every student is different and each situation is unique; therefore, student behavior cannot be matched to specific interventions. Good classroom management requires the ability to select appropriate interventions strategies from an array of alternatives. The following nonverbal and verbal interventions were explained in Henley, Ramsey, and Algonzzine (1993).

Nonverbal Intervention - The use of nonverbal interventions allows classroom activities to proceed without interruption. These interventions also enable students to avoid "power struggles" with teachers.

Body Language - Teachers can convey authority and command respect through body language. Posture, eye contact, facial expressions, and gestures are examples of body components that signal leadership to students.

Planned Ignoring - Many minor classroom disturbances are best handled through planned ignoring. When teachers ignore attention-seeking behaviors, students often do likewise.

Signal Interference - There are numerous nonverbal signals that teachers can use to quiet a class. Some of these include making eye contact, snapping fingers, giving a frown, shaking the head, or making a quieting gesture with the hand. A few teachers present signs like flicking the lights, putting a finger over the lips, or winking at a selective student.

Proximity Control - Teachers who move around the room often simply need to stand near a student or small group of students or gently place a hand on a student's shoulder to stop a disturbing behavior. Teachers who stand or sit as if rooted are compelled to issue verbal directions in order to deal with student disruptions.

Removal of Seductive Objects - Some students become distracted by objects. Removing seductive objects eliminates the need many students have to handle, grab, or touch objects that distract their attention. One way to accomplish this goal is to "fall in love" with the object. Teachers who take an interest in the child's distraction may state admiration of it and then ask to place it someplace safe (like the teacher's desk).

Verbal Interventions - Because nonverbal interventions are the least intrusive, they are generally preferred. Verbal interventions are useful after it is clear that nonverbal interventions have been unsuccessful in preventing or stopping disruptive behavior.

Humor - Some teachers have been successful in dispelling discipline problems with a quip or an easy comment that produces smiles or gentle laughter from students. This does not include sarcasm, cynicism, or teasing, which increase tension and often create resentment.

Sane Messages - Sane messages describe and model appropriate behavior. They help students understand how their behavior affects others. "Karol, when you talk during silent reading, you disturb everyone in your group," is an example of a sane message.

Restructuring - When confronted with student disinterest, the teacher may make the decision to change activities. This is an example of an occasion when restructuring is used by the teacher to regenerate student interest.

Hypodermic Affection - At times, students get frustrated, discouraged, and anxious in school. Hypodermic affection lets students know they are valued. Saying a kind word, giving a smile, or just showing interest in a child may give the encouragement that is needed.

Praise and Encouragement - Effective praise is directed at student behavior rather than the student personally. "Catching a child being good," is an example of an effective use of praise that reinforces positive classroom behavior. Comments like, "You are really trying hard," encourages student effort.

Alerting - Making abrupt changes from one activity to another can bring on behavior problems. Alerting helps students to make smooth transitions by giving them time to make emotional adjustments to change.

Accepting Student Feelings - Providing opportunities for students to express their feelings—even those that are distressful—helps them to learn to do so in appropriate ways. Role playing, class meetings or discussions, life space interviews, journal writings, and other creative modes help students to channel difficult feelings into constructive outlets.

Transfer Between Classes and Subjects

Teachers should always use class time efficiently. Doing so results in higher student subject engagement and greater subject matter retention. One way teachers use class time efficiently is through a smooth transition from one activity to another; this activity is also known as "management transition." Management transition occurs when the "teacher shifts from one activity to another in a systemic, academically oriented way."

One factor that contributes to efficient management transition is the teacher's management of instructional material. Effective teachers gather their materials during the planning stage of instruction. This way, the teacher avoids flipping through things looking for the items necessary for the current lesson, thereby avoiding lost momentum and poor student concentration.

Additionally, teachers who keep students informed of the sequencing of instructional activities maintain systematic transitions, as their students are prepared to move on to the next activity. For example, the teacher should say, "When we finish with this guided practice together, we will turn to page twenty-three and each student will do the exercises. I will then circulate throughout the classroom helping on an individual basis. Okay, let's begin."
Following an example such as this will lead to systematic smooth transitions between activities, because the students will be turning to page twenty-three when the class finishes the practice without a break in concentration.

Another method that leads to smooth transitions is done by moving students in groups and clusters rather than one-by-one. This is called "group fragmentation." For example, if some students do seat work while other students gather for a reading group, the teacher moves the students in pre-determined groups. Instead of calling the individual names of the reading group, which would be time consuming and laborious, the teacher simply says, "Will the blue reading group please assemble at the reading station. The red and yellow groups will quietly do the vocabulary assignment I am now passing out." As a result of this activity, the classroom is ready to move on in a matter of seconds rather than minutes.

Additionally, the teacher may employ academic transition signals, which are "teacher utterances that indicate movement of the lesson from one topic or activity to another by indicating where the lesson is and where it is going." For example, the teacher may say, "That completes our description of clouds, now we will examine weather fronts." Like the sequencing of instructional materials, this keeps the student informed on what is coming next; therefore, they will move to the next activity with little or no break in concentration.

Effective teachers manage transitions from one activity to another in a systematically oriented way by efficiently managing instructional matter, sequencing instructional activities, moving students in groups, and employing academic transition signals. Achievement is increased because students spend more class time engaged in on-task behavior.

Transition refers to changes in class activities that involve movement. Examples include:

- (a) Breaking up from large group instruction into small groups for learning centers and small-group instructions
- (b) Classroom to lunch, to the playground, or to elective classes
- (c) Finishing reading at the end of one period and getting ready for math the next period
- (d) Emergency situations such as fire drills

Successful transitions are achieved by using proactive strategies. Early in the year, the teacher should pinpoint the transition periods in the day and anticipate possible behavior problems (such as students habitually returning late from lunch). After identifying possible problems with the environment or the schedule, the teacher then plans proactive strategies to minimize or eliminate those problems.

Proactive planning gives the teacher the advantage of being prepared to address behaviors before they become problems and incorporate strategies into the classroom management plan right away. Transition plans can be developed for each type of transition, and the expected behaviors for each situation can be taught directly to the students.

Task Analysis

Teachers can use the set of behavioral specifications that are the result of a task analysis to prepare tests that will measure the student's ability to meet those specifications. These tests are referred to as criterion measurements. If task analysis identifies which skills will be needed to perform a task successfully, then the criterion measurements will further identify whether the student possesses the necessary skills or knowledge for that task. The level of performance that is acceptable is the "criterion level."

Criterion measurements must be developed along certain guidelines if they are to accurately measure a task and its sub-skills. Johnson and Morasky (1977) give the following guidelines for establishing criterion measurement:

1. Criterion measurement must directly evaluate a student's ability to perform a task.
2. Criterion measurements should cover the range of possible situations in order to be considered an adequate measure.
3. Criterion measurements should measure whether or not a student can perform the task without additional or outside assistance. They should not give any information that the student is expected to possess.
4. All responses in the criterion measurement should be relevant to the task being measured.

Behavioral objectives offer descriptive statements defining the student's task, state the conditions under which the task will occur, and show the criterion measurement required for mastery. The criterion measurement is the process for evaluating what the student can do. For the instruction to be meaningful, there must be a precise correspondence between the capabilities determined in a criterion measurement and the behavioral demands of the objective.

Data-based instruction is a model of instruction that combines elements of precision teaching, direct instruction, applied behavior analysis, and criterion-referenced instruction. It features direct and continuous measurement of student progress toward specific instructional objectives. (A detailed discussion of curriculum-based instruction appears in Mercer and Mercer). Curriculum-based measurement (CBM) assesses student progress through continuous rate samples taken from the student's curriculum. CBM is used to establish performance standards for a district or school, identify students who need special instruction interventions, and monitor student progress toward long-term goals.

In CBM data-based instruction, the teacher selects material at the level he or she expects the student to have mastered by the end of the school year. Material should be proportionately presented in alternate test forms. A norm-referenced database can be prepared by comparing the performance of all the students on the same measure. By using several samples, an average score can be computed for the group. Plotting the data for CBM scores can be done with a box plot to identify extremes. A box plot consists of:

- a) Ranking the scores form lowest to highest
- b) Calculating the percentage value of a single score by dividing 1 by the total number of scores in the sample
- c) Locating the 90 percent level, the 75 percent level, the 25 percent level, and the 10 percent level
- d) Calculating the median score (50th percentile)
- e) Plotting the points for individuals above and below the 90th and 10th percentiles
- f) Drawing the box for the 75th and 25th percentiles
- g) The box plot can be used to determine who should be in a low group and who should be in a high group

With this type of plot, low performers can be identified, students can be divided into groups, instructional programs can be planned, and long-range goals can be established. For low-performing or special education students, this system has applications in establishing a formative evaluation system. It does this by using successive higher-level or lower-level grade materials to calculate current levels of functioning from appropriate grade functioning by comparing the student to normative levels for those grades.

Individual data-based instruction can be done through direct measurement of relevant classroom behaviors, such as math computation rate. For permanent products (e.g., class assignments), measurement can be done daily and should be done at least twice weekly. Observational recordings (frequency, rate, duration, time sampling) are useful for classroom behaviors related to academic performance. Line graphs and bar graphs are commonly used to plot results. For rate data, ratio graphs plotted on a grid (e.g., correct/incorrect words read during a one-minute time sample) are often used in applied behavior analysis and precision teaching programs.

For monitoring progress toward long-term instructional goals, performance-monitoring charts should be prepared for each student. The baseline is the first three data collection points. A broken line (called the trend line) represents the rate of progress the student is expected to achieve by the first intervention period. If the student's actual performance is plotted and compared to the trend line, and if the student is not making sufficient progress, the teacher will know that a different intervention is needed. A new trend line is then established and the student's progress compared to the trend again. If the student meets the trend, the teacher may continue the instruction method. If the student exceeds the trend, then he or she is considered to have met the criterion, and new goal proficiency criterion is established.

Short-range goal performance monitoring can be plotted on a mastery-monitoring chart. Mastery monitoring is used with precision teaching programs; it charts student progress on a succession of short-term goals. The steps in mastery monitoring are:

- Select the target behavior by administering probe sheets that sample a behavior (e.g., multiplication facts to the fives). Several samples should be collected before the target behavior is established.
- Develop task sheets or probes for daily timed samples of student progress.
- Graph data two to five times weekly and decide on a standard of fluency as an instructional goal.
- Design the method of instruction.
- Analyze the data and make instructional decisions.

A proportional chart can show:

- Plots of incorrect responses
- Plots of correct responses
- Progress across several skills, with a vertical line to indicate the change to a new skill
- A numerical listing of the correct/incorrect responses next to the graph
- A space for writing the charted behaviors as well as the instructional goal

Data-based instruction and charting can show:

- Changes in level of performance when a new teaching intervention is used
- The change of rate in a trend line
- The consistency or variability in performance
- The measurement of the weekly rate compared to performance aim rate

Teachers can achieve the most effective use of data-based instruction by following these guidelines in the daily classroom routine:

- Use one-minute timings for ease of administration and charting
- Measure priority behaviors (at least initially)
- Data collection can be done for the whole group
- Set moderate to highly ambitious goals to encourage student achievement
- Use logical sequencing and the presentation of lower order skills and concepts before moving on to higher order or more complex skills and concepts

By considering the structure of the task to be learned and using task analysis to specify the sub-skills and sub-concepts necessary for reaching the goal or target behavior, a learning hierarchy can be developed. Successful learning depends on the presentation of skills in a logically sequenced curriculum, with the sequence extending from lower to higher order concepts and skills.

Task sequences may be forward chained or backward chained. Backward chaining is called descending task analysis, because it begins with a target task (the terminal behavior) and works backwards to prerequisite sub-skills.

In descending task analysis, the teacher first states the target task that identifies the sub-skills necessary for performing the target task. These sub-skills are further delineated until a sub-skill level at which the child is able to perform the tasks is reached. Descending task analysis works backward to subsidiary tasks on the theory that the successful mastery of the easier skills preceding them in the learning hierarchy.

In forward-chaining or ascending task analysis, the teacher initiates instruction on the first sub-skill of a task sequence. Once the designated criterion mastery is reached, instruction continues to the next sub-skill, linking it to the previously mastered response that now serves as a prerequisite. More complex sub-skills in the learning hierarchy are introduced as preceding sub-skills are mastered.

TEACHER CERTIFICATION STUDY GUIDE

Effectiveness of instruction is keyed to the teacher's ability to know when mastery criterion has been reached on each sub-skill in ascending order. If instruction on succeeding sub-skill levels begins before mastery of a lower level skill is achieved, performance gaps will weaken the chances of that student reaching the target task, or terminal behavior. Too slow a pace creates boredom and may lessen the student's enthusiasm for progressing through subsequent steps. Therefore, successful learning depends not only on presentation of skills in a logically sequenced learning hierarchy, but also upon the responsiveness to criteria mastery and appropriate movement through levels of difficulty.

Descending Task Analysis

TEACHER DOES

    Step 1 Statement of Target Task

    Step II Statement of Sub-skills

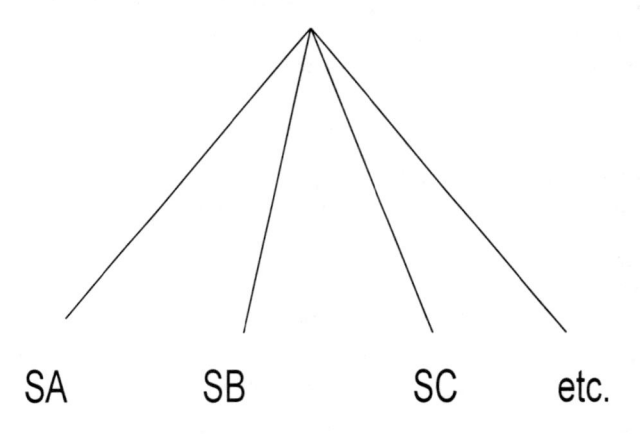

        SA   SB   SC   etc.

    Step III Statement of Sub-skills

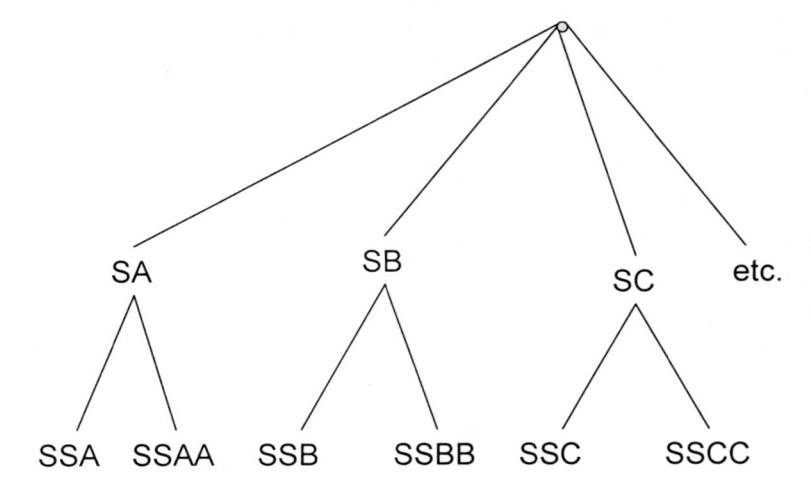

    SA   SB   SC   etc.

  SSA SSAA SSB SSBB SSC SSCC

TEACHER ASKS

Is it significant?
Is it relevant?

Are these sub-skills necessary for performing target tasks?

Are these sub-skills sufficient for performing target tasks?

Are these sub-skills relevant for performing target tasks?

Are there any missing or redundant sub-skills?

Can the child perform any of these tasks?
Are these sub-skills necessary for performing target tasks?

Are these sub-skills sufficient for performing target tasks?

Are these sub-skills relevant for performing target tasks?

Are there any missing or redundant sub-skills?

Can the child perform any of these tasks?

SPECIAL EDU. CROSS-CATEGORY

Diagnostic-Prescriptive Methods

Diagnostic and prescriptive teaching refer to the idea of using assessment data to diagnosis the difficulties the student may be having in a particular area. In the case of emotional disorders, this diagnosis may come from a variety of practitioners. Once the diagnosis is made and the problem has been clearly identified, the prescriptive teaching plan comes next. At this juncture, the educator looks at the specifics of the diagnosis and develops a plan to address all of the skills and issues. This method is quite similar to the approach a doctor takes with patients, in which the problem is found and a treatment is started to address the specific problem.

Behavioral Assessment

Cone and Hawkins (cited in Kerr & Nelson, 1983) conceptualize behavioral assessment as a process involving five phases: (1) screening and general disposition, (2) defining and generally quantifying the problem, (3) pinpointing target behaviors and designing interventions, (4) monitoring the problem, (5) following up on the purpose to identify the intervention priorities from a wide array of individuals and behaviors.

In general, screening devices are initially given to large numbers of students (similar to vision and hearing tests) as a means of identifying students at risk. These devices may be of a standardized, formal type, or they may be informal tools either produced commercially or made by the teacher. A teacher may select formal, standardized rating scales (e.g., Burk's Behavior Rating Scale, Devereux Child Behavior, or Adolescent, Elementary School Rating Scale), checklists of behaviors, self-concept scales (e.g., Piers-Harris Children's Self-Concept Scale), or the teacher may design and develop those types of tools him or herself. Self-inventories, questionnaires or self-reports (e.g., a self test, thinking about yourself), and sociometric devices (e.g., class pictures, a class play) may be used, or similar procedures designed by the teacher can be employed. Interviews may be held with the child or with others who possess knowledge about the child. Regardless, first level information is obtained and must be followed by a more extensive assessment when there is an indication of a problem.

The second phase involves comprehensive assessments to confirm or disprove screening results. Individual strengths and weaknesses are pinpointed, and interventions (including referral) are projected or formulated. Environmental variables (e.g., settings, persons, stimuli) that have an effect on the behaviors also need to be identified.

Target behaviors are selected in phase three, which need to be modified or taught. In order to be targeted, behaviors must be observable, measurable, and defined. Behavioral objectives are stated in a positive direction with behaviors, conditions, and criteria specified.

Student progress is monitored and evaluated during phase four. Instructional and behavioral plans are modified based on observed or recorded behavioral results. The frequency, duration, and magnitude of the behavior will influence the type of measurement system the teacher implements. The recording procedure will be largely determined by the person doing the observation (e.g., teacher, child, another teacher), the time available for observation (e.g., all day, one period, portions of periods), and the equipment available for measurement (e.g., wrist counter, timing device, pad and pen). Reliability may be determined by comparing and calculating agreements and disagreements of behavioral observations performed by the regular observer, and, on occasion, by an independent observer, as well.

During phase five, data is transferred onto visual graphs or charts and analyzed; data-based decisions and adjustments are then made possible. Formative (i.e., ongoing) and summative (i.e., occurring after teaching and learning) evaluations are mechanisms for documenting social and academic progress. Reversal (i.e., baseline, treatment) and comparison (i.e., baseline, treatment, and return to baseline) designs compare the behavior before and after treatment, with the latter demonstrating the effectiveness of the intervention. Multiple baselines are used to determine effects of interventions on two or more behaviors. The process is cyclical in that treatment may be adjusted, or if mastery is determined, other target behaviors can be pinpointed and interventions programmed.

The Individuals with Disabilities Education Act (IDEA) specifically calls for a functional behavior assessment when a child with a disability has his or her present placement modified for disciplinary reasons. IDEA does not elaborate on how a behavioral assessment should be conducted, as the procedures may vary dependent on the specific child.

TEACHER CERTIFICATION STUDY GUIDE

Essential Elements of Behavior Intervention Plans

A behavior intervention plan is utilized to reinforce or teach positive behavior skills. It is also known as a behavior support plan or a positive intervention plan. The child's team normally develops this plan, which includes the essential elements of:

- Skills training to increase the likelihood of appropriate behavior
- Modifications that will be made in classrooms or other environments to decrease or remove problem behaviors
- Strategies to take the place of problem behaviors
- Appropriate behaviors that serve the same function for the child
- Support mechanisms for the child to utilize for the most appropriate behaviors

The IEP team determines whether the school discipline procedures need to be modified for a child, or whether the penalties need to be different from those written into the policy. This decision should be based on an assessment and a review of the records, including the discipline records or any manifestation determination review(s) that have been concluded by the school.

A child's IEP or behavior intervention plan should concentrate on teaching skills. Sometimes, school discipline policies are not successful in rectifying problem behaviors—that is, the child does not learn what the school staff intended through the use of punishments such as suspension. The child may learn instead that problem behaviors are useful in meeting a need, such as being noticed by peers. When this is true, it is difficult to defend punishment, by itself, as effective in changing problem behaviors.

One of the most useful questions parents can ask when they have concerns about the discipline recommendations for their child is, "Where are the data that support the recommendations?" Special education decisions are based on data. If school staff wants to use a specific discipline procedure, they should check for data that support the use of the procedure.

Concepts Utilized in Behavior Modification Procedures

Behavior modification is a systematic approach to the modification of behavior. Its use has the effect of strengthening, maintaining, or weakening target behaviors. Concerns that have surfaced over the use of behavior modification pertain primarily to the concept of free will versus control by external forces. In addition, misunderstanding of behavioral procedures and misclassification of other types of treatment (e.g., electroconvulsive therapy) have perpetuated doubts about ethical use.

SPECIAL EDU. CROSS-CATEGORY 180

Factors that should be taken into consideration by educators who desire to use behavior modification in a responsible manner are as follows:

1. **Competency of teacher:** A responsible teacher who attempts to use behavior modification will have an understanding of the principles and techniques he or she is applying.
2. **Selection of appropriate goals:** Behaviors targeted for change should be those that will benefit and can be changed by the students.
3. **Accountability:** This implies being able to evaluate behaviorally stated goals, clearly described procedures, and results defined in terms of direct, functional relationships between interventions and behaviors.

Behavior modification is based on the premise that all behavior, regardless of its appropriateness, has been learned; therefore, it can be changed. The behavioral model deals with behaviors we can see, hear, or measure. After the behavior that is targeted for change has been identified and the reinforcers located, behavior can be systematically modified through behavior modification procedures.

Some of these procedures are used to increase behaviors (e.g., positive reinforcement, negative reinforcement, shaping and token economy), and other procedures are used to decrease behaviors (e.g., punishment, extinction). A procedure can be used to increase the rate of a desirable behavior while decreasing the rate of related but undesirable behaviors (i.e., differential reinforcement).

The ABCs of behavior modification are specified as the antecedent, the behavior, and the consequence. Stimuli that precede the behavior are referred to as antecedents; stimuli that follow the behavior are known as consequential events. All three are interactive components.

Certain environmental conditions or events become linked to particular behaviors over time. Any behavior is more likely to occur in the presence of the stimuli that accompanied the behavior when it was reinforced in the past. This is the principle of stimulus control, which describes a relationship between behavior and its antecedent stimuli (events or condition occurring before the behavior is performed).

Following the behaviors, consequential events occur. These events (i.e., reward, punishment) control the behavior of their effects. Behavior that is followed by a pleasant consequence tends to be increased or repeated. Behavior followed by an unpleasant consequence tends to show a decrease.

Consequential events have a functional relationship with behavior. Similarly, behavior that avoids or terminates an aversive stimulus will show an increase. For example, Jim avoids having his teacher frown at him by finishing his work. On another occasion, Jim terminates her disapproving scowl by returning to his desk and finishing his work.

Several approaches to student discipline are offered in this review. Examples are given to demonstrate principles of each. Teachers need to be familiar with these well-known approaches so that they can be used selectively when particular student behaviors and situations occur.

Life-Space Interview (Redl)
Life-space interview is a here-and-now intervention built around each child's life experience. It is applied in an effort to increase conscious awareness of distorted perceptions. These perceptions may be directed toward how one reacts to the behaviors and pressures of other persons. It is sometimes referred to as "emotional first aid."

> Example
>
> Jack, a 10-year-old fifth grader, is enrolled in Mr. Bird's resource room for students with behavior disorders. Jack's social behavior is creating difficulties for him, his classmates, and his teachers. Jack's unacceptable social behaviors have caused him to be ignored by some students, overly rejected by others, and used as a scapegoat by a few.
>
> Essentially, Jack believes he is unacceptable to his peers. He feels that others are making fun of him or rejecting him even when they are being friendly. When Jack feels he is being rejected, he immediately attempts to escape his discomfort. He tries to isolate himself by placing his backpack over his head, walking the hallways sideways with his face to the wall, and so on.
>
> Mr. Bird recognizes that eventually this behavior will affect all facets of Jack's functioning—including his academics. Involved staff discusses and agrees that life-space interviewing is an appropriate intervention in Jack's case. Each time Jack engages in the behavior, he is immediately removed by a supportive adult from the setting in which the behavior occurs.

The incident is reconstructed and discussed, and a plan for a more acceptable response by Jack to a classmate's smile, wave, and so on, is agreed on by Jack and the supportive adult. Jack returns to the setting in which the behavior occurred and continues his daily schedule.

Over time and after many life-space interviews, Jack increases his capacity to differentiate between social acceptance and rejection.

Interview Guidelines

1. Be polite to the individual. If the teacher doesn't have control of his or her emotions, it is best not to begin the interview.
2. Sit, kneel, or stand to establish eye contact. Talk with, never at, the individual being interviewed.
3. When unsure about the history of the incident, investigate. Do not conduct an interview on the basis of second- or third-hand information or rumors.
4. Ask appropriate questions to obtain a knowledgeable grasp of the incident. However, do not probe areas of unconscious motivation; limit the use of "why" questions.
5. Listen to the individual and attempt to comprehend his or her perception of the incident.
6. Encourage the individual to ask questions. Respond to the child's questions appropriately.
7. When the individual is suffering from apparent shame and/or guilt because of the incident, attempt to reduce and minimize these feelings.
8. Facilitate the individual's efforts to communicate what he or she wishes to do.
9. Work carefully and patiently with the individual to develop a mutually acceptable plan of action for immediate or future implementation.

Reality Therapy
In reality therapy, the therapist or teacher takes present behavior and confronts students about whether their behavior is helping them or hurting them. Confrontational questions assist the individual in taking responsibility for his or her behavior. Responsibility is seen as the ability to fulfill one's personal needs in a manner that does not deprive other individuals of their ability to fulfill their own needs. The teacher acts as a facilitator as her or he assists the individual is developing a plan by which to resolve troublesome behavior. The person generally feels more responsible for enacting the plan if it is written and signed. In summary, reality therapy is the process of teaching an individual to face existing reality, to function responsibly, and, as a result, to fulfill personal needs.

Example

Kyle, a tenth-grade student at Greenwood High School, had superior academic potential. However, he was flunking several subjects. It became evident that Kyle's future relative to graduation and college was being affected by his behavior.

Mr. Scott, Kyle's favorite teacher, decided he needed to help the boy. He did not want Kyle to jeopardize his future. Mr. Scott decided to use the reality therapy approach with Kyle. After all, he and Kyle were friends; he cared about the boy; and he knew Kyle could improve with help.

In their first session, Mr. Scott confronted Kyle with questions like "What are you doing?" "Is it helping you?" "If not, what else could you do to help yourself?" It was found that Kyle would not work in any subject area if he did not like the teacher. If the teacher was too demanding, unfriendly, and so on, Kyle just gave up—he refused to study.

Kyle recognized that his behavior was only harmful to himself. He and Mr. Scott developed a plan of action. During the next few months, they met regularly to monitor Kyle's progress and to write and revise the plan as needed. Kyle learned to accept responsibility for his behavior. His grades improved dramatically.

Interview Guidelines

1. Be personal. Demonstrate to the individual that a teacher can be a friend who cares about the individual and who is interested in his or her welfare.
2. Focus the therapeutic process on the individual's present behavior, not his or her past behavior. Accept the individual's expressed feelings, but do not probe into unconscious motivators. Confront by asking "what," "how," and "who" questions. Limit asking "why" questions.
3. Do not preach, moralize, or make value judgments about the individual's behavior.
4. Help the individual formulate a practical plan to increase responsible behavior.
5. Encourage the individual to overtly make a commitment to the mutually agreed-upon plan.
6. Do not accept the individual's excuses for irresponsible behavior. When a plan fails or cannot be implemented, develop another.
7. Do not punish the individual for irresponsible behavior. As a general principle, allow the individual to realize the logical consequences of irresponsible behavior unless the consequences are unreasonably harmful.
8. Provide the individual with emotional support and security throughout the therapeutic process.

Transactional Analysis (Berne & Harris)
Transactional analysis is considered a rational approach to understanding human behavior. It is based on the assumption that individuals can learn to have trust in themselves, think for themselves, make their own decisions, and express personal feelings. According to this approach, there are different persons within us. Our day-to-day experiences serve as stimuli that evoke memories of past situations and cause a person to relive the events with recorded images and feelings.

This behavioral intervention provides the teacher with a framework for viewing what is said to and by students. The principles of this intervention can be applied on the job, in the home, in the classroom, and in the neighborhood—wherever people deal with people. Although transactional analysis procedures are primarily intellectual or cognitive, the person using them gains emotional as well as intellectual insight into self and others.

The personality is composed of three ego states: (1) the parent, (2) the child, and (3) the adult. Individuals are in the parent state when acting, thinking, and feeling as they observed their parents doing. Individuals are in the adult ego state when dealing with current reality, gathering facts, and computing objectively.

Individuals are in the child ego state when they are feeling and acting as they did when they were children.

Ego states are most evident and observable in an individual's interactions and exchanges with others. The process of transactional analysis is primarily the examination of exchanges between the individual and others in the environment.

Although there are many specific types of transaction, there are three major ones:

1. <u>Complementary transaction.</u> These are predictable reactions received from a person in response to an act. For example, the usual response of a child to a parent requesting him or her to clean a room is that the child grumbles a little but does it.
2. <u>Cross - transactions</u>. These transactions occur when an individual receives an unpredictable response from another individual. For example, an unexpected response from a child who usually cleans his room might be, "No way, I won't do it. You're the mother, and it's your job." An unexpected response from a colleague who is usually helpful in emergencies when requested to substitute might be, "Forget it. I have enough to do. It's your emergency, your class, and your problem, not mine."
3. <u>Ulterior transactions</u>. These transactions have a hidden message in which what is stated is not the real message being sent. For example, imagine a man who is both husband and a father painting his large family house. He would like and needs help. Instead of saying, "Hey, people, I need help," he complains about the work, his tiredness and muscle aches, his age, the size of the house, and so on. His purpose is really to obtain help, not sympathy.

All humans have a personality composed of the three ego states, which are a result of our reactions to stimulation from others in the environment. This reaction is a result of reinforcement, or strokes, from others in the environment. A stroke is a form of recognition, or attending to, that is necessary for all human beings. Strokes may be verbal or physical, positive or negative.

Four life positions that predominate in a person's personality are:

1. I'm not okay; you're okay.
2. I'm not okay; you're not okay.
3. I'm okay; you're not okay.
4. I'm okay; you're okay.

The fourth position—we are both okay—is only entered because of a conscious and verbal decision. Transactional analysis is designed to help the individual attain this position.

SPECIAL EDU. CROSS-CATEGORY

Role-playing and Psychodrama (Moreno & Raths)

Psychodrama was originally developed for therapeutic purposes. Role playing can help to clarify feelings and emotions as they relate to existing reality in three ways.

1. It can focus on real occurrences. An incident may be reenacted and the participants told to attend to the feelings aroused, or an incident may be reenacted with the participants changing roles and attending the feelings of the aroused by these new roles. An individual may be directed to deliver a soliloquy (monologue) to re-create an emotionally loaded event. Emphasis here is on expressing feelings that were hidden or held back when the event first occurred.
2. It can focus on significant others. The individual may portray a significant person in his or her life about whom a great amount of conflict is felt.
3. It can focus on processes and feelings occurring in new situations. Directions for this type of role playing may be very specific, with the participants provided with special characters and actions, or directions may be vague, allowing the participants to form their own characters.

Role playing and psychodrama techniques have been incorporated into effective education programs concerned with clarification of values and standards.

Example

George, a 13-year old eighth grader, was shorter than the other boys in his grade. First the girls and then the boys grew several inches, while George's height seemed to stay the same. His classmates were constantly making fun of his size. They called him "runt," "shorty," "midget," and "dwarf." Each day, someone came up with a new name to call him.

George was a sensitive person, and whenever he was called a name, he withdrew. More and more, his teacher began seeing George sitting alone while the others played. Mrs. Wright was very concerned about George's mental well-being and his classmates' lack of consideration and empathy overall. She believed that role playing might be a method of helping the whole class, including George, gain insight into their behavior.

As the students began to empathize with the feelings of the characters they were role playing, George became more accepted and less a target of their hurtful behavior. George began playing with the others more readily during free time.

SPECIAL EDU. CROSS-CATEGORY

The Principle of Contingency Management

The term contingency refers to the planned, systematic relationship established between a behavior and a consequence. As such, contingency management is an approach that teachers use to attempt to modify behavior by managing the contingencies, or consequences, of those behaviors. Contingency management incorporates the systematic use of reinforcement and punishment to develop, maintain, or change behavior. The following guidelines may be used in developing a contingency management plan.

1. <u>Decide what to measure</u>. A desired target behavior is specified and defined.
2. <u>Select a measurement strategy</u>. The behavior must be observable and measurable, as in frequency and duration.
3. <u>Establish a baseline</u>. The level of the behavior prior to implementing a treatment plan or an intervention must be established.
4. <u>Design a contingency plan.</u> Reinforcers or punishers are selected that correspond with behavioral consequences.
5. <u>Implement the contingency plan</u>. Collect data, provide reinforcement or punishment for the behavioral occurrences in accordance with the schedule selected for use, and record behavioral measurements on a graph.
6. <u>Evaluate the program</u>. Modify the contingency management plan as needed. Modifications can be achieved by (1) a reversal to baseline to determine effect of treatment on behavior, (2) changing the reinforcer or punisher if needed, or (3) implementing a new treatment.

A contingency management plan can be very useful in the classroom setting. In most classrooms, teachers specify what behaviors are expected and the contingencies for performing those behaviors. Contingencies are stated in the form of "If...then..." statements. Contingency management may take the form of various treatment techniques, such as token economies, contingency contracting, and precision teaching.

Students may be involved in the process of designing, implementing, and evaluating a contingency management plan. They can decide on behaviors that are in need of modification, select their reinforcers, assist in data collection, record the data on graphs, and evaluate the effectiveness of the contingency or treatment plan.

The ultimate goal in allowing students to participate in contingency management is to encourage their use of the procedures they have been taught to manage their own behavior. As with self-recording, the transition from teacher-managed to student-managed programs must be gradual, and students should be explicitly taught how to use self-reinforcement or self-punishment.

TEACHER CERTIFICATION STUDY GUIDE

The Method and Application of Backward-Chaining

Behavioral chaining is a procedure in which individual responses are reinforced for occurring in sequence to form a complex behavior. Each link is subsequently paired with its preceding one, thus each link serves as a conditioned reinforcer for the link immediately preceding it. Behavior chains can be acquired by having each step in the chain verbally prompted or demonstrated. The prompts can then be faded and the links combined, with reinforcement, occurring after the last link has been performed.

In backward chaining, the components of the chain are acquired by reversing the order of the steps (or sub-skills) necessary to successfully complete the target task. The task is modeled in correct order by the teacher, and then each sub-skill is modeled in reverse order from beginning to end. The student practices the modeled sub-skill, and upon mastery of it, reverses back to the correct order until the task is completed. In this way, the final link or target behavior is consistently reinforced, and preceding links are built up, one at a time.

An example of backward chaining is evident when teaching a child to dress himself. The child is given the instruction, "Jimmy, take your jacket off," and his jacket is unzipped and lifted off the shoulders and down the arms until only the cuffs remain on Jimmy's wrists. If he does not pull the jacket the rest of the way off, he is physically guided to do so. He is given a reinforcer following removal of the garment. During the next session, the procedure is repeated, but the sleeve is left on his arms. In subsequent sessions, both arms are left in the sleeves, and then the jacket is left zipped. The instruction, "Jimmy, take your jacket off" is always presented, and a reinforcer is given only when the task is completed. The removal of each garment is taught in this manner; and the component steps are combined until an instruction like, "Jimmy, take your jacket off" has acquired stimulus.

Backward chaining may be used to teach other self-help skills such as toileting, grooming, and eating. Many academic and pre-academic readiness skills can be effectively taught using this procedure, as well. Steps until the final one are provided, with prompting occurring on the last step, and reinforcements delivered following the behavior. Each step in the program is prompted until the student can perform the entire sequence by him or herself. The backward chaining procedure may be of greatest assistance when a student experiences limited receptive abilities or imitative behavior.

Assertive Discipline

Assertive discipline, developed by Canter and Canter, is an approach to classroom control that allows the teacher to constructively deal with misbehavior and maintain a supportive environment for the students. The assumptions behind assertive discipline are:

- Behavior is a choice
- Consequences for not following rules are natural and logical, not a series of threats or punishments.
- Positive reinforcement occurs for desired behavior
- The focus is on the behavior and the situation, not the student's character

The assertive discipline plan should be developed as soon as the teacher meets the students. The students can become involved in developing and discussing the needs for the rules. Rules should be limited to four to six basic classroom rules that are simple to remember and positively stated (e.g., "Raise hand to speak" instead of "Don't talk without permission").

1. *Recognize and remove roadblocks to assertive discipline.* Replace negative expectations with positives, and set reasonable limits for students.
2. *Practice an assertive response style.* That is, clearly state teacher expectations and expect the students to comply with them.
3. *Set limits.* Take into consideration the students' behavioral needs, the teacher's expectations, and set limits for behavior. Decide ahead of time what to do when the rules are broken or followed.
4. *Follow through promptly with consequences when students break the rules.* However, the students should clearly know in advance what to expect when a rule is broken. Conversely, follow through with the promised rewards for compliance and good behavior. This reinforces the concept that individuals choose their behavior and that there are consequences for their behavior.
5. *Devise a system of positive consequences.* Positive consequences do not always have to be food or treats. However, rewards should not be promised if it is not possible to deliver them.

All teachers who work with special education have a need for knowledge that includes skills required for classroom management. It is the teacher's responsibility to use whatever techniques and strategies he or she can to develop each child's learning potential to the fullest. In order to accomplish this goal, a teacher must know how to make a learning environment attractive, comfortable, safe, and motivating.

Careful structuring of the classroom environment and attention to variables (such as student scheduling, time of day allotments, and use of equipment and materials) is essential to effective management of the classroom. The teacher must know which factors promote selective attention and facility in learning. Above all, he or she must remain an effective facilitator for children who may otherwise become discouraged in the school environment.

Competencies in this section emphasize preventive discipline, behavior modification, social skills instruction, and techniques for enhancing the self-concept of students. Identification of inappropriate behaviors, along with knowledge of procedures for the modification of behavior, must be known and used consistently in order to obtain results. The conditions under which antecedent and consequent stimuli influence behaviors in the educational setting must be thoroughly understood. Therefore, the teacher must be able to apply behavior analysis in a scientific manner with a view toward understanding behavior and its functional relationship to environmental events.

Additionally, students must be able to practice newly learned social skills in a learning environment that support and accepts their attempts. The teacher must sometimes use other counseling and discipline approaches that are effective if applied in a systematic manner. Self-concept training is generally needed for students who have experienced frustration and failure. The effective teacher will acquire conceptual understanding of these principles, model them, and utilize them in a wide range of teaching situations. In this way, students will be assisted toward generalizing behaviors across settings.

COMPETENCY 26.0 UNDERSTAND STRATEGIES AND TECHNIQUES USED TO IMPROVE STUDENTS' TRANSITION TO ADULT LIFE ROLES

For example: strategies and techniques that promote care for self and others, positive health and fitness habits, and travel and mobility routines; strategies for increasing students' understanding of the responsibilities associated with friendship, human sexuality, family life, and parenting; strategies for promoting students' ability to advocate for themselves and obtain assistance as necessary (e.g., from family, government agencies, consumer organizations, advocacy groups); sensitivity to ways that cultural diversity may affect students' attitudes toward and strategies for self-advocacy; and techniques for promoting independent and community living skills, citizenship skills, multicultural awareness, and participation in civic, leisure, and recreational activities.

- *Please refer to Competencies 24.0, 23.0, and 27.0 for information that is applicable to this skill.*

TEACHER CERTIFICATION STUDY GUIDE

COMPETENCY 27.0 UNDERSTAND PRINCIPLES OF AND PROCEDURES FOR SUPPORTING STUDENTS' TRANSITION FROM SCHOOL TO EMPLOYMENT AND/OR POST-SECONDARY EDUCATION AND TRAINING

For example: techniques and settings for promoting career and vocational awareness, exploration, and preparation; strategies for providing work experience and career planning services to students; and appropriate goals, objectives, activities, benchmarks, programs, and support to promote transition into employment and/or post-secondary education.

Transition Planning and Student Independence

Transition planning is mandated in the Individuals with Disabilities Education Act (IDEA). The transition planning requirements ensure that planning is begun at age 14 and continued through high school. Transition planning and services focus on a coordinated set of student-centered activities designed to facilitate the student's progression from school to post-school activities. Transition planning should be flexible and focus on the developmental and educational requirements of the student at different grades and times.

Transition planning is a student-centered event that necessitates a collaborative endeavor. In reference to secondary students, the responsibilities are shared by the student, parents, secondary personnel, and postsecondary personnel, who are all members of the transition team.

In most cases when transition is mentioned, it refers to a child 14 or over; however, in some cases, children younger than 14 may need transition planning and assistance. Depending on the child's disability and its severity, a child may need assistance with transitioning to school from home, or to school from a hospital or institution (or any other setting). In these cases, the members of the transition team may also include doctors or nurses, social workers, speech therapist, and physical therapists.

It is important that the student play a key role in transition planning. This will entail asking the student to identify preferences and interests and to attend meetings on transition planning. The degree of success experienced by the student in postsecondary educational settings depends on the student's degree of motivation, independence, self-direction, self-advocacy, and academic abilities developed in high school. Student participation in transition activities should be implemented as early as possible, and no later than age 16.

In order to contribute to the transition planning process, the student should Understand his or her learning disability and the impact it has on learning and work; implement achievable goals; present a positive self-image by emphasizing strengths, while understanding the impact of the learning disability; know how and when to discuss and ask for needed accommodations; be able to seek instructors and learning environments that are supportive; and establish an ongoing personal file that consists of school and medical records, individualized education program (IEP), resume, and samples of academic work.

The primary function of parents during transition planning is to encourage and assist students in planning and achieving their educational goals. Parents should also encourage students to cultivate independent decision-making and self-advocacy skills.

Transition planning involves input from four groups: the student, parents, secondary education professionals, and postsecondary education professionals. The result of effective transition from a secondary to a postsecondary education program is a student with a learning disability who is confident, independent, self motivated, and eager to achieve career goals. This effective transition can be achieved if the team consisting of the student, parents, and professional personnel work as a group to create and implement effective transition plans. The transition team of a student entering the workforce may also include community members, organizations, company representatives, vocational education instructors, and job coaches.

Transition Services

Transition services are different for each student. They must take into account the student's interests and preferences. Evaluation of career interests, aptitudes, skills, and training may also be considered.

The transition activities that have to be addressed, unless the IEP team finds it uncalled for, are: (a) instruction, (b) community experiences, and (c) the development of objectives related to employment and other post-school areas.

   a) Instruction – The instruction part of the transition plan deals with school instruction. The student should have a portfolio completed upon graduation. Students should research and plan for further education and/or training after high school. Education can be in a college setting, technical school, or vocational center. Goals and objectives created for this transition domain depend on the nature and severity of the student's disability, the student's interests in further education, plans made for accommodations needed in future education and training, and identification of post-secondary institutions that offer the requested training or education.

b) Community experiences – This part of the transition plan investigates how the student utilizes community resources. Resources entail places for recreation, transportation services, agencies, and advocacy services. It is essential for students to deal with the following areas:

- Recreation and leisure (examples: movies, YMCA, religious activities)
- Personal and social skills (examples: calling friends, religious groups, going out to eat)
- Mobility and transportation (examples: passing a driver's license test or utilizing Dial-A-Ride)
- Agency access (examples: utilizing a phone book and making calls)
- System advocacy (example: have a list of advocacy groups to contact)
- Citizenship and legal issues (example: registering to vote)

c) Development of employment – This segment of the transition plan investigates becoming employed. Students should complete a career-interest inventory and have the opportunity to investigate different careers. Many work skill activities can take place within the classroom, home, and community. Classroom activities may concentrate on employability skills, community skills, mobility, and vocational training. Home and neighborhood activities may concentrate on personal responsibility and daily chores. Community based activities may focus on part-time work after school and in the summer, cooperative education or work-study, individualized vocational training, and volunteer work.

d) Daily living skills – This segment of the transition plan is also important, although it is not essential to the IEP. Living away from home can be an enormous undertaking for people with disabilities. Numerous skills are needed to live and function as an adult. In order to live as independently as possible, a person should have an income, know how to cook, clean, shop, pay bills, get to a job, and have a social life. Some living situations may entail independent living, shared living with a roommate, supported living, or group homes. Areas that may need to be looked into include personal and social skills, living options, income and finances, medical needs, community resources, and transportation.

Self-Advocacy

Learning about one's self involves the identification of learning styles, strengths and weakness, interests, and preferences. For students with mild disabilities, developing an awareness of the accommodations includes those necessary for finding a job and in postsecondary education. Students can also help identify alternative ways they can learn.

Self-advocacy involves the ability to effectively communicate one's own rights, needs, and desires. It also includes the ability to take responsibility for making decisions that impact one's life.

There are many elements in developing self-advocacy skills in students who are involved in the transition process. Helping the student to identify future goals or desired outcomes in transition planning areas is a good place to start. Self-knowledge is critical for the student in determining the direction that transition planning will take.

The role of the teacher in promoting self-advocacy should include encouraging the student to participate in the IEP process as well as other key parts of educational development. Self-advocacy issues and lessons are effective when they are incorporated into the student's daily life. Teachers should listen to the student's problems and ask the student for input. The teacher should talk with the student about possible solutions, discussing the pros and cons of doing something. A student who self-advocates should feel supported and encouraged. Good self-advocates know how to ask questions and get help from other people. They do not let other people do everything for them.

Students need to practice newly acquired self-advocacy skills. Teachers should have students role play various situations (such as setting up a class schedule, moving out of the home, and asking for accommodations needed for a course).

The impact of transition planning on a student with a disability is very great. The student should be an active member of the transition team, as well as the focus of all activities. Students often think that being passive and relying on others to take care of them is the way to get things done. However, students should be encouraged to express their opinions throughout the transition process. They need to learn how to express themselves so that others listen and take them seriously. These skills should be practiced within a supportive and caring environment.

TEACHER CERTIFICATION STUDY GUIDE

DOMAIN IV. WORKING IN A COLLABORATIVE LEARNING COMMUNITY

COMPETENCY 28.0 UNDERSTAND HOW TO ESTABLISH PARTNERSHIPS WITH OTHER MEMBERS OF THE SCHOOL COMMUNITY TO ENHANCE LEARNING OPPORTUNITIES FOR STUDENTS WITH SPECIAL NEEDS

For example: consultation, collaboration, and communication skills and strategies for working with other school staff and support service providers, including general education teachers, to solve problems and promote student achievement; and strategies for effectively providing services in a variety of educational contexts (e.g., coordinating instruction with other teaching professionals).

How to Advocate Effectively for Students with Disabilities and for the Special Education Program

Because of the unique needs of each student with disabilities, special education teachers frequently act as advocates for their students and the special education program in general.

In order to be an effective advocate, the teacher must be knowledgeable in a number of areas. First, the special educator must understand the general education program. Factors such as student expectations (learning standards), materials, and teacher training and in-service provide a starting point. If the special educator is familiar with the goals and overall program for all students at a specific grade level, he or she will have a clear picture of the direction to be working with his or her students with disabilities.

The special educator should also have a clear understanding of each student's strengths and needs. He or she must consider how each student can participate in the general education curriculum to the extent that it is beneficial for that student (IDEA 2004). For example, the teacher should know when services and instruction should take place outside of the general education classroom.

In addition, special educators should have an understanding of alternate materials that are useful or necessary for students, as well as what resources for materials are available.

Knowledge of the Individuals with Disabilities Education Act (IDEA 2004) and NCLB (No Child Left Behind) provides an outline of legislative mandates for special education.

A clear understanding of the above points will allow the special educator to most effectively advocate for the most appropriate placement, programming, and materials for each student. The teacher must be able to advocate for research-based methods with measurable outcomes.

Oftentimes, advocacy happens between regular and special education teachers. A special educator may see modification or accommodation possibilities that could take place in the general education classroom. It is his or her responsibility to advocate those practices. The special education teacher may also offer to make supplementary materials or to work with a group of students in the general education setting to achieve that goal. When students with disabilities are in an inclusion classroom, give and take on the part of both teachers as a team is crucial.

The special education teacher may need to be an advocate for the program (or the needs of an individual student) with the administration. Although success for all students is important to administration, the teacher may be required to explain the need for comparable materials written at the different reading level, for assistance in the classroom, or for the availability of specific classes or therapies.

Occasionally, the local school district cannot provide an appropriate educational setting. The special educator must then advocate with the school district for appropriate placement of the child in another, more suitable environment.

A Plan for Working with Classroom Aides and Volunteers

Teacher aides and volunteers can become an integral part of the classroom teaching process. Teacher aides may be full-time or part-time. Generally, programs serving the more severely disturbed have an aide that exclusively works with one teacher. Otherwise, teachers need to maximize the benefit of the time that the aide comes to the classroom. Classroom duties may be categorized as follows:

Paperwork: Classroom aides can correct student's homework, seatwork, and tests. They can observe and collect data on behavior, as well as chart student progress on graphs. Aides can also prepare materials (such as flash cards and worksheets) for tutoring and learning centers. If the teacher needs to modify a textbook for a student, the aide can help with this task by tape recording or highlighting texts. The aide can also be used for "housekeeping" duties such as making bulletin boards, photocopying, and filing.

Classroom Instruction: Classroom aides can help individual students with making up work after an absence, or they may tutor students who need extra practice with a difficult assignment. They can help conduct activities like listening to students as they read, read aloud, or tell stories to student groups, and help the teacher with hands-on activities.

The special educator is trained to work in a team approach. This occurs from the initial identification of students who appear to deviate from the normal performance or behavior for particular age- and grade-level students. The special education teacher serves as a consultant (or as a team member, depending on the school district) to the student support team. If the student is referred, the special education teacher may be asked to collect assessment data for the forthcoming comprehensive evaluation. This professional then generally serves on the multidisciplinary eligibility, individualized educational planning, and placement committees. If the student is placed in a special education setting, the special educator continues to coordinate and collaborate with regular classroom teachers and support personnel at the school-based level.

Teachers of exceptional students are expected to manage many roles and responsibilities, not only as they concern their students, but also with respect to students' caregivers and other involved educational, medical, therapeutic, and administrative professionals. Because the needs of exceptional students are by definition multidisciplinary, a teacher of exceptional children often serves as the hub of a many-pronged wheel, communicating, consulting, and collaborating with the various stakeholders in a child's educational life. Managing these relationships effectively can be a challenge, but is central to successful work in exceptional education.

Paraprofessionals and General Education Teachers

Paraprofessionals and general education teachers are important collaborators with teachers of exceptional students. Although they may not have the theoretical experience to assure their effective interaction with exceptional students, they often have daily exposure to them. They also bring valuable perspective to, and opportunities for breadth and variety in, an exceptional child's educational experience.

General education teachers offer curriculum and subject matter expertise and a high level of professional support, while paraprofessionals may provide insights born of their particular familiarity with individual students. CEC suggests that teachers can best collaborate with general education teachers and paraprofessionals by:

- Offering information about the characteristics and needs of children with exceptional learning needs
- Discussing and brainstorming ways to integrate children with exceptionalities into various settings within the school community
- Modeling best practices, instructional techniques, and accommodations and coaching others in their use
- Keeping communication about children with exceptional learning needs and their families confidential
- Consulting with these colleagues in the assessment of individuals with exceptional learning needs.
- Engaging these colleagues in group problem solving and in developing, executing, and assessing collaborative activities
- Offering support to paraprofessionals by observing their work with students, and offering feedback and suggestions

Related Service Providers and Administrators

Related service providers and administrators offer specialized skills and abilities that are critical to an exceptional education teacher's ability to advocate for his or her student and meet a school's legal obligations. Related service providers—speech, occupational, and language therapists; psychologists; and physicians—offer expertise and resources unparalleled in meeting a child's developmental needs. Administrators are often experts in the resources available at the school and local education agency levels, knowledgeable about the culture and politics of a school system, and powerful partners in meeting the needs of exceptional education teachers and students.

A teacher's most effective approach to collaborating with these professionals includes:

- Confirming mutual understanding of the accepted goals and objectives of the student with exceptional learning needs as documented in IEP
- Soliciting input about ways to support related service goals in classroom settings
- Understanding the needs and motivations of each and acting in support whenever possible
- Facilitating respectful and beneficial relationships between families and professionals
- Regularly and accurately communicating observations and data about the child's progress or challenges

SPECIAL EDU. CROSS-CATEGORY

Collaborative Planning with General Educators and Other Professionals

Research has shown that educators who collaborate become more diversified and effective in the implementation of curriculum and assessment of effective instructional practices. The ability to gain additional insight into how students learn and modalities of differing learning styles can increase a teacher's capacity to develop proactive instruction methods. Teachers who team teach or have daily networking opportunities can create a portfolio of curriculum articulation and inclusion for students.

People in business are always encouraged to network in order to further their careers. The same can be said for teaching. If English teachers get together and discuss what is going on in their classrooms, those discussions make the "whole" much stronger than the parts. Even if there are not formal opportunities for such networking, it's wise for schools or even individual teachers to develop and seek them.

Effective Collaboration and the Exceptional Student's Learning Environment

Collaboration
- Special educators are part of the instructional or planning team
- Teaming approaches are used for problem solving and program implementation
- Regular teachers, special education teachers, and other specialists collaborate (e.g., co-teach, team teach, work together on teacher assistance teams)

To ensure the greatest possibility of the child's educational success, all concerned parties must collaborate to discuss appropriate modifications to the learning environment. Each professional should bring forth information from his or her area of expertise and share it with the remainder of the team. Members should also share their knowledge of the child from previous interactions. For example, the child's previous teacher maybe able to offer some suggestions about modifications that were previously successful. The team then discusses the best accommodations for the child depending on the child's exceptionality and strengths and weaknesses. The team should communicate often to verify the success or failure of the modifications and adjust or add modifications as needed.

Scheduling
Scheduling is a very important topic to consider when thoroughly discussing each student. Not only is it important to ensure the child is receiving the necessary classes and extra assistance needed, but the time of the day each subject should be taught is also vital. For example, if the student is more alert and focused in the afternoon, he or she may need to take his or her weakest academic courses in the afternoon. Additionally, the nurse may know that the child takes medication after lunch that makes him or her drowsy, so that child may need to take his or her weakest academic courses in the morning.

Physical Arrangement
Physical arrangement is another important area to discuss with other professionals. The special education teacher and the previous teacher may offer suggestions based on their prior knowledge of the child. The child may function better in the front of the class or away from windows. A physical therapist may suggest the child is seated near the door. Therefore, it is essential that the team collaborates to discuss potential modification of the child's learning environment to address the needs of the whole child.

The role of the special education teacher and the general education teacher is to work together to ensure that students with disabilities are able to attain their educational objectives in the least restrictive environment. Some students are best served in the general education setting with additional accommodations, while other students may be best served in the special education setting. The educators must work together to decide what educational program is best suited for the student and where the student can best meet his or her goals and objectives.

These decisions should be made during the student's IEP meeting. It is important that the special education teacher, the general education teacher, and other interested professionals (such as speech teacher) are in attendance at the meeting so they can discuss and collaborate on their roles in helping the student.

Students with disabilities often experience insufficient access to and a lack of success in the general education curriculum. To promote improved access to the general curriculum for all learners, information should be presented in various formats using a variety of media forms; students should be given numerous methods to express and demonstrate what they have learned, and they should be provided with multiple entry points to engage their interest and motivate their learning.

Printed reading materials can be challenging to individuals with disabilities. Technology can help alleviate some of these difficulties by providing a change from printed text to electronic text that can be modified, enhanced, programmed, linked, and searched.

Text styles and font sizes can be changed as required by readers with visual disabilities. Text can be read aloud with computer-based text-to-speech translators and combined with illustrations, videos, and audio. Electronic text provides alternative formats for reading materials that can be tailored to match learner needs and structured in ways that enhance the learning process to expand both physical and cognitive access.

Collaborative Management of the Exceptional Student's Daily Routine
Effective collaboration among teachers and other professionals allows them to feel supported by other teachers in their mission to better meet the needs of their students. When collaboration is done successfully, teachers feel comfortable admitting what they do not know, as it is assumed that everyone is faced with challenges and has knowledge to bring to the situation.

When teachers are able to share challenges and difficulties, as well as successful teaching strategies, they can effectively evaluate teaching practices in school and provide a variety of resources for use in the classroom. For example, through collaboration, teachers can discuss effective techniques for dealing with transition time, so that what is done effectively in one class can be shared and tried in other settings.

When teachers share ideas for successful teaching practices with one another, they gain a wider base of knowledge to bring to the classroom. A variety of pedagogical approaches are available, and the teacher has a resource on which to rely when they need additional input or advice. Additionally, if a teacher is part of a community of sharing, that teacher is more likely to value the benefits of the support and knowledge created in such a community.

The teacher who places importance on collaboration, sharing, and peer-oriented learning often attempts to create a similar community in his or her class. A community of sharing within the classroom permits students to feel safe sharing ideas, challenges, and achievements with peers.

Depending on a student's disability and the school setting, special education teachers need to work with speech pathologists, school psychologists, occupational therapists, social workers, general education teachers, and community workers to plan the most optimal education program for each student. Special education teachers who work in inclusive settings or who co-teach or team-teach with general education teachers must spend enough time to sufficiently plan, develop, and put into practice an educational situation that is stimulating and suitable for all the students in the class.

Parents are also a significant part of the collaboration team. They are the experts on their children. Both parents and teachers have a lot to give in the educational planning for students with disabilities—if they work together, they can be a strong team.

Collaboration and working together require time, which is in short supply in the educational setting. Educators never have enough time to do everything that they want to do. In order to work effectively, special education teachers need the time to work and plan with parents and other professionals.

Collaborative Management of the Exceptional Student's Functional Integration

Review of Student Needs with Inclusion Teacher and Support Staff

It may be determined at a student's IEP meeting that some time in the general education setting is appropriate. The activities and classes listed for inclusion may include field trips, lunch, recess, physical education, music, library, art, computers, math, science, social studies, spelling, reading, and/or English. The IEP specifies which classes and activities and the amount of time that the student will be with general education peers. The IEP also lists any modifications or accommodations that will be needed.

Modifications that may be considered for the general education classroom include the amount of work or type of task required. Modifications for a student with a learning disability might include a learning a reduced number of spelling words or writing the vocabulary word that goes with a given definition instead of writing the definition that goes with a given word.

Accommodations are defined as changes to the school environment or the use of necessary equipment to overcome a disability. An accommodation for a student with a hearing impairment might include the use of an auditory trainer or asking another student to serve as a note taker.

Prior to the student starting in a general education placement (regardless of the minutes on the IEP), the general education teacher and support staff (if any) should be in-serviced on the student's disability and needs according to his or her IEP. Sometimes, this in-servicing happens as the student's IEP is developed. Other times it is done at a later date.

Student Expectations in the Inclusion Setting

The student with a disability should be well aware of his or her responsibilities in the general education setting. These expectations should include a combination of behavior and task performance issues. Although the student should be aware of needed accommodations and modifications—and should be a self-advocate for such—he or she should not use disability as an excuse for not fulfilling the expectations.

Students may benefit from previewing material, using a checklist to keep track of materials and assignments, keeping an assignment notebook, reviewing materials after the lesson, and using study aids such as flashcards. Sometimes, a behavior tracking chart may also be used.

Monitoring Student progress in the Inclusion Setting

Once the student is in the general education setting for the time and activities listed on the IEP, the special education teacher needs to monitor student progress. This can be done through verbal follow up with the general education teacher or by asking the teacher to complete a progress form. Of course, grades and the student's ability to restate learned information or answer questions are also indicators.

Evaluation of Student's Future Placement in the Inclusion Setting

If the student is successful in the general education activities and classes listed on the IEP, the special education teacher may consider easing back on modifications and accommodations on the next IEP. He or she may also consider adding minutes or classes for students' general education inclusion.

If the student has some difficulty, the special educator may consider adding more modifications or accommodations on the next IEP. If the student has significant difficulty, he or she may need to receive more services in the special education classroom.

Effective Instructional Planning with Other Educators

According to IDEA 2004, students with disabilities are to participate in the general education program to the extent that it is beneficial for them. As these students are included into a variety of general education activities and classes, the need for collaboration among teachers grows.

Co-Teaching

One model used for general education and special education teachers to collaborate is co-teaching. In this model, both teachers actively teach in the general education classroom. For example, both teachers might conduct a small science experiment group at the same time, switching groups at some point in the lesson. Perhaps in social studies, one teacher will lecture while the other teacher writes notes on the board or points out information on a map.

In the co-teaching model, the general education teacher and special educator often switch roles back and forth within a class period or at the end of a chapter or unit.

Push-In Teaching

In the push-in teaching model, the special educator teaches parallel material in the general education classroom. For example, when the regular education teacher teaches word problems in math, the special educator may be working with some students on setting up the initial problems and having them complete the computation. Another example would be in science: the general education teacher can ask review questions for a test, and the special educator can work with a student who has a review study sheet to show the answer from a group of choices.

In the push-in teaching model, it may appear that two versions of the same lesson are being taught, or that two types of student responses and activities are being monitored on the same material. The push-in teaching model is considered one type of differentiated instruction in which two teachers are teaching simultaneously.

Consultant Teaching

In the consultant teaching model, the general education teacher conducts the class after planning with the special educator about how to differentiate activities so the needs of the student with a disability are met.

In a social studies classroom using the consultant teaching model, both teachers may discuss what the expectations are for a student with a learning disability and fine motor difficulty when the class does reports on states. They may decide that doing a state report is appropriate for the student; however, he or she may use the computer to write the report so that he or she can utilize the spell check feature and create legible work.

Effective Curricula Planning Across Disciplines

The Individuals with Disabilities Education Act (1997) requires the collaboration of educational professionals in order to provide equitable opportunities for students with disabilities.

Collaboration in a school environment can take place between a variety of advocates for the students, including general educators, special education teachers, school psychologists, speech and language pathologists, interpreters, administrators, parents, and other professionals serving students with special needs. Using only sporadic communication between mainstream educators and other educational professionals damages the educational experience given to students.

Students with disabilities develop greater self-images and recognize their own academic and social strengths when included in the mainstream classroom and serviced by teams of educational professionals. In addition, this method finds staff with higher rates of professional growth, personal support, and enhanced teaching motivation. However, creating teacher-assistance teams to provide intervention support to the general educator often fails due to time constraints and the lack of commitment given to collaboration.

Every member of a collaborative team has precise knowledge of his or her discipline, and transdisciplinary teams integrate these areas. For example, an ESL teacher can provide knowledge regarding the development of language skills and language instruction methodology. Counselors and psychologists can impart knowledge as human development specialists and show their expertise in conducting small-group counseling and large-group interventions. School staff and instructors can benefit from what mainstream teachers add in the areas of performance information and knowledge of measures and benchmarks. Special education teachers can provide insight into designing and implementing behavior management programs as well as share strategies for effective instruction to students with special needs. Speech pathologists can contribute their knowledge of speech and language development and provide insight into the identification of learning disabilities in language-minority students.

Transdisciplinary teaming requires team members to build on the strengths and the needs of their particular populations. In this way, each professional can contribute when it comes to developing and implementing appropriate curricula.

Determination of Student Need for Assistive Technology
Oftentimes, the special educator will identify the need for consultation or testing in an area that a student is having difficulty. Testing or other professional evaluation may result in the trial or ongoing use of some form of assistive technology as listed on the student's IEP.

Training of School Personnel on Use of Assistive Technology
Although special educators are often trained in using a variety of assistive devices, advances in technology make it necessary for professionals to participate in ongoing training for new or unfamiliar equipment. This training may be conducted by a knowledgeable therapist or consultant in the school district, or school personnel may need to attend a workshop off campus.

Collaborative Techniques for Working with Classroom Paraprofessionals, Aides, and Volunteers

This section will specifically address the working relationship teachers should have with their colleagues in the classroom environment. There are six basic steps in having a rewarding collaborative relationship, whether working with paraprofessionals, aides, or volunteers.

While it is understood that there are many titles to those who may be assisting in the classroom, this section summarizes their titles as "classroom assistant."

1) *Get to know each other*
   The best way to start a relationship with anyone is to find time alone to get to know him or her. Give a new classroom assistant the utmost respect and look at this as an opportunity to share talents. Remember that this is an opportunity to find places of agreement and disagreement, which can help maintain and build a working relationship. Good working relationships require the knowledge of where each others strengths and weaknesses are. Share your strengths and weaknesses and listen to theirs. This knowledge may create one of one of the best working relationships you have ever had.

2) *Remember communication is a two-way street*
   As a professional educator, it is important to remember that you must actively communicate with others. This is especially important with a classroom assistant. Let them see you listening. Pay attention and make sure that your classroom assistant sees that you care what he or she thinks. Encourage them to engage in conversation. Also remember that asking your classroom assistant for details and insights may help you further meet the needs of your students.

   It is also your responsibility to remove and prevent communication barriers in your working relationship. You must be the one to avoid giving negative criticism or put downs. Do not "read" motivations into the actions of your classroom assistant. Learn about him or her through open communication.

3) *Establish clear roles and responsibilities*
The Access Center for Improving Outcomes of All Students K-8 has defined these roles in the chart on the next page. (Note that it is also often helpful to write out what roles and expectations you have for the classroom assistant together in a contract-type fashion.)

	Teacher Role	**Classroom Assistant Role**	**Areas of Communication**
Instruction	<ul><li>Plan all instruction, including the goals and objectives you expect in your small groups</li><li>Provide instruction in whole-class settings</li></ul>	<ul><li>Work with small groups of students on specific tasks, including review or re-teaching of content</li><li>Work with one student at a time to provide intensive instruction or remediation on a concept or skill</li></ul>	<ul><li>Teachers provide specific content and guidance about curriculum, students, and instructional materials</li><li>Classroom assistants note student progress and give feedback to teachers</li></ul>
Curriculum & Lesson Plan Development	<ul><li>Develop all lesson plans and instructional materials</li><li>Ensure alignment with standards, student needs, and IEPs</li></ul>	<ul><li>Provide assistance in development of classroom activities, retrieval of materials, and coordination of activities</li></ul>	<ul><li>Mutual review of lesson plan components prior to class</li><li>Teachers provide guidance about specific instructional methods</li></ul>
Classroom Management	<ul><li>Develop and guide class-wide management plans for behavior and classroom structures</li><li>Develop and monitor individual behavior management plans</li></ul>	<ul><li>Assist with the implementation of class-wide and individual behavior management plans</li><li>Monitor hallways, study hall, and other activities outside normal class</li></ul>	<ul><li>Teachers provide guidance about specific behavior management strategies and student characteristics</li><li>Classroom Assistants note student progress and activities and give feedback to teachers</li></ul>

("Working Together: Teacher-Paraeducator Collaboration" The Access Center for Improving Outcomes of All Students K-8, http://www.k8accesscenter.org/documents/RESOURCELIST3-1.doc)

SPECIAL EDU. CROSS-CATEGORY

4) *Plan together*
   Planning together lets your classroom assistant know you consider them valuable. It also provides a timeline of expectations that will aid both of you in your classroom delivery to students. It gives the impression to your students that you are on the same page and that you both know what is going to happen next.

5) *Show a united front*
   It is essential to let your students know that both adults in the room deserve the same amount of respect. Have a plan in place on how you should address negative behaviors individually as well as together. DO NOT make a statement in front of your students that your classroom assistant is wrong. Take time to address issues you may have regarding class time privately, not in front of the class.

6) *Reevaluate your relationship*
   Feedback is wonderful! Stop every now and then and discuss how you are working as a team. Be willing to listen to suggestions. Taking this time may be your opportunity to improve your working relationship.

Additional Reading:

"Creating a Classroom Team" http://www.aft.org/pubs-reports/psrp/classroom team.pdf

"Working Together: Teacher-Paraeducator Collaboration" The Access Center for Improving Outcomes of All Students K-8, http://www.k8accesscenter.org/documents/RESOURCELIST3-1.doc

TEACHER CERTIFICATION STUDY GUIDE

Enhancing Educational Opportunities through School Personnel

Communication

When implementing a behavior intervention plan, it is important that the plan is put into place with input from all the people who work with the student. This includes the student's parent, teachers, support teachers, and other interested parties. Through communication, all parties involved can agree on expectations as well as rewards or consequences.

If a reward or punishment is established in the school, it must be reinforced in the home setting so the student sees consistency and the behavior plan can flow between settings.

It is important that all parties ensure ongoing communication on a weekly (if not daily) basis to ensure that proper feedback and follow-up is taking place. The behavior intervention plan should define behaviors and consequences, and it should be adaptable to different places (such as the classroom, playground, after-school program, daycare, etc). In order for consistency to take place, proper communication must take place on an ongoing basis. Consistency helps the student learn what is expected of him or her.

The behavior intervention plan should be evaluated to make sure that it is being followed and is working effectively. The plan should be reviewed at least annually, but can be reviewed whenever any member of the team feels it is necessary.

At intervals scheduled by the IEP team, the behavioral intervention case manager, parent/guardian, and others shall evaluate the effectiveness of the behavioral intervention plan.

If the IEP team determines that major changes in the behavioral intervention plan are necessary, the teacher and behavioral intervention case manager conduct additional functional analysis assessments and propose changes.

The parent/guardian and the behavioral intervention case manager (or qualified designee) may make minor modifications in accordance with law without an IEP team meeting. The IEP team also may include in the plan contingency schedules for altering specified procedures, their frequency, or their duration without reconvening the IEP team.

Effective Attitudes for Optimum Student Programming and Success

Influence of Teacher Attitudes

The attitude of the teacher can have both a positive or negative impact on student performance. A teacher's attitude can impact the expectations that the teacher has toward the student's potential performance, as well as how the teacher behaves toward the student. This attitude, combined with expectations, can impact a student's self-image as well as his or her academic performance.

Negative teacher attitudes toward students with disabilities are detrimental to the handicapped students mainstreamed in general education classrooms. The phenomenon of a *self-fulfilling prophecy* is based on the attitude of the teacher. A self-fulfilling prophecy means that what one expects to happen is usually what ends up happening.

In the context of education, this can mean that the predictions of a teacher about the ability of a student to achieve or not to achieve educational objectives are often proven to be correct. In subtle ways, teachers communicate their expectations of individual students. In turn, the students may adjust their behavior to match the teacher's expectations.

Researchers in psychology and education have investigated this occurrence and discovered that many people are sensitive to verbal and nonverbal cues from others regarding how they expect to be treated. As a result, they may consciously and subconsciously change their behaviors and attitudes to conform to another person's hopes. Depending on the expectation, this can be either advantageous or detrimental.

The teacher's attitude toward a student can be shaped by a number of variables including race, ethnicity, disability, behavior, appearance, and social class. All of these variables can impact the teacher's attitude toward the student and how the student will achieve academically.

The teacher has a responsibility to not allow his or her negative attitudes toward the student to impact how he or she perceives or interacts with the student. If the teacher is able to communicate to all of the students that they have great potential (and is optimistic regarding this), then the students should excel in some aspect of their educational endeavors.

It can be hard for teachers to maintain a positive attitude at all times with all students, but it is important to at least be encouraging to all students at all times. Every student has the potential to be successful in school. Consistent encouragement can help turn a C student into a B or even A student, while negative feedback can lead to failure and loss of self-esteem.

Teachers should utilize their verbal communication skills to ensure that the things they communicate to students are said in the most positive manner possible. For example, instead of saying, "You talk too much," it would be more positive to state, "You have excellent verbal communication skills and are very sociable."

Teachers have a major influence on what happens in the classroom because they are the primary decision makers and they set the tone for how the information they distribute is absorbed.

For teachers to rise above their prejudices and preset attitudes, it is important that they are given training and support services to enable them to deal with students who come from challenging backgrounds or present challenging behaviors.

Develop the Capacity of Staff, Students, and Families to Intervene
Schools should provide the entire school community—teachers, students, parents, support staff—with training and support in responding to imminent warning signs, preventing violence, and intervening safely and effectively. Interventions must be monitored by professionals who are competent in the approach.

A continuum of educational services must be made available by the LEA. Children must be placed in their least restrictive environment and, insofar as possible, with regular classmates.

Communication Strategies
Effective communication strategies are required when dealing with families and students with disabilities. The communication strategies should be flexible and respond to the individual needs of the families.

Teachers traditionally communicate their educational philosophies to families through parent workshops or newsletters. These methods have their drawbacks; however, as in many cases, workshops may have low attendance as parents have problems with work schedules or with getting outside help to take care of a student with disability.

In addition, newsletters may be thrown away or not read thoroughly, and those that are only written in English distance parents for whom English is not their first language.

Family school partnerships are developed when families are encouraged to spend more time in the classroom and offered more information about their child's education. When families are in the classroom, they have a chance to observe teacher-student interactions, ask the teacher questions, and give feedback on curriculum or development. They also have an opportunity to meet other families.

As the structure of families in today's societies continue to change, teachers may need to try different family outreach strategies that target the new family structure. Teachers need to have a range of strategies for contacting parents, including using the telephone, email, letters, newsletters, classroom bulletin boards, and parent teacher conferences.

Teachers also need to be familiar with the student's home culture and have an appreciation for diversity. (One way in which to do this is to plan lessons and activities that are inclusive of the multi-cultural classroom.) Through effective communication, teachers can involve parents as leaders and decision makers in the school. As more students with disabilities are included in the general education curriculum, both special and regular educators will need training that focuses on effectively interacting with parents of children with disabilities to involve them as equal partners in the educational planning and decision-making process.

COMPETENCY 29.0 UNDERSTAND HOW TO PROMOTE STRONG SCHOOL-HOME RELATIONSHIPS

For example: strategies for establishing and maintaining communication with families from a diversity of backgrounds; how to recognize and overcome barriers to communication with families; how to work collaboratively with families to promote their participation in planning and implementing their children's education; and how to provide information, training, support, counseling, and referrals to families whose children have special needs.

Demonstrating Familiarity with Typical Concerns of Parents and Guardians of Students with Disabilities and with Strategies for Planning an Individualized Program that Addresses these Concerns

All parents share some basic goals for their children. They want their children to grow up to be healthy, happy members of society who lead independent lives with productive employment. Parents of students with disabilities are no different, although the path that their children take may have additional turns and obstacles along the way.

Health
Many children with disabilities have associated health problems or are at risk for health problems. Many also routinely take medication(s) for health or behavioral conditions.

Parents of students with disabilities are usually concerned with their children's long-range health, the cost of health care (as children and later as adults), and the effects of medication on their child's behavior, health, and school work.

It is not uncommon for special education students to take some medication while at school. Providing the school with the needed medication may be a financial strain for the family. The simple fact that others will be aware of the child's health and medications can also be a parental concern.

Parents are often concerned because their children have difficulty identifying changes in their health and in communicating possible changes in medication reactions. IEPs often include objectives for the child to participate in this type of communication.

Happiness

The quality of life for more severely disabled children is different than that of the general population. Even students with less severe physical conditions (for example, a learning disability) may have lower self-esteem because they feel "stupid" or "different." Students with disabilities often have difficulties making friends, which can also impact happiness.

Parents of students with disabilities (as all parents) feel the emotional impact of the disability on their children. Most parents are anxious to help their children feel good about themselves and fit in with the general population of their peers.

Social goals may be included on the IEP. Some students (particularly those on the autism spectrum) may have time set aside to meet with a speech and language pathologist to work on social language. Other students may meet regularly with social workers to discuss situations from the classroom or general school setting.

Independence

Initially, parents of students with disabilities may be somewhat overprotective of their children. However, most parents are eventually able to focus on ways to help the child function independently.

Young children with disabilities may be working on self-care types of independence such as dressing, feeding, and toilet use. Elementary students may be working on asking for assistance, completing work, and being prepared for class with materials (books, papers, etc.). High school students may be working on driving, future job skills, or preparation for post-secondary education.

Job Training

IDEA 2004 addresses the need for students with disabilities to be prepared for jobs or post-secondary education in order to be independent, productive members of society.

Job training goals and objectives for the student with a disability may be vocational (such as food service, mechanical work, carpentry, etc.) or they may include appropriate high school coursework to prepare for a college program.

Productivity

Ultimately, the goal of parent and school is for the student to become a productive member of society who can support him or herself financially and live independently. This type of productivity happens when the student becomes an adult with a measure of good health, positive self-esteem, the ability to interact positively with others, independent personal and work skills, and job training.

Particular Stages of Concern

Parents of students with special needs often deal with increased concerns at times when the child is going into a new stage of development. Some of these times include: when the child is first identified as having a disability, entrance into an early childhood special education program, kindergarten (when it is evident that the disability remains despite services received thus far), third grade (when the student is expected to use more skills independently), junior high school, and entrance into high school.

Additional IEP goals and objectives may be warranted at these times, as the student is expected to use a new set of skills or may be entering a new educational setting.

It should be noted that parents are often concerned when a younger, non-disabled sibling surpasses the child with the disability in some skill (such as feeding or reading). Previously, the parents may not have fully been aware of what most children can do at a particular age.

Parental Rights Regarding the IEP of the Exceptional Student

A special educator must have knowledge of parental rights in order to communicate them to parents.

Notification of Rights (Procedural Safeguards)

The distribution of this publication is mandated by federal law. It outlines the procedures of evaluation/identification, placement, review, and dispute resolution of the child with a disability. It also outlines parental rights at each of these steps.

This publication is to be given to parents prior to any meeting (in the areas above). It is vital that school personnel conducting any type of IEP-related meeting verify that parents have received this publication and ascertain whether or not they have questions concerning it.

In the case of parents who do not speak English as their primary language, a copy of the procedural safeguards document should be provided in their native language.

Evaluation Consent

Parental consent must be given prior to the evaluation of a student for special education eligibility. This consent must be given in writing (a signature) on a form that outlines the evaluation components.

Notification of Meetings

Parents must be provided notification (in writing) of any IEP related meeting ten days prior to that meeting. In addition, a total of three communications (preferably all in writing) of the meeting must be made and documented by special education staff.

In the case of a meeting that is scheduled sooner than ten days from notification, the meeting may happen only with parental signature waiving their right to ten day consent.

This is sometimes an option agreed upon by both sides (school and parents) when there is an imminent need for change in an IEP or placement or when scheduling conflicts make this desirable.

Right for Representation at Meetings

Parents of the student with disabilities may bring another person(s) to the IEP meetings. This type of representation may include an advocate or professional in a related field.

In the case of the advocate, the person may offer additional insight, ask questions, or simply takes notes for later review by the parent.

Providing the School with Additional Information

Oftentimes, students with disabilities see a number of professionals at school and in the community. This includes therapists and doctors. If parents supply information from these professionals to the IEP team, it is a valuable component to establishing the best program for the student.

At times, outside professionals request that the school complete an evaluation on a specific student. (For example, a student with a diagnosis of ADHD by a doctor may also have a request from that doctor for evaluation of eligibility of special education services.)

While it is most likely that the school will decide to honor such a request, it is not required that they do so.

TEACHER CERTIFICATION STUDY GUIDE

Parent Request for an IEP Meeting

Because of the behavioral component of an emotional disturbance, parental rights may be exercised more often in these cases. For example, a student with a learning disability who receives language and reading instruction may only have the IEP reviewed annually.

At any time, a parent may request an IEP meeting. Some common reasons to request an IEP meeting include: the location of services (regular vs. special education classroom), specific goals and objectives, disciplinary matters, support services/therapies (speech, occupational, physical, vision, art, music), amount of time/services from a paraprofessional, testing considerations, and transportation arrangements.

Right to Review Hearing/Due Process
At times there will be disagreements between parents and school regarding some aspect of the student's IEP and related program.

Although the parent has the right to request a review/hearing, the issues of concern should first be addressed at the service level (teacher and special education director meeting with the parents).

Understand How to Promote Strong School-Home Relationships

All parents hope that the world will embrace their child and treat him or her with fairness and compassion. Parents of children with emotional disturbances are no different. They, too, long to know that teachers understand their child and see the positive benefit he or she will offer the world. All too often, the communication between school and home regarding a child with emotional disturbance only focuses on inappropriate behaviors and the need for remediation.

The typical special educator communicates with parents of his or her emotionally disturbed students throughout the year. It is important that this communication begin on a positive note. To support this, the educator may consider sending a welcome letter prior to the school year, emphasizing his or her desire to have a positive, growing year with the students.

It is also wise to initiate communication about something positive the student has done prior to a note or a call home about negative behavior. Many special educators find it good practice to start all communication (report card comments, IEP levels of functioning, phone conversations, etc.) with a positive comment before offering constructive suggestions for change.

SPECIAL EDU. CROSS-CATEGORY

Demonstrate an Understanding of Ways to Communicate with Parents to Enhance Strong Home-School Relationships

Communication Notebook
A communication notebook is a notebook passed from teacher to parent (or other person involved with the student) to discuss the student's behavior. This ensures the generalization of skills, and it can also be used to discuss the individual's social, interpersonal, behavioral, and academic skills across settings.

Phone Calls
Phone calls offer a personal way to communicate with parents regarding positive news or school/behavioral concerns. Difficulty can arise when both parents work or are for other reasons unavailable for calls. If the special educator uses phone calls to communicate with parents, it is important that he or she keep documentation of the date and call details.

E-mail
Sometimes it is more convenient to use the internet for communication. If the student's parents have internet access in their home, this type of communication is convenient and offers a built in record of the contact.

Behavior Checklists
Often, the behavior of an emotionally disturbed student is recorded on a checklist that is sent home to parents on a daily or weekly basis.

Student Progress Reports
The special educator and any therapists providing services to the student with an emotional disturbance are required to report progress on IEP goals and objectives. This reporting is done quarterly on a form provided by the school district and is attached to the student's current IEP.

Report Cards
As all students, the student with an emotional disturbance receives a report that indicates quarterly grades, attendance, and general teacher comments.

Parent Newsletter
Many teachers use a weekly newsletter to communicate with parents regarding upcoming activities, school holidays, instructional topics, and tests. The parent newsletter is a means of keeping the parent informed. It acknowledges that parents and educators work together on the same educational team.

Teacher/School Web Page
Increased use of technology has resulted in teacher and/or school websites where parents can access newsletter information, school contact information, homework assignments, and details of upcoming events. Because not every family can access online information, it is wise that the special educator also provide a paper copy to students.

Workshops and Speakers
Sometimes school districts offer classes, workshops, and speaker presentations for parents of emotionally disturbed students. These educational activities include the parents as part of the educational team working with the student. Topics for these workshops/speakers might include discipline, behavioral interventions, study strategies, or further education about types of emotional disabilities.

Parent Lending Library
Parenting books and DVDs, as well as informational materials about specific emotional disturbances, are often offered through parent lending libraries. These libraries may be set up in a classroom, office, school library, or regional facility.

Parent Support Groups
These groups offer the chance for school personnel and parents to talk about the needs of the emotionally disturbed child and his or her family. Discipline, respite care, self-control (parent and child), advocacy, financial planning, and preparing for the world of adulthood (and jobs) are a few topics that may be covered in parent support groups.

The Purpose of School-Home Communication

Communication of Expectations

Effective and safe schools make persistent efforts to involve parents by: informing them routinely about school discipline policies, procedures, and rules, and about their children's behavior (both good and bad); involving them in making decisions concerning school-wide disciplinary policies and procedures; and encouraging them to participate in prevention.

It is also crucial for school personnel and parents to communicate about social skills, behaviors, and academic issues that are currently being addressed. This allows for support, practice, and feedback from both sides.

Communication of Progress

It is important for the special educator to keep parents informed about the emotionally disturbed student's progress on day-to-day activities and behavior, as well as IEP goals and objectives.

Communication of Consequences

Because of the impulsive nature and difficulty of interpersonal skills of many students with emotional disturbances, the special educator must frequently award consequences for inappropriate behaviors. It is important to use consistency with the student and communication with parents about behaviors (good and bad) and their resulting consequences. Although the teacher does not need to report every slight infraction of the school/classroom rules, he or she should be thorough in reporting major or reoccurring behavioral concerns to parents.

Cultural Diversity and School-Home Relationships

Effective teaching and learning for students begins with teachers who can demonstrate sensitivity for diversity in teaching and in relationships within school communities.

Student portfolios should include work that has a multicultural perspective. Classroom inclusion where students share cultural and ethnic life experiences in their learning is also important. Teachers must be responsive to including cultural and diverse resources in their curriculum and instructional practices.

One way to demonstrate inclusion of multiple cultures is to expose students to culturally sensitive room decorations and posters. Teachers should also continuously make cultural connections that are relevant and empowering for all students. Cultural sensitivity can be communicated beyond the classroom with parents and community members to establish and maintain relationships.

Diversity can be further defined as the following:

- Differences among learners, classroom settings, and academic outcomes
- Acceptance of varied biological, sociological, ethnic, socioeconomic, psychological, and learning backgrounds
- Differences in classroom settings that promote learning opportunities (such as collaborative, participatory, and individualized learning groupings)
- Expected learning outcomes that are theoretical, affective, and cognitive for students

In a culturally sensitive classroom, teachers maintain equity and fairness in student interactions and curriculum implementation. Teachers establish a classroom climate that is culturally respectful and engaging for students. Assessments include cultural responses and perspectives that become further learning opportunities for students. Other artifacts that could reflect teacher/student sensitivity to diversity might consist of the following:

- Student portfolios reflecting multicultural/multiethnic perspectives
- Journals and reflections from field trips and guest speakers from diverse cultural backgrounds
- Printed materials and wall displays from multicultural perspectives
- Parent/guardian letters in a variety of languages reflecting cultural diversity
- Projects that include cultural history and diverse inclusions
- Disaggregated student data reflecting cultural groups
- Classroom climate of professionalism that fosters diversity and cultural inclusion

The target of diversity allows teachers a variety of opportunities to expand their experiences with students, staff, community members, and parents from culturally diverse backgrounds. These experiences can then be proactively applied in promoting cultural diversity inclusion in the classroom. Teachers are then also able to engage and challenge students to develop and incorporate their own diversity skills in building character and relationships with cultures beyond their own. In changing the thinking patterns of students to become more cultural inclusive, teachers are addressing the globalization of our world.

The teacher should be familiar with the effects of cultural stereotypes and racism on the development of students with disabilities. The teacher should know that variations in beliefs, traditions, and values exist across and within cultures. The teacher should also be familiar with the characteristics and biases of his or her own culture and how these biases can impact their teaching, behavior, and communication.

TEACHER CERTIFICATION STUDY GUIDE

Other cultural considerations include:

- The teacher should include multicultural perspectives in lessons and convey to students how knowledge is developed from the vantage point of a particular culture.

- Educators need to ensure they demonstrate positive regard for the culture, religion, gender, and varying abilities of students and their families. This includes showing sensitivity to students with different cultural and ethnic backgrounds when designing the curriculum.

- Teachers who use themes with a multicultural perspective should ensure that they are not teaching material that could be considered culturally insensitive or offensive.

- For professional development training programs to be successful, it is crucial that teachers develop an in-depth understanding of the influence of culture and language on students' academic performance. This will help them to differentiate between genuine learning problems and cultural differences.

- Culturally sensitive teaching creates a helpful, receptive, and enriched educational setting that permits all students to feel comfortable as they look at their attitudes and share their thoughts.

- As members of a culturally pluralistic society, students and educators must develop healthy and open-minded attitudes and interpersonal skills to communicate and collaborate across cultures and to function successfully in many situations.

- Multicultural activities and lessons are important for all students and teachers; in unbiased classrooms, students hear the voices of a variety of different cultural groups. This enables students to be able to understand the world from multiple ethnic and cultural perspectives, instead of just agreeing with the point of view of the mainstream culture.

- As cultures place varying value on education or on the role of genders, different views may be taken of individuals with disabilities, appropriate education, career goals, and the individual's role in society.

- It is important for the special educator to consider the possible need for a translator for IEP meetings and parent conferences. He or she may also need to seek the means necessary to translate written communication such as notes and newsletters.

Demonstrate Understanding of the Importance of the School-Home Relationship to IEP Meetings

IEP related meetings involve a team of parents and school personnel who could meet for the following reasons: initial case-study evaluation, annual review of IEP, triennial review of student's eligibility and IEP program, IEP amendment, manifestation determination, or post-secondary transition.

According to IDEA 2004, the IEP team includes the parents of a child with a disability; not less than one regular education teacher of such child (if the child is, or may be, participating in the regular education environment); not less than one special education teacher (or, where appropriate, not less than one special education provider of such child); a representative of the local educational agency; an individual who can interpret the instructional implications of evaluation results; at the discretion of the parent of the agency, other individuals who have knowledge or special expertise regarding the child, including related services personnel; and, whenever appropriate, the child with a disability.

Parental involvement must occur in the development of the child's educational program. According to the law, parents must:

1. Be notified before initial evaluation or any change in placement. This is done with a written notice in their primary language describing the proposed school action, the reasons for it, and the available educational opportunities.
2. Consent, in writing, before the child is initially evaluated.

Parents may:

3. Request an independent educational evaluation if they feel the school's evaluation is inappropriate.
4. Request an evaluation at public expense if a due process hearing decision is that the public agency's evaluation was inappropriate.
5. Participate on the committee that considers the evaluation, placement, and programming of the student.

Involving the special education student (when appropriate) and his or her family in setting instructional goals is necessary to develop a well-rounded IEP. When families help set goals for things that are important to the special education student, subsequent increased family cooperation and involvement are usually evident. Typically, the parent of the child knows the child best, so meshing the school goals and those of the family will provide a program that is most thorough in meeting the student's needs.

Progress on these mutually accepted goals—as well as those initiated by the school—can be charted or measured in a variety of ways. The method used to track the goals should be those indicated in the goals and objectives section of the IEP.

Demonstrate an Understanding of the Importance of School-Home Communication Regarding Medication

Students with disabilities who take medications often experience medication side effects that can impact their behavior and educational development. Teachers may perceive the child is unmotivated or drowsy, not fully understanding the cognitive effects that medications can have on a child.

Some medications may impair concentration, which can lead to poor processing ability, lower alertness, and drowsiness and hyperactivity. Students who take several medications may have an increased risk of behavioral and cognitive side effects.

If educators are aware of the types of medication that their students are taking, along with the myriad of side effects, they will be able to respond more positively when some of the side effects of the medication change their students' behaviors, response rates, and attention spans.

In strong school-home communication, the student's parents should let the school know when the student is beginning or changing medication, allowing educators to look out for possible side effects. Conversely, the special educator has a responsibility to communicate effects and changes in behavior and class work that may be the result of medication (changes in amount or missed dosages).

TEACHER CERTIFICATION STUDY GUIDE

COMPETENCY 30.0   UNDERSTAND HOW TO ENCOURAGE SCHOOL-COMMUNITY INTERACTIONS THAT ENHANCE LEARNING OPPORTUNITIES FOR STUDENTS WITH SPECIAL NEEDS

For example: strategies for accessing and working effectively with agencies and services that can help meet the needs of students with special needs.

Demonstrate an Understanding of the Importance of School-Community Interactions for Effective Learning for Students with Emotional Disabilities

According to Walther-Thomas et al (2000), "Collaboration for Inclusive Education," ongoing professional development that provides teachers with opportunities to create effective instructional practice is vital and necessary: "A comprehensive approach to professional development is perhaps the most critical dimension of sustained support for successful program implementation." The inclusive approach incorporates learning programs that include all stakeholders in defining and developing high quality programs for students.

The figure below shows how an integrated approach of stakeholders can provide the optimal learning opportunity for all students.

Integrated Approach to Learning

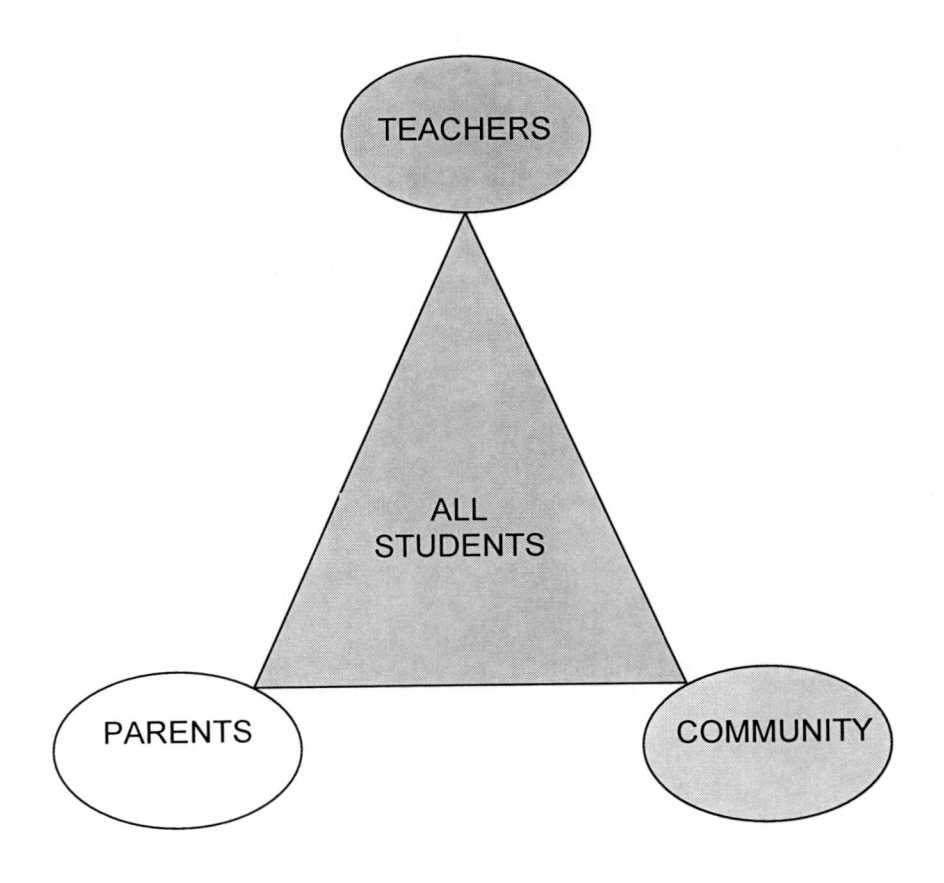

[Diagram: A triangle labeled "ALL STUDENTS" with three ovals at its vertices — "TEACHERS" at the top, "PARENTS" at the bottom left, and "COMMUNITY" at the bottom right.]

In the integrated approach to learning, teachers, parents, and community support members become the integral apexes to student learning. The focus and central core of the school community is triangular as a representation of how effective collaboration can work in creating success for student learners. The goal of student learning and achievement is the heart of the school community. The direction of teacher professional development in constructing effective instruction is clearly articulated in a greater understanding of facilitating learning strategies that develop skills and education equity for students.

Demonstrate an Understanding of Ways to Enhance Student Learning at Various Ages through School-Community Interaction

Even the very young exceptional child (unless the severity of the behavior precludes such) can benefit from field trips and activities in the community. The special education teacher is encouraged to look for opportunities that are age-appropriate and will provide the opportunity to interact with typically functioning peers.

Some community activities to consider for a young emotionally disturbed student include visiting a pumpkin farm or apple orchard, going to visit Santa, touring the zoo, going to the circus, watching a play/puppet show, or attending a concert.

In addition to field trips and community outings, a young emotionally disturbed student may benefit from school assemblies, classroom presenters (such as a firefighter, police officer, or anti-drug representative), or simply a musical presentation.

These types of events may even be incorporated in the emotionally disturbed child's rewards for appropriate behavior and school work.

TEACHER CERTIFICATION STUDY GUIDE

Demonstrate Understanding of the Purposes and Components of Transition Planning for the Student with Emotional Disturbances into the Post-Secondary Community

As many factors are considered in the student's initial placement into special education, so should the complete picture of the student be considered when establishing appropriate community resources for a smooth transition from high school to the community.

As with each level of education, the responsibility of the special educator is to prepare students for the next stage of learning and functioning. A major focus of special education is to prepare students to become working, independent members of society. IDEA 2004 also includes these types of requisites. Certain skills beyond academics are needed to attain the level of functioning desired by teachers, parents, and IDEA.

Beginning when a student is 14, and annually thereafter, the student's IEP must contain a statement of his or her transition service needs. These focus on the student's courses of study (e.g., vocational education or advanced placement) and, when appropriate, include interagency responsibilities and links for possible future assistance

Beginning at least one year before the student reaches the age of majority under state law, the IEP must contain a statement that the student has been informed of the rights under the law that will transfer to him or her upon reaching the age of majority.

Post-School Transition CSE
Unfortunately, this type of CSE is often pushed aside and its importance ignored. However, this last CSE before a student leaves the school district "umbrella" of special education services can be the one that provides lasting opportunities for the student. Since the student was 15 years old, transitional evaluations and statements have been important. This is the transitional CSE. It is here that students and their parents should be given lasting resources and supports that will grow as the young adult with special needs steps out into society.

One of the most basic of resources that teachers need to think of is the test modifications of their students. Test modifications can follow students through life and provide several occupational opportunities.

TEACHER CERTIFICATION STUDY GUIDE

Demonstrate an Understanding of Ways the Special Educator can Build Effective Interaction with Community Resources

Agencies and resources in the community are important resources for the teacher of the emotionally disturbed student, the students themselves, and their families.

Social Service Agency Resource File
In order for the special educator to effectively work with community resources for the transition of emotionally disturbed students, he or she must be aware of the what resources are available. Organizing a resource file that includes brochures and contact information of key individuals is important. Some special educators find it helpful to create a secondary resource file that can be accessed by students and their families.

Agency categories that can be included in such a file are: medical assistance, food pantries, housing, counseling, emergency shelters, employment, vocational rehabilitation, drug awareness, and advocacy. Information should also be kept on a wide variety of post-secondary training options (vocational and college).

Speaker's Bureau
The special educator may participate in a speaker's bureau or invite other professionals in the field to speak at the school (for parents, other educators, or students). When inviting speakers from the community, the teacher may wish to consider representatives from the above agencies, professionals from post-secondary educational institutions and training programs, or those from the medical and legal fields.

Committee Memberships and Advisory Boards
The special educator may wish to serve on a community agency advisory board or work with the school district to create one for the program. This type of activity establishes a strong community tie for student transition and serves as a sounding board for program considerations.

Professional Membership
The special educator should also consider appropriate professional memberships that will provide the opportunity for further professional growth and networking.

Invitation for Consultation/Participation in Transition Team
Based on the information from and interaction with professionals from community agencies, the special education may invite consultative input (while guarding individual student confidentiality) or, in some cases, invite the community professional to the student's transition meeting.

Understand Educator Resources Relevant to the Education of Exceptional Students

A number of resources are available for educators working with students with emotional disabilities. Some resources are professional or parent organizations that require membership. Others are agencies that provide information without membership.

The benefits of these organizations includes websites, message boards, newsletters, journals, workshops, and conferences.

Resource organizations may be in the field of special education (e.g., emotional disturbance), social services, legal assistance, housing information and assistance, employment training and job search help, or health services (including mental health).

The professional associations representing the spectrum of those available for individuals with disabilities are listed here. Some of these organizations date from the pioneer times of special education and are still in active service. Divisional organizations under the Council for Exceptional Children (CEC) are included and are listed separately, along with information about their professional publications.

Organization	Members	Mission
Alexander Graham Bell Association for the Deaf and Hard of Hearing 3417 Volta Place, N.W. Washington, D.C. 27.0 http://www.agbell.org	Teachers of the deaf, speech-language pathologists, audiologists, physicians, hearing aid dealers	To promote the teaching of speech, lip reading, and use of residual hearing to persons who are deaf; encourage research; and work to further better education of persons who are deaf.
Alliance for Technology Access 1304 Southpoint Blvd., Suite 240, Petaluma, CA 94954 Phone: (707) 778-3011 Fax: (707) 765-2080 TTY (707) 778-3015 Email: atainfo@ataccess.org http://www.ataccess.org	People with disabilities, family members, and professionals in related fields; organizations that work within communities	To **increase the use of technology** by **children and adults with disabilities and functional limitations**.

TEACHER CERTIFICATION STUDY GUIDE

Organization	Members	Mission
American Council of the Blind 1155 15th Street NW Ste 1004 Washington, DC 200055.0 Phone: (202) 467-5081 (800) 424-8666 Fax: (202) 467-5085 http://acb.org		To improve the well-being of all blind and visually impaired people by: serving as a representative national organization of blind people and conducting a public education program to promote greater understanding of blindness and the capabilities of blind people.
American Council on Rural Special Education (ACRES) Utah State University 2865 Old Main Hill Logan, Utah 84322 Phone: (435) 797-3728 http://www.acres-sped.org/	Open to anyone interested in supporting their mission	To provide leadership and support that will enhance services for individuals with exceptional needs, their families, and the professionals who work with them, and for the rural communities in which they live.
American Society for Deaf Children 3820 Hartzdale Drive, Camp Hill, PA 17011 Phone: (717) 703-0073 (866) 895-4206 Fax: (717) 909-5599 Email: asdc@deafchildren.org http://www.deafchildren.org	Open to all who support the mission of the association	To provide support, encouragement, and information to families raising children who are deaf or hard of hearing.
American Speech-Language-Hearing Association 10801 Rockville Pike Rockville, MD 20852	Specialists in speech-language pathology and audiology	To advocate for the provision of speech-language and hearing services in school and clinic settings; advocate for legislation relative to the profession; and work to promote effective services and development of the profession.

Organization	Members	Mission
Asperger Syndrome Education Network (ASPEN) 9 Aspen Circle Edison, NJ 08820 Phone: (732) 321-0880 Email: info@AspenNJ.org http://www.aspennj.org		Provides families and individuals whose lives are affected by autism spectrum disorders and nonverbal learning disabilities with education, support, and advocacy.
Attention Deficit Disorder Association 15000 Commerce Pkwy, Suite C Mount Laurel, NJ 08054 Phone: (856) 439-9099 Fax: (856) 439-0525 http://www.add.org/	Open to all who support the mission of ADDA	Provides information, resources, and networking to adults with AD/HD and to the professionals who work with them.
Autism Society of America 7910 Woodmont Avenue, Suite 300 Bethesda, Maryland 20814 Phone: (800) 328-8476 http://www.autism-society.org	Open to all who support the mission of ASA	To increase public awareness about autism and the day-to-day issues faced by individuals with autism, their families, and the professionals with whom they interact. The Society and its chapters share a common mission of providing information and education, and supporting research and advocating for programs and services for the autism community.
Brain Injury Association of America 8201 Greensboro Drive Suite 611 McLean, VA 22102 Phone: (703) 761-0750 http://www.biausa.org	Open to all	Provides information, education and support to assist the 5.3 million Americans currently living with traumatic brain injury and their families.

Organization	Members	Mission
Child and Adolescent Bipolar Association (CABF) 1187 Wilmette Ave. P.M.B. #331 Wilmette, IL 60091 http://www.bpkids.org	Physicians, scientific researchers, and allied professionals (therapists, social workers, educators, attorneys, and others) who provide services to children and adolescents with bipolar disorder or do research on the topic	**Ed**ucates families, professionals, and the public about pediatric bipolar disorder; **connects** families with resources and support; **advocates** for and **empowers** affected families; and **supports research** on pediatric bipolar disorder and its cure.
Children and Adults with Attention Deficit/ Hyperactive Disorder (CHADD) 8181 Professional Place - Suite 150 Landover, MD 20785 Phone: (301) 306-7070 Fax: (301) 306-7090 Email: national@chadd.org http://www.chadd.org	Open to all	Providing resources and encouragement to parents, educators, and professionals on a grassroots level through CHADD chapters
Council for Exceptional Children (CEC) 1110 N. Glebe Road Suite 300 Arlington, VA 22201 Phone: (888) 232-7733 TTY: (866) 915-5000 Fax: (703) 264-9494 http://www.cec.sped.org	Teachers, administrators, teacher educators, and related service personnel	Advocate for services for [disabled] and gifted individuals. A professional organization that addresses service, training, and research relative to exceptional persons.
Epilepsy Foundation of America (EFA) 8301 Professional Place Landover, MD 20785 Phone: (800) 332-1000 http://www.epilepsyfoundation.org	A non-membership organization	Works to ensure that people with seizures are able to participate in all life experiences; and to prevent, control and cure epilepsy through research, education, advocacy, and services.

Organization	Members	Mission
Family Center on Technology and Disability (FCTD) 1825 Connecticut Avenue, NW 7th Floor Washington DC 20009 Phone: (202) 884-8068 Fax: (202) 884-8441 Email: fctd@aed.org http://www.fctd.info/	Non member association	A resource designed to support organizations and programs that work with families of children and youth with disabilities.
Hands and Voices P.O. Box 371926 Denver CO 80237 Phone: (866) 422-0422 Email: parentadvocate@handsandvoices.org http://www.handsandvoices.org	Families, professionals, other organizations, pre-service students, and deaf and hard of hearing adults who are all working toward ensuring successful outcomes for children who are deaf and hard of hearing	To support families and their children who are deaf or hard of hearing, as well as the professionals who serve them. A resource designed to support organizations and programs that work with families of children and youth with disabilities.
The International Dyslexia Association Chester Building, Suite 382 8600 LaSalle Road Baltimore, Maryland 21286 Phone: (410) 296-0232 Fax: (410) 321-5069 http://www.interdys.org	Anyone interested in IDA and its mission can become a member	Provides information and referral services, research, advocacy, and direct services to professionals in the field of learning disabilities.
Learning Disabilities Association of America (LDA) 4156 Library Road Pittsburgh, PA 15234 Phone: (412) 341-1515 Fax: (412) 344-0224 http://www.ldanatl.org/	Anyone interested in LDA and its mission can become a member	Provides cutting edge information on learning disabilities, practical solutions, and a comprehensive network of resources.

Organization	Members	Mission
National Association of the Deaf (NAD) 8630 Fenton Street, Suite 820, Silver Spring, MD Phone: (209) 210-3819 TTY: (301) 587-1789 Fax: (301) 587-1791 Email: NADinfo@nad.org http://nad.org	Anyone interested in NAD and its mission can become a member	To promote, protect, and preserve the rights and quality of life of deaf and hard of hearing individuals in the United States of America.
National Mental Health Information Center P.O. Box 42557 Washington, DC 2001515.0 Phone: (800) 789-2647 http://www.mentalhealth.samhsa.gov	Government agency	Developed for users of mental health services and their families, the general public, policy makers, providers, and the media.
National Dissemination Center for Children with Disabilities (NIHCY) P.O. Box 1492 Washington, DC 2001313.0 Phone: (800) 695-0285 Fax: (202) 884-8441 Email: **nichcy@aed.org** http://www.mentalhealth.samhsa.gov	Non-membership association	A central source of information on: • disabilities in infants, toddlers, children, and youth, • IDEA, which is the law authorizing special education, • No Child Left Behind (as it relates to children with disabilities), and research-based information on effective educational practices.
US Department of Education Office of Special Education and Rehabilitative Services http://www.ed.gov/about/offices/list/osers/index.html	Government resource	Committed to improving results and outcomes for people with disabilities of all ages.

Organization	Members	Mission
Wrights Law Email: webmaster@wrightslaw.com http://wrightslaw.com	Non-membership organization	Parents, educators, advocates, and attorneys come to Wrightslaw for accurate, reliable information about special education law, education law, and advocacy for children with disabilities.
TASH **(Formerly The Association for Persons with Severe Handicaps)** 29 W. Susquehanna Ave., Suite 210 Baltimore, MD 21204 Phone: (410) 828-8274 Fax: (410) 828-6706 http:// www.tash.org	Anyone interested in TASH and its mission can become a member	To create change and build capacity so that all people, no matter their perceived level of disability, are included in all aspects of society.
American Psychological Association 750 First Street, NE, Washington, DC 200022.0-4242 Phone: (800) 374-2721 Fax: (202) 336-5500 TTY: (202) 336-6123 http://www.apa.org	Psychologists and professors of psychology	Scientific and professional society working to improve mental health services and to advocate for legislation and programs that will promote mental health; facilitate research and professional development.
Association for Children and Adults with Learning Disabilities 4156 Library Road Pittsburgh, PA 15234 http://www.acldonline.org/	Parents of children with learning disabilities and interested professionals	Advance the education and general well-being of children with adequate intelligence who have learning disabilities arising from perceptual, conceptual, or subtle coordinative problems, sometimes accompanied by behavior difficulties.

Organization	Members	Mission
The Arc of the United States 1010 Wayne Avenue Suite 650 Silver Springs, MD 20910 Phone: (301) 565-3842 Fax: (301) 565-3843 http://www.the arc.org	Parents, professionals, and others interested in individuals with mental retardation	Work on local, state, and national levels to promote treatment, research, public understanding, and legislation for persons with mental retardation; provide counseling for parents of students with mental retardation.
National Association for Gifted Children 1707 L Street, NW Suite 550 Washington, DC 20036 Phone: (202) 785-4368 Fax: (202) 785-4248 Email: nagc@nagc.org http://nagc.org	Parents, educators, community leaders, and other professionals who work with gifted children.	To address the unique needs of children and youth with demonstrated gifts and talents.
Council for Children with Behavioral Disorders Two Ballston Plaza 1110 N. Glebe Road Arlington, VA 22201 Phone: (800) 224-6830 Fax: (703) 264-9494	Members of the Council for Exceptional Children who teach children with behavior disorders or who train teachers to work with those children	Promote education and general welfare of children and youth with behavior disorders or serious emotional disturbances; promote professional growth and research on students with behavior disorders and severe emotional disturbances.

TEACHER CERTIFICATION STUDY GUIDE

Organization	Members	Mission
Council for Educational Diagnostic Services Two Ballston Plaza 1110 N. Glebe Road Arlington, VA 22201	Members of the Council for Exceptional Children who are school psychologists, educational diagnosticians, and social workers who are involved in diagnosing educational difficulties	Promote the most appropriate education of children and youth through appraisal, diagnosis, educational intervention, implementation, and evaluation of a prescribed educational program. Work to facilitate the professional development of those who assess students. Work to further development of better diagnostic techniques and procedures.
Council for Exceptional Children Two Ballston Plaza 1110 N. Glebe Road Arlington, VA 22201	Teachers, administrators, teacher educators, and related service personnel	Advocate for services for [disabled] and gifted individuals. This is a professional organization that addresses service, training, and research relative to exceptional persons.
Council of Administrators of Special Education Two Ballston Plaza 1110 N. Glebe Road Arlington, VA 22201	Members of the Council for Exceptional Children who are administrators, directors, coordinators, or supervisors of programs, schools, or classes for exceptional children; college faculty who train administrators	Promote professional leadership; provide opportunities for the study of problems common to its members; communicate through discussion and publications information that will facilitate improved services for children with exceptional needs.

SPECIAL EDU. CROSS-CATEGORY

TEACHER CERTIFICATION STUDY GUIDE

Organization	Members	Mission
Division for Children with Communication Disorders Two Ballston Plaza 1110 N. Glebe Road Arlington, VA 22201	Members of the Council for Exceptional Children who are speech-language pathologists, audiologists, teachers of children with communication disorders, or educators of professionals who plan to work with children who have communication disorders	Promote the education of children with communication disorders. Promote professional growth and research.
Division for Early Childhood Two Ballston Plaza 1110 N. Glebe Road Arlington, VA 22201	Members of the Council for Exceptional Children who teach preschool children and infants or educate teachers to work with young children	Promote effective education for young children and infants. Promote professional development of those who work with young children and infants. Promote legislation and research.
Division for the Physically Handicapped Two Ballston Plaza 1110 N. Glebe Road Arlington, VA 22201	Members of the Council for Exceptional Children who work with individuals who have physical disabilities or educate professionals to work with those individuals	Promote closer relationships among educators of students who have physical impairments or are homebound. Facilitate research and encourage development of new ideas, practices, and techniques through professional meetings, workshops, and publications.
Division for the Visually Handicapped Two Ballston Plaza 1110 N. Glebe Road Arlington, VA 22201	Members of the Council for Exceptional Children who work with individuals who have visual disabilities or educate professionals to work with those individuals	Work to advance the education and training of individuals with visual impairments. Work to bring about better understanding of educational, emotional, or other problems associated with visual impairment. Facilitate research and development of new techniques or ideas in education and training of individuals with visual problems.

SPECIAL EDU. CROSS-CATEGORY

TEACHER CERTIFICATION STUDY GUIDE

Organization	Members	Mission
Division on Career Development Two Ballston Plaza 1110 N. Glebe Road Arlington, VA 22201	Members of the Council for Exceptional Children who teach or in other ways work toward career development and vocational education of exceptional children	Promote and encourage professional growth of all those concerned with career development and vocational education. Promote research, legislation, information dissemination, and technical assistance relevant to career development and vocational education.
Division on Mental Retardation Two Ballston Plaza 1110 N. Glebe Road Arlington, VA 22201	Members of the Council for Exceptional Children who work with students with mental retardation or educate professionals to work with those students	Work to advance the education of individuals with mental retardation, research mental retardation, and the training of professionals to work with individuals with mental retardation. Promote public understanding of mental retardation and professional development of those who work with persons with mental retardation.
Gifted Child Society P.O. Box 120 Oakland, NJ 07436	Parents and educators of children who are gifted	Train educators to meet the needs of students with gifted abilities, offer assistance to parents facing special problems in raising children who are gifted, and seek public recognition of the needs of these children.
National Association for the Education of Young Children 1313 L St. N.W. Suite 500, Washington DC 200055.0 Phone: (800) 424-2460 Email: webmaster@naeyc.org http://www.naeyc.org		Promote service and action on behalf of the needs and rights of young children, with emphasis on provision of educational services and resources.
National Association for Retarded Citizens 5101 Washington Ave., N.W. Washington, D.C http://www.thearc.org		Work to promote the general welfare of persons with mental retardation; facilitate research and information dissemination relative to causes, treatment, and prevention of mental retardation.

SPECIAL EDU. CROSS-CATEGORY

Organization	Members	Mission
National Easter Seal Society 230 West Monroe Street, Suite 1800 Chicago, IL 60606 Phone: (800) 221-6827 TTY: (312) 726-1494 http://www.easterseals.com	State units (49) and local societies (951); no individual members	Establish and run programs for individuals with physical impairments, usually including diagnostic services, speech therapy, preschool services, physical therapy, and occupational therapy.
The National Association of Special Education Teachers 1201 Pennsylvania Avenue, N.W., Suite 300 Washington D.C. 200044.0 Phone: (800) 754-4421 Fax: (800) 424-0371 Email: contactus@naset.org	Special education teachers	To render all possible support and assistance to professionals who teach children with special needs; to promote standards of excellence and innovation in special education research, practice, and policy in order to foster exceptional teaching for exceptional children.

COMPETENCY 31.0 UNDERSTAND THE HISTORY AND PHILOSOPHY OF SPECIAL EDUCATION, KEY ISSUES AND TRENDS, ROLES AND RESPONSIBILITIES, AND LEGAL AND ETHICAL ISSUES RELEVANT TO SPECIAL EDUCATION

For example: the historical and philosophical foundations of special education; ways in which approaches to special education have changed over time; legal and ethical issues in special education (e.g., confidentiality, personal involvement with students and families, student discipline and suspension); roles and responsibilities of teachers; mediation techniques; and application of special education related laws (e.g., Section 504 of the Rehabilitation Act, the Americans with Disabilities Act [ADA], the Individuals with Disabilities Education Act [IDEA]), regulations, and guidelines (e.g., regarding identification, referral, evaluation, eligibility, program development, delivery of services, procedural safeguards).

Demonstrating Knowledge of Ethical Practices in Instruction and Other Professional Activities (e.g., interactions with students, use of copyrighted educational materials, use of information technology) Related to the Education of Students with Disabilities

The special educator is expected to demonstrate ethical practice in all areas of his or her teaching responsibilities.

With regards to interaction with students, teaching and discipline practices should reflect practices that are respectful of the student as a person. Researched-based methods should be employed that provide measurable outcomes.

The ethics of special education goes beyond methods to include materials. With students of a variety of age and/or ability levels (and often limited funding), appropriate materials can become difficult to obtain. If possible, students should be included in the head count for ordering general education materials. When alternative materials are needed, it is important to secure those through special education funding sources in the school.

It is important to note that teaching materials that are copyrighted may not be photocopied unless they are specifically intended for such use as printed on the book. The same is true for musical materials that have a copyright. If materials are intended for reproduction, it will be stated.

Technology brings a world of information to the special educator and students in the classroom. Careful consideration should be given, however, to the validity of the information before it is incorporated into practice or curricular material. Reputable sources for education practices have connections to recognized organizations for special educators (such as the Council for Exceptional Children or to teacher training programs).

SPECIAL EDU. CROSS-CATEGORY

TEACHER CERTIFICATION STUDY GUIDE

Likewise, students should be guided in finding and using valid sites for research and learning. It is important to teach the philosophy that not everything on the internet is true.

Ethical practice in communication is an additional expectation of all educators—especially of those teaching students with disabilities. Confidentiality is crucial. Specific information regarding a student's disability and IEP should be discussed only with the team of professionals working with the student and his or her family. When an exchange of information is needed with another school district, physician, therapist, or other professional outside of the school district, it is necessary to get written permission from the student's parent. Often, forms for such are available from the school district.

Demonstrating Knowledge of the Standards and Policies of the Profession (e.g., The Codes of Ethics of the Council for Exceptional Children [CEC] and other organizations)

The special educator is expected to use accepted teaching practices with measurable outcomes. He or she is also expected to use professionalism and confidentiality in the role of a teacher. Professional organizations provide a structure for understanding those expectations.

The Council for Exceptional Children (CEC) is a national professional organization (with state chapters) that encompasses teaching in all areas of disability. The CEC has established a *Code of Ethics for Educators of Persons with Exceptionalities.* In brief, the code charges educators with continuing to learn best practices in the education of students with disabilities, providing a quality educational program that will best meet the needs of students and their families, and abiding by legal and ethical guidelines of the profession. The CEC Code of Ethics is on the following page.

CEC Code of Ethics
for
Educators of Persons with Exceptionalities

We declare the following principles to be the Code of Ethics for educators of persons with exceptionalities. Members of the special education profession are responsible for upholding and advancing these principles. Members of The Council for Exceptional Children agree to judge and be judged by them in accordance with the spirit and provisions of this Code.

1. Special education professionals are committed to developing the highest educational and quality of life potential of individuals with exceptionalities.

2. Special education professionals promote and maintain a high level of competence and integrity in practicing their profession.

3. Special education professionals engage in professional activities which benefit individuals with exceptionalities, their families, other colleagues, students, or research subjects.

4. Special education professionals exercise objective professional judgment in the practice of their profession.

5. Special education professionals strive to advance their knowledge and skills regarding the education of individuals with exceptionalities.

6. Special education professionals work within the standards and policies of their profession.

7. Special education professionals seek to uphold and improve where necessary the laws, regulations, and policies governing the delivery of special education and related services and the practice of their profession.

8. Special education professionals do not condone or participate in unethical or illegal acts, nor violate professional standards adopted by the Delegate Assembly of CEC.

The Council for Exceptional Children. (1993). CEC Policy Manual, Section Three, part 2 (p. 4). Reston, VA: Author.

Demonstrating the Ability to Exercise Objective Professional Judgment

The special education teacher comes to the job with past experiences as well as personal opinions and beliefs. It is vital that he or she not let those personal persuasions guide him or her professionally. Objective professional judgment is important in all areas of the teacher's role.

Objective professional judgment should be exercised when considering the cultural, religious, and sexual orientations of the special educator's students and their families. An unbiased approach to communication maintains positive interaction and increased cooperation between home and school. The result is a better educational program that will meet the individual student's needs.

Objectivity should also be exercised when considering assessment of possible disability. Educator preference for a particular assessment should be secondary to matching the needs of the child with a specific instrument. Assessment tools should be researched-based and determined to be appropriate for the needs of the specific student.

When establishing the special education program, the specific student's IEP must be followed. If the special educator determines that the goals and objectives of the IEP no longer fit the child's needs, an IEP meeting should be called to review and possibly revise the document. Again, the revision of the IEP should be based on the needs of the child as determined objectively—not on the personal preference of the teacher for a particular type of program or schedule. This objectivity should include materials, scheduling, activities, and evaluation.

The student's IEP should also be focused on the learning standards established by the state. In particular, learning activities should be employed that provide measurable outcomes. Such data provides objective evaluation of student progress and mastery of the targeted standards.

Professional objectivity is crucial in communication with administration for the representation of students' needs for placement, programming, materials, scheduling, and staffing. When documented, data-driven information is presented, optimum decisions are made for students with disabilities and for the school community in general.

Identifying Ways to Address One's Own Cultural Biases and Differences to Ensure Positive Regard for the Culture, Religion, Gender, and Sexual Orientation of Individual Students

The role of the special education teacher is to advocate for the most appropriate education for students, guide them in discovering new knowledge, and help them in developing new skills to the best of their potential. According to IDEA 2004, the teacher is to prepare them for future, purposeful work in society with the possibility of post-secondary education or training.

Although each special educator is also a person with a set of experiences, opinions, and beliefs, it is important the he or she remain unbiased and positive. In order to do so, the special educator should avail him or herself of opportunities to learn about various cultures, religions, genders, and sexual orientations. This can be accomplished through reading, classroom awareness activities as appropriate, and teacher in-service.

Reading to increase awareness and acceptance of cultural differences may be done through professional, adult literature as well as through books to be read with the class. Cultural activities in the classroom are especially well-received, and foods, dress, and games are easily added to the curriculum.

The special educator is charged with academic, social, communicative, and independent skills instruction. Education or influence in other areas is not appropriate.

When the special educator remains unbiased in this way, he or she is better able to meet the needs of students and not react to additional factors. The students and their families are also more open to school-related suggestions.

The teacher's reaction to differences with students and their families models the commonly taught character education trait of respect. When an educator demonstrates respect for all individuals in a program, it is likely that respect will also be practiced by students, parents, and administration.

TEACHER CERTIFICATION STUDY GUIDE

Legal Issues Relevant to Special Education

Background

The U.S. Constitution does not specify protection for education. However, all states provide education, and thus individuals are guaranteed protection and due process under the 14th Amendment. The basic source of law for special education is the Individuals Disabilities Education Act (IDEA) and its accompanying regulations. IDEA represents the latest phase in the philosophy of educating children with disabilities. Initially, children with disabilities did not go to school the majority of the time. When they did, they were segregated into special classes in order to avoid disrupting the regular class. Their education usually consisted of simple academics and later, training for manual jobs.

By the mid-1900s, advocates for handicapped children argued that segregation was inherently unequal. By the time of P.L. 94-142, about half of the estimated 8 million handicapped children in the United States were either not being appropriately served in school or were excluded from schooling altogether. There were a disproportionate number of minority children placed in special programs. Identification and placement practices and procedures were inconsistent, and parental involvement was generally not encouraged. After segregation on the basis of race was declared unconstitutional in Brown v, Board of Education, parents and other advocates filed similar lawsuits on behalf of children with handicaps.

The culmination of their efforts resulted in P.L. 94-142. This section is a brief summary of that law and other major legislation, which affect the manner in which special education services are delivered to handicapped children.

Significant Legislation with an Impact on Exceptional Student Education

<u>Brown v. Board of Education, 1954</u>
While this case specifically addressed the inequality of "separate but equal" facilities on the basis of race, the concept that segregation was inherently unequal—even if facilities were provided—was later applied to handicapping conditions.

<u>Diana v. the State Board of Education, 1970</u>
This case resulted in the decision that all children must be tested in their native language.

<u>Wyatt v. Stickney, 1971</u>
This case established the right to adequate treatment (education) for institutionalized persons with mental retardation.

Pennsylvania Association for Retarded Citizens (PARC) v. Commonwealth of Pennsylvania, 1972
Special education was guaranteed to children with mental retardation. The victory in this case sparked other court cases for children with other disabilities.

Mills v. Board of Education of the District of Columbia, 1972
The right to special education was extended to all children with disabilities, not just mentally retarded children. Judgments in PARC and Mills paved the way for P.L. 94-142.

Public Law 93-112 (Rehabilitation Amendments of 1973)
This is the first comprehensive federal statute to specifically address the rights of disabled youth. It prohibited illegal discrimination in education, employment, or housing on the basis of a disability.

Section 504, Rehabilitation Act of 1973
Section 504 expands an older law by extending its protection to other areas that receive federal assistance, such as education. Protected individuals must (a) have a physical or mental impairment that substantially limits one or more major life activities (such as self-care, walking, seeing, breathing, working, and learning); (b) have a record of such an impairment; and (c) be regarded as having such an impairment. A disability in itself is not sufficient grounds for a complaint of discrimination. The person must be otherwise qualified, or able to meet, the requirements of the program in question.

Public Law 93-380 (Education Amendments of 1974
Public Law 94-142 is the funding portion of this act. It requires the states to provide full educational opportunities for children with disabilities. It addressed identification, fair evaluation, alternative placements, due process procedures, and free, appropriate public education.

Public Law 94-142 (Education for all Handicapped Children Act), 1975
Provided for a free, appropriate public education for all children with disabilities, defined special education and related services, and imposed rigid guidelines on the provisions of those services. It paralleled the provision for a free and appropriate public education in Section 504 of Public Law 94-142, and extended these services to preschool children with disabilities (ages three to five) through provisions to preschool incentive grants.

TEACHER CERTIFICATION STUDY GUIDE

Public Law 94-142 (Education for All Handicapped Children Act), 1975
The philosophy behind this pieces of legislation is that education is to be provided to all children aged six to eighteen who meet age eligibility requirements. All children are assumed capable of benefiting from education. For children with severe or profound handicaps, "education" may be interpreted to include training in basic self-help skills and vocational training as well as academics.

The principles of IDEA also incorporate the concept of "normalization." Within this concept, persons with disabilities are allowed access to everyday patterns and conditions of life that are as close as possible or equal to their non-disabled peers. There are seven fundamental provisions of IDEA.

Goss v. Lopez, 1975
This case ruled that the state could not deny a student education without following due process. While this decision is not based on a special education issue, the process of school suspension and expulsion is obviously critical in assuring an appropriate public education to children with disabilities.

Public Law 95-56 (Gifted and Talented Children's Act), 1978
This case defined the gifted and talented population and focused on this exceptionally category, which was not included in Public Law 94-142.

Larry P. v. Riles, 1979
This case ordered the reevaluation of black students enrolled in classes for educable mental retardation (EMR) and enjoined the California State department of Education from the use of intelligence tests in subsequent EMR placement decisions.

Parents in Action on Special Education (PASE) v. Hannon, 1980
This ruled that IQ tests are necessarily biased against ethnic and racial subcultures.

Board of Education v. Rowley, 1982
Amy Rowley was a deaf elementary school student whose parents rejected their school district's proposal to provide a tutor and speech therapist services to supplement their daughter's instruction in the regular classroom. Her parents insisted on an interpreter, even though Amy was making satisfactory social, academic, and educational progress without one. In deciding in favor of the school district, the Supreme Court ruled that school districts must provide those services that permit a student with disabilities to benefit from instruction. Essentially, the court ruled that the states are obligated to provide a "basic floor of opportunity"—that is, to *reasonably* allow the child to benefit from social education.

SPECIAL EDU. CROSS-CATEGORY 250

Public Law 98-199 (Education of the Handicapped Act [EHA] Amendments), 1983

Public Law 94-142 was amended to provide added emphasis on parental education and preschool, secondary, and post-secondary programs for children and youth with disabilities.

Irving Independent School District v. Tatro, 1984

IDEA lists health services as one of the "related services" that schools are mandated to provide to exceptional students. Amber Tatro, who had spina bifida, required the insertion of a catheter on a regular schedule in order to empty her bladder. The issue was specifically over the classification of clean, intermittent catheterization (CIC) as a medical service (not covered under IDEA) or a "related health service" (which would be covered). In this instance, the catheterization was not declared a medical service, but a "related service" necessary for the student to have in order to benefit from special education. The school district was obliged to provide the service. The Tatro case has implications for students with other medical impairments who may need services to allow them to attend classes at the school.

Smith v. Robinson, 1984

This 1984 case concerned reimbursement of attorney's fees for parents who win litigation under IDEA. At the time of this case, IDEA did not provide for such reimbursement. Following this ruling, Congress passed a law awarding attorney's fees to parents who win their litigation.

Public Law 99-372 (Handicapped Children's Protection Act of 1985)

This law allows parents who are unsuccessful in due process hearings or reviews to seek recovery of attorney's fees.

Public Law 99-457, 1986

Beginning with the 1991-1992 school year, special education programs were required for children ages three to five, with most states offering outreach programs to identify children with special needs from birth to age three. In place of, or in addition to an annual IEP, the entire family's needs are addressed by an Individual Family Service Plan (IFSP), which is reviewed with the family every six months.

Public Law 99-457 (Education of the Handicapped Act Amendments of 1986)

This re-authorized existing EHA, amended Public Law 94-142 to include financial incentives for states to educate children three to five years old by the 1990-1991 school years, and established incentive grants to promote programs serving infants with disabilities (birth to two years of age).

Public Law 99-506 (Rehabilitation Act Amendments of 1986)

This authorized formula grant funds for the development of supported employment demonstration projects.

School Board of Nassau County v. Arline, 1987
This established that contagious diseases are a disability under Section 504 of the Rehabilitation Act and that people with them are protected from discrimination, if otherwise qualified (actual risk to health and safety of others may make persons unqualified).

Honig v. Doe, 1988
Essentially, students may not be denied education or be excluded from school when their misbehavior is related to their handicap. The "stay put" provision of IDEA allows students to remain in their current educational setting pending the outcome of administrative or judicial hearings. In the case of behavior that is a danger to the student or others, the court allows school districts to apply their normal procedures for dealing with dangerous behavior, such as time-out, loss of privileges, detention, or study carrels. Where the student has presented an immediate threat to others, that student may be temporarily suspended for up to 10 school days to give the school and the parent's time to review the IEP and discuss possible alternatives to the current placement.

Americans with Disabilities Act (ADA) 1990
This bars discrimination in employment, transportation, public accommodations, and telecommunications in all aspects of life, not just those receiving federal funding. Title II and Title III are applicable to special education because they cover the private sector (such as private schools) and require access to public accommodations. New and remodeled public buildings, transportation vehicles, and telephone systems now must be accessible to the handicapped. ADA also protects individuals with contagious diseases, such as AIDS, from discrimination.

Public Law 101-336 (American with Disabilities Act ADA), 1990
This gives civil rights protection to individuals with disabilities in private sector employment, all public services, public accommodations, transportation, and telecommunications. Patterned after Section 504 of the Rehabilitation Act of 1973.

In 1990, the U.S. House of Representatives
opened for citizen comment the issue of a separate exceptionality category for students with attention deficit disorders. The issue was tabled without legislative action.

Public Law 101-476 (Individuals with Disabilities Education Act IDEA), 1990
This reauthorized and renamed existing EHA. This amendment to EHA changed the term "handicapped" to "disability," expanded related services, and required individual education programs (IEPs) to contain transitional goals and objectives for adolescents (ages 16 and above, special situations).

Florence County School Dist Four v. Shannon Carter, 1993

This established that when a school district does not provide FAPE for a student with disability, the parents may seek reimbursement for private schooling. This decision has encouraged districts to be more inclusive of students with autism who receive ABA/Lovaas therapy.

IDEA 97 Reauthorization

The amendment retains the major provisions of previous federal laws and also includes modifications to the law. Some of the changes include: participation of students with disabilities in statewide assessment programs with accommodations when required; changes to the IEP with emphasis on students with disabilities participating in the general curriculum and regular education teachers taking part in developing the IEP; lowering of the age to begin focusing on transition service needs from 16 to 14; and a guarantee that no student with a disability can be deprived of continuing educational services because of behavior.

No Child Left Behind Act (NCLB), 2002

This created strong standards in each state for what every child should know and learn in reading and math for grades three through eight. Student progress and achievement are measured for every child annually. Test results are made available in annual report. Schools are accountable for improving performance of all student groups. Parents with children in chronically failing schools are permitted to transfer their child to a better-performing school. Special education teachers must teach students to a level of proficiency; if a special education teacher teaches a core subject, he or she must meet the standard of a highly qualified teacher in that subject.

M.L. v. Federal Way School District (WA) in the Ninth Circuit Court of Appeals, 2004

This case ruled that the absence of a regular education teacher on an IEP team was a serious procedural error.

TEACHER CERTIFICATION STUDY GUIDE

No Child Left Behind

No Child Left Behind, Public Law 107-110, was signed on January 8, 2002. It addresses the accountability of school personnel for student achievement with the expectation that every child will demonstrate proficiency in reading, math, and science. The first full wave of accountability will take place 12 years from the start date, when children who attended school under NCLB graduate. However, the process to meet that accountability begins now.

In fact, as students progress through the school system, testing shows if an individual teacher has effectively met the needs of his or her students. Through testing, each student's adequate yearly progress or lack thereof is tracked.

NCLB affects regular and special education students, gifted students and slow learners, and children of every ethnicity, cultural background, and environment. NCLB is a document that encompasses every American educator and student.

Educators are affected as follows. Elementary teachers (K-3) are responsible for teaching reading and using different, scientific-based approaches, as needed. Elementary teachers of upper grades teach reading, math, and science. Middle and high school teacher teach to higher standards. Sometimes, they have the additional task of playing catch up with students who did not have an adequate education in earlier grades.

Special educators are responsible for teaching students to a level of comparable proficiency to that of their non-disabled peers. This raises the bar of academic expectations throughout the grades. For some students with disabilities, the criteria for getting a diploma is more difficult. Although a small percentage of students with disabilities will need alternate assessment, they still need to meet grade-appropriate goals.

In order for special education teachers to meet the professional criteria of this act, they must be *highly qualified*—that is, certified or licensed in their area of special education—and show proof of a specific level of professional development in the core subjects that they teach. As special education teachers received specific education in the core subjects they teach, they are better prepared to teach to the same level of learning standards as general education teachers.

SPECIAL EDU. CROSS-CATEGORY 254

TEACHER CERTIFICATION STUDY GUIDE

Major Components Retained and Changes of IDEA 2004

The second revision of IDEA occurred in 2004, when IDEA was re-authorized as the Individuals with Disabilities Education Improvement Act of 2004 (IDEIA 2004). It is commonly referred to as IDEA 2004 and became effective on July 1, 2005.

It was the intention to improve IDEA by adding the philosophy and understanding that special education students need preparation for further study beyond the high school setting. Accordingly, IDEA 2004 provided a close tie to P.L. 89-10, the Elementary and Special Education Act of 1965, and stated that students with special needs should have maximum access to the general curriculum. "Maximum access" was defined as the amount necessary for an individual student to reach his or her fullest potential. Full inclusion was stated not to be the only option by which to achieve this; IDEA specified that skills should be taught to compensate students later in life in cases where inclusion was not the best setting.

IDEA 2004 also added a new requirement for special education teachers in the secondary level by enforcing NCLB's *highly qualified* requirements for the subject area of each teacher's curriculum. The rewording in this part of IDEA states that they shall be *no less qualified* than teachers in the core areas.

Free and Appropriate Public Education (FAPE) was revised by mandating that students must have maximum access to appropriate general education. Additionally, LRE placement for those students with disabilities must have the same school placement rights as those students who are not disabled. IDEA 2004 recognizes that due to the nature of some disabilities, appropriate education may vary in the amount of participation and/or placement in the general education setting.

For some students, FAPE means a choice as to the type of educational institution they attend (e.g., private school), any of which must provide the special education services deemed necessary for the student through the IEP.

The definition of *assistive technology devices* was amended to exclude devices that are surgically implanted (e.g., cochlear implants) and clarified that students with assistive technology devices shall not be prevented from having special education services. Assistive technology devices may need to monitored by school personnel, but schools are not responsible for the implantation or replacement of such devices surgically.

The definition of *child with a disability,* the term used for children ages three to nine with a developmental delay, was changed to allow for the inclusion of Tourette's Syndrome.

SPECIAL EDU. CROSS-CATEGORY

IDEA 2004 recognized that all states must follow the National Instructional Materials Accessibility Standards, which states that students who need materials in a certain form will get those at the same time their non-disabled peers receive their materials. Teacher recognition of this standard is important.

Changes in Requirements for Evaluations
The clock/time allowance between the request for an initial evaluation and the determination of whether or not a disability is present was changed to state that the finding or determination must occur within 60 calendar days of the request. This is a significant change, as it was previously interpreted to mean 60 school days. Parental consent is also required for any evaluations or prior to the start of special education services.

No single assessment or measurement tool may now be used to determine special education qualification. Assessments and measurements should be in *language and form* that will give the most accurate picture of the child's abilities.

IDEA 2004 recognized that there exists a disproportionate representation of minorities and bilingual students in special education programs. It also determined that pre-service interventions that are scientifically based on early reading programs, positive behavioral interventions and support, and early intervening services may prevent some of those children from needing special education services. This understanding led to a child not being considered to have a disability if he or she has not had appropriate education in math or reading. A child can also not be considered to have a disability if the reason for his or her delays is speaking English as a second language.

When determining a specific learning disability, the criteria may or may not use a discrepancy between achievement and intellectual ability, instead focusing on whether not the child responds to scientific research-based intervention. In general, children who were not found eligible for special education (via testing) but are known to need services (via functioning, excluding lack of instruction) are still eligible for special education services. This change allows input for evaluation to include state and local testing, classroom observation, academic achievement, and related developmental needs.

Changes in Requirements for IEPs

Individualized Education Plans (IEPS) continue to have multiple sections. One section, present levels, now addresses academic achievement and functional performance. Annual IEP goals must address the same areas.

IEP goals should be aligned to state standards; thus, short term objectives are not required on every IEP. Students with IEPs must not only participate in regular education programs to the full extent possible, but they must show progress in those programs. This means that goals should be written to reflect academic progress.

For students who must participate in alternate assessment, there must be alignment to alternate achievement standards.

Significant changes were made in the definition of the IEP team, as well. Not less than one teacher from each of the areas of special education and regular education must be present.

IDEA 2004 also recognizes that the amount of required paperwork placed on teachers of students with disabilities should be reduced wherever possible. To accomplish this, a pilot program has been developed in which some states participate using multi-year IEPs. Individual student inclusion in this program requires consent by both the school and the parent.

TEACHER CERTIFICATION STUDY GUIDE

POST-TEST

1. Jonathan has attention deficit hyperactivity disorder (ADHD). He is in a regular classroom and appears to be doing okay. However, his teacher does not want John in her class because he will not obey her when she asks him to stop doing a repetitive action such as tapping his foot. The teacher sees this as distractive during tests. John needs: *(Competency 1) (Easy Rigor)*

   A. An IEP
   B. A 504 Plan
   C. A VESID evaluation
   D. A more restrictive environment

2. According to IDEA, a child whose disability is related to being deaf and blind may not be classified as: *(Competency 1) (Rigorous)*

   A. Multiple disabilities
   B. Other health impaired
   C. Having mental retardation
   D. Visually Impaired

3. A child may be classified under the special education "umbrella" as having a traumatic brain injury (TBI) if he/she does not have which of the following causes? *(Competency 1) (Rigorous)*

   A. Stroke
   B. Anoxia
   C. Encephalitis
   D. Birth trauma

4. Children with visual-spatial difficulties may not accomplish some developmental tasks, such as: *(Competency 1) (Rigorous)*

   A. Answering when called upon.
   B. Demonstrating characteristics of certain letter in print
   C. A delay in achieving the "th" sound
   D. Recognition of the permanence of print

5. A developmental delay may be indicated by a: *(Competency 1) (Rigorous)*

   A. Second grader having difficulty buttoning clothing
   B. Stuttered response
   C. Kindergartner not having complete bladder control
   D. Withdrawn behavior

6. Parents are more likely to have a child with a learning disability if: *(Competency 2) (Average Rigor)*

   A. They smoke tobacco
   B. The child is less than five pounds at birth
   C. The mother drank alcohol on a regular basis until she planned for a baby
   D. The father was known to consume large quantities of alcohol during the pregnancy

SPECIAL EDU. CROSS-CATEGORY

7. Echolalia (repetitive stereo-typed actions) and a severe disorder of thinking and communication are indicative of: *(Competency 2) (Average Rigor)*

    A. Psychosis
    B. Schizophrenia
    C. Autism
    D. Paranoia

8. Which behavioral disorder is difficult to diagnose in children because the symptoms are manifested quite differently than in adults? *(Competency 2) (Rigorous)*

    A. Anorexia
    B. Schizophrenia
    C. Paranoia
    D. Depression

9. Tom's special education teacher became concerned about her ability to deliver the adaptations and services he needs when she heard him begin to talk to someone who was not there. He also responds to questions in a nonsensical manner. Tom's teacher is concerned because she thinks he may be exhibiting symptoms of: *(Competency 2) (Easy Rigor)*

    A. Sensory perceptual disorder
    B. Mental illness
    C. Depression
    D. Tactile sensory deprivation

10. Of the following, which does not describe the term delinquency? *(Competency 2) (Average Rigor)*

    A. Behavior that would be considered criminal if exhibited by an adult
    B. Socialized aggression
    C. Academic truancy
    D. Inciting fights with verbal abuse

11. Janice is a new student in your self-contained class. She is extremely quiet and makes little, if any, eye contact. Yesterday she started to "parrot" what another student said. Today you became concerned when she did not follow directions and seemed not to even recognize your presence. Her cumulative file arrived today; when you review the health section, it will most likely state that she is diagnosed with: *(Competency 2) (Average)*

    A. Autism
    B. Central processing disorder
    C. Traumatic brain injury
    D. Mental retardation

12. Students who engage in gang activity, are often in fights, and are often truant could be said to be: *(Competency 2) (Average Rigor)*

    A. Socially maladjusted
    B. Emotionally disturbed
    C. Learning disabled
    D. Depressed

13. A student who has issues with truancy, gang membership, low school performance, and drug use is displaying: *(Competency 2) (Average Rigor)*

    A. Emotionally disturbed behaviors
    B. Symptoms of self-medication
    C. Average adolescent behavior
    D. Warning signs of crisis

14. Which of these explanations would not likely account for the lack of a clear definition of behavior disorders? *(Competency 3) (Rigorous)*

    A. Problems with measurement
    B. Cultural and/or social influences and views of what is acceptable
    C. The numerous types of manifestations of behavior disorders
    D. Differing theories that use their own terminology and definitions

15. Mark is receiving special education services within a 12:1:1. His teacher recommends that he be placed in a more restrictive setting, such as a residential placement. She presents good reasoning. What will the committee most likely recommend? *(Competency 3) (Average Rigor)*

    A. 8:1:1
    B. BOCES school placement
    C. 1:1 Aide
    D. Return to placement

16. What is the highest goal a teacher should aim for while preparing a student for success? *(Competency 3) (Average Rigor)*

    A. Reading
    B. Budgeting
    C. Cooking
    D. Self-advocacy

17. Modeling of a behavior by an adult who verbalizes the thinking process, overt self-instruction, and covert self-instruction are components of: *(Competency 3)(Rigorous)*

    A. Rational-emotive therapy
    B. Reality therapy
    C. Cognitive behavior modification
    D. Reciprocal teaching

18. Cognitive modeling is an excellent transition to: *(Competency 3) (Rigorous)*

    A. Covert Self-instruction
    B. Overt self-guidance
    C. Self-monitoring
    D. Self-reinforcement

19. Across America there is a toxic substance that is contributing to the creation of disabilities in our children. What is it? *(Competency 4) (Average Rigor)*

    A. Children's aspirin
    B. Fluoride water
    C. Chlorine gas
    D. Lead

20. Children who are characterized by impulsivity generally: *(Competency 4) (Easy Rigor)*

   A. Do not feel sorry for their actions
   B. Blame others for their actions
   C. Do not weigh alternatives before acting
   D. Do not outgrow their problem

21. A person who has a learning disability: *(Competency 4) (Easy Rigor)*

   A. Has an IQ two standard deviations below the norm
   B. Has congenital abnormalities
   C. Is limited by the educational environment
   D. Has a disorder in one of the basic psychological processes

22. What is considered the most effective when teaching children with special needs new concepts in math? *(Competency 4)(Rigorous)*

   A. Problem solving
   B. Direct instruction
   C. Repetition
   D. Ongoing assessment

23. Mr. Ward notes that Jennifer, a 9th grade student, understands the concept for three-step equations but seems unable to do problems successfully. When he reviews Jennifer's work, he notes that her addition and subtraction is not correct. What strategy would be most appropriate? *(Competency 4)(Average Rigor)*

   A. Basic multiplication and addition charts
   B. Checks for understanding
   C. Private instruction on adding and subtracting
   D. Calculator usage

24. All of these are effective in teaching written expression EXCEPT: *(Competency 4) (Easy Rigor)*

   A. Exposure to various styles and direct instruction in those styles
   B. Immediate feedback from the teacher with all mistakes clearly marked
   C. Goal setting and peer evaluation of written products according to set criteria.
   D. Incorporating writing with other academic subjects

25. Those with learning disabilities that are not physically noticeable continue to feel the stigma of the label "Special Education." Part of the reason for this is…
(Competency 5) (Average Rigor)

   A. The media rarely portrays people with learning disabilities that are not physically noticeable.
   B. The label "stupid" often accompanies the label "special."
   C. There is a very low percentage of people with special needs that are not visually noticeable.
   D. The appearance of "normal" is difficult to maintain.

26. Women who smoke during pregnancy are more likely to have a child with a learning disability as their children are born with: *(Competency 6) (Easy Rigor)*

   A. low birth weight.
   B. nicotine addiction.
   C. jaundice.
   D. low oxygen intake rate.

27. You checked the IEP for more information when you received a new student. Unfortunately, the IEP only provided the label "Mental Retardation." You are looking for an IQ level or a level of retardation to verify your own conclusions. The student has difficulty communicating his thoughts difficulty receiving communication. He has difficulty with tasks that require fine motor skills. He requires hand over hand assistance to wash his hands. It is likely that the student is: *(Competency 6) (Rigorous)*

   A. Mildly Retarded
   B. Moderately Retarded
   C. Severely Retarded
   D. Profoundly Retarded

28. Which of the following traits is NOT typical of a student who is labeled as orthopedically impaired or as Other Health Impaired?
(Competency 8) (Rigorous)

   A. Frequent speech and language defects; communication may be prevented
   B. echolatia orthosis may be present
   C. Periods of confusion and loss of memory
   D. Emotional (psychological) problems, which require treatment

29. A good assessment of whether a child may have ADHD in your classroom would include a(n) _____. *(Competency 10) (Average Rigor)*

    A. Baseline
    B. Monetary time sampling
    C. Age-based norm criteria
    D. Construct validity

30. Criteria for choosing behaviors to measure by frequency include all but those that: *(Competency 10) (Average Rigor)*

    A. Have an observable beginning
    B. Last a long time
    C. Last a short time
    D. Occur often

31. Criteria for choosing behaviors to measure by duration include all but those that: *(Competency 10) (Easy Rigor)*

    A. Last a short time
    B. Last a long time
    C. Have no readily observable beginning or end
    D. Do not happen often

32. The basic tools necessary to observe and record behavior may include all BUT: *(Competency 10) (Average Rigor)*

    A. Cameras
    B. Timers
    C. Counters
    D. Graphs or charts

33. You are working with a functional program and have placed a student in a vocational position at a coffee house. You need to perform a task analysis of making coffee. Which task should be first in the analysis? *(Competency 10) (Average Rigor)*

    A. Filling the pot with water
    B. Taking the order
    C. Measuring the coffee
    D. Picking the correct coffee

34. The extent that a test measures what it claims to measure is called: *(Competency 10) (Rigorous)*

    A. Reliability
    B. Validity
    C. Factor analysis
    D. Chi Square

35. A best practice for evaluating student performance and progress on IEPs is: *(Competency 10) (Rigorous)*

    A. Formal assessment
    B. Curriculum-based assessment
    C. Criterion-based assessment
    D. Norm-referenced evaluation

36. Statements like "Darren is lazy," are not helpful in describing his behavior for all but which of these reasons? *(Competency 10) (Average Rigor)*

    A. There is no way to determine if any change occurs from the information given
    B. The student—not the behavior—becomes labeled
    C. Darren's behavior will manifest itself clearly enough without any written description
    D. Constructs are open to various interpretations among the people who are asked to define them

37. Marcie is often not in her seat when the bell rings. She may be found at the pencil sharpener, throwing paper away, or fumbling through her notebook. Which of these descriptions of her behavior can be described as a pinpoint? *(Competency 10) (Easy Rigor)*

    A. Is tardy
    B. Is out of seat
    C. Is not in seat when late bell rings
    D. Is disorganized

38. Which is NOT an example of a standard score? *(Competency 10) (Rigorous)*

    A. T-score
    B. Z-score
    C. Standard deviation
    D. Stanine

39. Criteria for choosing behaviors that are in the most need of change involve all but the following: *(Competency 10) (Average Rigor)*

    A. Observations across settings to rule out certain interventions
    B. Pinpointing the behavior that is the poorest fit in the child's environment
    C. The teacher's concern about what is the most important behavior to target
    D. Analysis of the environmental reinforcers

40. Alternative assessments include all of the following EXCEPT: *(Competency 10) (Average Rigor)*

    A. Portfolios
    B. Interviews
    C. Teacher-made tests
    D. Performance-based tests

41. The most direct method of obtaining assessment data, and perhaps the most objective, is: *(Competency 10) (Rigorous)*

    A. Testing
    B. Self-recording
    C. Observation
    D. Experimenting

42. When a teacher is choosing behaviors to modify, the issue of social validity must be considered. Social validity refers to: *(Competency 10) (Easy Rigor)*

    A. The need for the behavior to be performed in public
    B. Whether the new behavior will be considered significant by those who deal with the child
    C. Whether there will be opportunities to practice the new behavior in public
    D. Society's standards of behavior

43. Which of these would be the least effective measure of behavioral disorders? *(Competency 10) (Average Rigor)*

    A. Alternative assessment
    B. Naturalistic assessment
    C. Standardized test
    D. Psychodynamic analysis

44. Which would not be an advantage of using a criterion-referenced test? *(Competency 10) (Rigorous)*

    A. Information about an individual's ability level is too specific for the purposes of the assessment
    B. It can pinpoint exact areas of weaknesses and strengths
    C. You can design them yourself
    D. You do not get comparative information

45. Measurement of adaptive behavior should include all but: *(Competency 10) (Rigorous)*

    A. The student's behavior in a variety of sett*ings*
    B. *The student's skills displayed in a* variety of settings
    C. Comparative analysis to other students in the class
    D. Analysis of the student's social skills

46. Grading should be based on all of the following EXCEPT: *(Competency 10) (Average Rigor)*

    A. Clearly-defined mastery of course objectives
    B. A variety of evaluation methods
    C. Performance of the student in relation to other students
    D. Assigning points for activities and basing grades on a point total

47. Anecdotal records should? *(Competency 10) (Average Rigor)*

    A. Record observable behavior
    B. End with conjecture
    C. Record motivational factors
    D. Note previously stated interests

48. A good naturalistic assessment requires: *(Competency 11) (Rigorous)*

   A. Communication notebooks
   B. Portfolios
   C. Long-range planning
   D. Diverse responses

49. Otumba is a 16 year old in your class who recently came from Nigeria. The girls in your class have come to you to complain about the way he treats them in a sexist manner. When they complain, you reflect that this is also the way he treats adult females. You have talked to Otumba before about appropriate behavior. You should first? *(Competency 11) (Rigorous)*

   A. Complain to the principal
   B. Ask for a parent-teacher conference
   C. Check to see if this is a cultural norm in his country
   D. Create a behavior contract for him to follow

50. If a child does not qualify for classification under special education, the committee shall: *(Competency 11) (Average Rigor)*

   A. Refer the parental interventions to the 504 Plan
   B. Provide temporary remedial services for the student
   C. Recommend to the parent possible resources outside of the committee for which the child may qualify
   D. Give the parents the information about possible reviews by an exterior source

51. What is required of a special education teacher when approaching an administrator regarding a request to change placement of a student? *(Competency 11) (Rigorous)*

   A. Observation
   B. Objectivity
   C. Assessments
   D. Parent permission

52. Which of the following statements was not offered as a rationale for inclusion? *(Competency 11) (Average Rigor)*

   A. Special education students are not usually identified until their learning problems have become severe
   B. Lack of funding will mean that support for the special needs children will not be available in the regular classroom
   C. Putting children in segregated special education placements is stigmatizing
   D. There are students with learning or behavior problems who do not meet special education requirements but who still need special services

53. What is required of a special education teacher when approaching an administrator regarding a request to change placement of a student? *(Competency 11) (Rigorous)*

   A. Observation
   B. Objectivity
   C. Assessments
   D. Parent permission

54. Mr. Johnson asks his students to score each of their classmates in areas such as with whom they would prefer to play and work. A Likert-type scale with non-behavioral criteria is used. This is an example of: *(Competency16) (Rigorous)*

   A. Peer nomination
   B. Peer rating
   C. Peer assessment
   D. Sociogram

55. Mrs. Taylor takes her students to a special gymnastics presentation that the P.E. coach has arranged in the gym. The students get a chance to perform some of the simple stunts. They all easily go through the movements except for Sam, who is known as the class klutz. Carl, another student of Mrs. Taylor's, helps Sam, who does not give up and finally completes the stunts. His classmates cheer him on with comments like, "Way to go!" What kind of teaching technique was implemented? *(Competency 16) (Average Rigor)*

   A. Group share
   B. Modeling
   C. Peer tutoring
   D. All of the above

56. Ms. Denario was planning on using graphic organizers with the new book the students would be reading. When would be a good time to use a graphic organizer? *(Competency 16) .(Average Rigor)*

   A. Before the lesson
   B. During the lesson
   C. Before, during and, after the lesson.
   D. Before and after the lesson

57. Kareem's father sounds upset and is in the office demanding to see his son's cumulative record. You should: *(Competency 17) (Average Rigor)*

   A. Tell him that he will have to make an appointment
   B. Bring the record to a private room for him to review with either an administrator or yourself
   C. Take the record to the principal's office for review
   D. Give the record to the parent

58. Standards of accuracy for a student's spelling should be based on the student's: *(Competency 17) (Rigorous)*

   A. Grade level spelling list
   B. Present reading book level
   C. Level of spelling development
   D. Performance on an informal assessment

59. Which of these techniques is least effective in helping children correct spelling problems? *(Competency 17) (Easy Rigor)*

   A. The teacher models the correct spelling in a context
   B. Students see the incorrect and the correct spelling together in order to visualize the correct spelling
   C. Positive reinforcement as the child tests the rules and tries to approximate the correct spelling
   D. Copying the correct word five times

60. Teacher feedback, task completion, and a sense of pride over mastery or accomplishment of a skill are examples of: *(Competency 18) (Average Rigor)*

   A. Extrinsic reinforcers
   B. Behavior modifiers
   C. Intrinsic reinforcers
   D. Positive feedback

61. Which of the following does NOT have an important effect on the spatial arrangement (physical setting) of your classroom? *(Competency 18) (Average Rigor)*

   A. Adequate physical space
   B. Ventilation
   C. Window placement
   D. Lighting adequacy

62. A suggested amount of time for a large-group instruction lesson for a sixth or seventh grade group would be: *(Competency 18) (Rigorous)*

    A. 5 to 40 minutes
    B. 5 to 50 minutes
    C. 5 to 30 minutes
    D. 5 to 15 minutes

63. Cooperative learning does NOT utilize: *(Competency 18) (Average Rigor)*

    A. Shared ideas
    B. Small groups
    C. Independent practice
    D. Student expertise

64. Which of these techniques is least effective in helping children correct spelling problems? *(Competency 18) (Rigorous)*

    A. The teacher models the correct spelling in a context
    B. Student sees the incorrect and the correct spelling together in order to visualize the correct spelling
    C. Positive reinforcement as the child tests the rules and tries to approximate the correct spelling
    D. Copying the correct word five times

65. A typical one to one teaching/tutoring model is typically found in a …. *(Competency 18) (Average Rigor)*

    A. 12:1:1
    B. 6:1:1
    C. Inclusive classroom
    D. Resource Room

66. The phonics approach to teaching children how to read utilizes what method? *(Competency 19) (Average Rigor)*

    A. Reading for meaning
    B. Reading for letter combinations
    C. Identifying words by their position and context
    D. Word configurations

67. Marisol has been mainstreamed into a 9th grade language arts class. Although her behavior is satisfactory, and she likes the class, Marisol's reading level is about two years below grade level. The class has been assigned to read *Great Expectations* and write a report. What intervention would be LEAST successful in helping Marisol complete this assignment? *(Competency 19) (Average Rigor)*

   A. Having Marisol listen to a taped recording while following the story in the regular text
   B. Giving her a modified version of the story
   C. Telling her to choose a different book that she can read
   D. Showing a film to the entire class and comparing and contrasting it with the book

68. A teacher should consider all of the following when evaluating a student's reading comprehension EXCEPT: *(Competency 19)(Average Rigor)*

   A. Past experience
   B. Teacher-prepared preset questions on text
   C. Level of content
   D. Oral language comprehension.

69. Task related attending skills include: *(Competency 19) (Rigorous)*

   A. Compliance to requests
   B. Writing the correct answer on the chalk board
   C. Listening to the assignment
   D. Repeating instructions

70. Organizing ideas by use of a web or outline is an example of which writing activity? *(Competency 20) (Easy Rigor)*

   A. Revision
   B. Drafting
   C. Prewriting
   D. Final draft

71. Ryan is working on a report about dogs. He uses scissors and tape to cut and rearrange sections and paragraphs. He then photocopies the paper so he can continue writing. In which stage of the writing process is Ryan? *(Competency 20) (Easy Rigor)*

   A. Final draft
   B. Prewriting
   C. Revision
   D. Drafting

72. Celia, who is in fourth grade, asked, "Where are my ball?" She also has trouble with passive sentences. Language interventions for Celia would target: (Competency 20) (Rigorous)

    A. Morphology
    B. Syntax
    C. Pragmatics
    D. Semantics

73. Teaching techniques that stimulate active participation and understanding in the mathematics class include all but which of the following? (Competency 21) (Easy Rigor)

    A. Having students copy computation facts for a set number of times
    B. Asking students to find the error in an algorithm
    C. Giving immediate feedback to students
    D. Having students chart their progress

74. One of the skills necessary for problem solving is: (Competency 21) (Easy Rigor)

    A. Identifying the main idea
    B. Order of operations
    C. Algebraic comprehension
    D. Written expression

75. Children enter school with many skills. Generally they have all the skills below, EXCEPT: (Competency 21) (Rigorous)

    A. Classifying
    B. Numerical Notation
    C. Comparing
    D. Equalizing

76. Many special education students may have trouble with the skills necessary to be successful in algebra and geometry for all but one of these reasons: (Competency 22 (Average Rigor)

    A. Prior instruction focused on computation rather than understanding
    B. Unwillingness to problem solve
    C. Lack of instruction in prerequisite skills
    D. Large amount of new vocabulary

77. Which of the following sentences will NOT test recall? (Competency 22) (Average Rigor)

    A. What words in the story describe Goldilocks?
    B. Why did Goldilocks go into the three bears' house?
    C. Name in order the things that belonged to the three bears that Goldilocks tried.
    D. What did the three bears learn about leaving their house unlocked?

78. Which is not indicative of a handwriting problem? *(Competency 23) (Rigorous)*

   A. Errors persisting over time
   B. Little improvement on simple handwriting tasks
   C. Fatigue after writing for a short time
   D. Occasional letter reversals, word omissions, and poor spacing

79. Laura is beginning to raise her hand first instead of talking out. An effective schedule of reinforcement should be: *(Competency 23) (Average Rigor)*

   A. Continuous
   B. Variable
   C. Intermittent
   D. Fixed

80. To facilitate learning instructional objectives in spelling: *(Competency 23) (Average Rigor)*

   A. They should include a grade level spelling list
   B. They should be written and shared
   C. They should be arranged in order of similarity
   D. They should be taken from a scope and sequence

81. Transfer of learning occurs when? *(Competency 23) (Rigorous)*

   A. Experience with one task influences performance on another task
   B. Content can be explained orally
   C. Student experiences the "I got it!" syndrome
   D. Curricular objective is exceeded

82. Teacher modeling, student-teacher dialogues, and peer interactions are part of which teaching technique designed to provide support during the initial stages of instruction? *(Competency 23) (Rigorous)*

   A. Reciprocal teaching
   B. Scaffolding
   C. Peer tutoring
   D. Cooperative learning

83. Functional curriculum focuses on all of the following EXCEPT: *(Competency 23) (Rigorous)*

   A. Skills needed for social living
   B. Occupational readiness
   C. Functioning in society.
   D. Remedial academic skills

84. Kenny is a 9th grader enrolled in Wood Shop; he is having difficulty grasping fractions. You know that Kenny has difficulty with abstract concepts. What would be a good method to teach this concept?
(Competency 23) (Rigorous)

   A. Pie blocks that proportionately measure whole, half, 1/4, 1/8, etc.
   B. Strips of paper that proportionately measure whole, half, 1/4, 1/8, etc.
   C. One-on-one review of the worksheet
   D. Working in the wood shop, privately showing him how to measure

85. Sam is working to earn half an hour of basketball time with his favorite P.E. teacher. At the end of each half hour, Sam marks his point sheet with an X if he reached his goal of no call-outs. When he has received 25 marks, he will receive his basketball free time. This behavior management strategy is an example of: *(Competency 24) (Average)*

   A. Self-recording
   B. Self-evaluation
   C. Self-reinforcement
   D. Self-regulation

86. Mark has been working on his target goal of completing his mathematics class work. Each day he records, on a scale of 0 to 3, how well he has done his work, and his teacher provides feedback. This self-management technique is an example of: *(Competency 24) (Average Rigor)*

   A. Self-recording
   B. Self reinforcement
   C. Self-regulation
   D. Self-evaluation

87. Children with behavior disorders often do not exhibit stimulus control. This means they do not display:
(Competency 25) (Average Rigor)

   A. Culturally correct behaviors
   B. Understanding of where and when certain behaviors are appropriate
   C. Acceptance of others
   D. Listening skills

88. Which of the following is NOT a feature of effective classroom rules? *(Competency 25) (Easy Rigor)*

   A. They are about four to six in number
   B. They are negatively stated
   C. Consequences are consistent and immediate
   D. They can be tailored to individual teaching goals and teaching styles

SPECIAL EDU. CROSS-CATEGORY 273

89. When would proximity control not be a good behavioral intervention? *(Competency 25) (Easy Rigor)*

   A. Two students are arguing
   B. A student is distracting others
   C. One student threatens another
   D. Involve fading and shaping

90. Which of the following should be avoided when writing goals for social behavior? *(Competency 25) (Average Rigor)*

   A. Non-specific adverbs
   B. Behaviors stated as verbs
   C. Criteria for acceptable performance
   D. Conditions where the behavior is expected to be performed

91. In a positive classroom environment, errors are viewed as: *(Competency 25) (Average Rigor)*

   A. Symptoms of deficiencies
   B. Lack of attention or ability
   C. A natural part of the learning process
   D. The result of going too fast

92. Which of the following is NOT the best way to encourage and strengthen a social skill? *(Competency 25) (Average Rigor)*

   A. Role playing
   B. Field trips
   C. Student story telling
   D. Reading a book on the topic

93. Distractive behavior, verbal outbursts, and passive aggressiveness should be addressed using: *(Competency 25) (Rigorous)*

   A. Time-outs
   B. Response cost
   C. Planned ignoring
   D. Rule reminders

94. A student with a poor self-concept may manifest in all of the ways listed below EXCEPT: *(Competency 25) (Average Rigor)*

   A. Withdrawn actions
   B. Aggression
   C. Consistently announcing his/her achievements
   D. Shyness

95. Mr. Brown finds that his chosen consequence does not seem to be having the desired effect of reducing the target misbehavior. Which of these would LEAST LIKELY account for Mr. Brown's lack of success with the consequence?
(Competency 25) (Rigorous)

   A. The consequence was aversive in Mr. Brown's opinion, but not the students'
   B. The students were not developmentally ready to understand the connection between the behavior and the consequence
   C. Mr. Brown was inconsistent in applying the consequence
   D. The intervention had not previously been shown to be effective in studies

96. Token systems are popular for all of these advantages EXCEPT:
(Competency 25) (Average Rigor)

   A. The number needed for rewards may be adjusted
   B. Rewards are easy to maintain
   C. They are effective for students who generally do not respond to social reinforcers
   D. Tokens reinforce the relationship between desirable behavior and reinforcement

97. An effective classroom behavior management plan includes all but which of the following? *(Competency 25) (Average Rigor)*

   A. Transition procedures for changing activities
   B. Clear consequences for rule infractions
   C. Concise teacher expectations for student behavior
   D. Strict enforcement

98. Teaching children skills that will be useful in their home lives and neighborhoods is the basis of: *(Competency 27) (Average Rigor)*

   A. Curriculum-based instruction
   B. Community-based instruction
   C. Transition planning
   D. Academic curriculum

99. An important goal of collaborative consultation is: *(Competency 27) (Easy Rigor)*

   A. Mainstream as many ESE students as possible
   B. Guidance on how to handle ESE students from the ESE teacher
   C. Mutual empowerment of both the mainstream and the ESE teacher
   D. Document progress of mainstreamed students

100. Transition services that are mandatory to be addressed include all of the following EXCEPT: *(Competency 27) (Easy Rigor)*

    A. Instruction
    B. Community experience
    C. Development of employment
    D. Self-Advocacy

101. You are having continual difficulty with your classroom assistant. A good strategy to address this problem would be: *(Competency 28) (Rigorous)*

    A. To address the issue immediately
    B. To take away responsibilities
    C. To write a clearly established role plan for discussion
    D. To speak to your supervisor

102. Which of the following is a responsibility that can NOT be designated to a classroom aide? *(Competency 28) (Average Rigor)*

    A. Small group instruction
    B. Small group planning
    C. Coordination of an activity
    D. Assist in BIP implementation

103. The key to success for the exceptional student placed in a regular classroom is: *(Competency 28) (Average Rigor)*

    A. Access to the special aids and materials
    B. Support from the ESE teacher
    C. Modification in the curriculum
    D. The mainstream teacher's belief that the student will profit from the placement

104. Ability to supply specific instructional materials, programs, and methods and to influence *environmental learning variables* are advantages of which service model for exceptional students?
(Competency 28) (Rigorous)

    A. Regular classroom
    B. Consultant teacher
    C. Itinerant teacher
    D. Resource room

105. A consultant teacher should be meeting the needs of his/her students by: *(Competency 28) (Easy Rigor)*

    A. Pushing in to do small group instruction with regular education students
    B. Asking the student to show his/her reasoning for failing
    C. Meeting with the teacher before class to discuss adaptations and expectations
    D. Accompanying the student to class

106. Students with disabilities develop greater self-images and recognize their own academic and social strengths when they are: *(Competency 28)(Easy Rigor)*

    A. Included in the mainstream classroom
    B. Provided community-based internships
    C. Socializing in the hallway
    D. Provided 1:1 instructional opportunity

107. When a teacher is choosing behaviors to modify, two issues must be considered. What are they? *(Competency 28) (Average Rigor)*

    A. The need for the behavior to be performed in public *and* the culture of acceptance
    B. The culture of the child *and* society's standards regarding the behavior
    C. Evidence that the behavior can be changed *and* society norms
    D. Standards of the student's community *and* school rules

108. A BIP (Behavior Intervention Plan) is written to teach positive behavior. Which element listed below is NOT a standard feature of the plan? *(Competency 28) (Rigorous)*

    A. Identification of behavior to be modified
    B. Strategies to implement the replacement behavior
    C. Statement of distribution
    D. Team creation of BIP

109. By November, Annette's 7th grade teacher is concerned with her sporadic attendance. What action should take place next? *(Competency 28)(Average Rigor)*

A. Notify CPS
B. Notify the police of non-compliance with compulsory attendance
C. Question parents about the absences
D. Notify the administrator

110. You have a group of 8th grade students in an English class. Sheryl sits in the back of the room by choice and rarely answers questions. You believe that she has a learning disability and begin to modify her worksheets. You are: *(Competency 28) (Average Rigor)*

A. Planning for success of the student
B. Creating a self-fulfilling prophecy
C. Developing a student-centered curriculum
D. Testing her ability

111. Parents of children with disabilities may seek your advice on several aspects regarding their children. A mother calls you and complains she can't keep her son on task and she has to keep sending her son back to the bathroom until he finishes getting prepared for the day. What advice should you give her? *(Competency 28) (Average Rigor)*

A. Request an educational evaluation
B. Recommend close supervision until he does all tasks together consistently
C. Create a list of tasks to be completed in the bathroom
D. Ask for outside coordination of services advocacy that can assist with this type of issue

112. Which is not a goal of collaboration for a consult teacher? *(Competency 28) (Average Rigor)*

A. To have the regular education teacher understand the student's disability
B. Review content for accuracy
C. Review lessons for possible necessary modifications
D. Understanding of reasons for current grade

SPECIAL EDU. CROSS-CATEGORY 278

113. You have documented proof that Janice performs higher with the use of a computer on both class work and tests. Which kind of CSE/IEP Conference should be held? *(Competency 29) (Easy Rigor)*

   A. Manifestation determination
   B. Post-school transition to insure provision of a laptop by outside services
   C. Amendment; change of program/placement
   D. Annual

114. Diversity can be identified in students by: *(Competency 29) (Average Rigor)*

   A. Biological factors
   B. Socioeconomic status (SES)
   C. Ethnicity
   D. All of the above

115. Kara's mother has requested a computer for her child to do class work and homework; the CSE does not agree. Kara complains to you. You should: *(Competency 29) (Easy Rigor)*

   A. Tell her you agree with her
   B. Recommend an outside source that may provide a free laptop computer
   C. Tell Kara's mother she can still fight the CSE's decision by requesting a due process hearing
   D. Tell the parent to call a lawyer

116. Shyquan is in your inclusive class, and she exhibits a slower comprehension of assigned tasks and concepts. Her first two grades were Bs but she is now receiving failing marks. She has seen the resource teacher. You should: *(Competency 29) (Rigorous)*

   A. Ask for a review of current placement
   B. Tell Shyquan to seek extra help
   C. Ask Shyquan if she is frustrated
   D. Ask the regular education teacher to slow instruction

117. The integrated approach to learning utilizes all resources available to address student needs. What are the resources? *(Competency 30) (Average Rigor)*

    A. The student, his/her parents, and the teacher
    B. The teacher, the parents, and the special education team
    C. The teacher, the student, and an administrator to perform needed interventions
    D. The student, his/her parents, the teacher, and community resources

118. Which of these characteristics is NOT included in the IDEA definition of emotional disturbance? *(Competency 31) (Average Rigor)*

    A. General pervasive mood of unhappiness or depression
    B. Social maladjustment manifested in a number of settings
    C. Tendency to develop physical symptoms, pains, or fear associated with school or personal problems
    D. Inability to learn that is not attributed to intellectual, sensory, or health factors

119. IDEA 2004 changed the IEP by? *(Competency 31) (Rigorous)*

    A. Not requiring short-term objectives
    B. Requiring an inclusive activity
    C. Requiring parents to participate in the CSE
    D. Establishing new criteria to be classified as learning disabled

120. According to IDEA 2004, students with disabilities are to do what? *(Competency 31) (Average Rigor)*

    A. Participate in the general education program to the fullest extent that it is beneficial for them
    B. Participate in a vocational training within the general education setting
    C. Participate in a general education setting for physical education
    D. Participate in a modified program that meets their needs

121. Teachers in grades K-3 are mandated to teach what to all students using scientifically based methods with measurable outcomes? *(Competency 31) (Average Rigor)*

    A. Math
    B. Reading
    C. Citizenship
    D. Writing

SPECIAL EDU. CROSS-CATEGORY 280

122. What legislation started FAPE? *(Competency 31) (Average Rigor)*

   A. Section 504
   B. EHCA
   C. IDEA
   D. Education Amendment 1974

123. The revision of Individuals with Disabilities Education Act in 1997: *(Competency 31) (Rigorous)*

   A. Required collaboration of educational professionals in order to provide equitable opportunities for students with disabilities
   B. Removed the requirement for short-term objectives with objectives with goals
   C. Required school administrator approval for an IEP to be put into place
   D. Required FBAs and BIPs for all students that were suspended for six days

124. Taiquan's parents are divorced and have joint custody. They have both requested to be present at the CSE. You call to make sure that they received the letter informing them of the upcoming CSE. Taiquan's father did not receive the notification and is upset. You should: *(Competency 31) (Rigorous)*

   A. Tell him that you could review the meeting with him later
   B. Ask him if he can adjust his schedule
   C. Tell him you can reschedule the meeting
   D. Ask him to coordinate a time for the CSE to meet with his ex-wife

125. According to IDEA 2004, an FBA must be: *(Competency 31) (Average Rigor)*

   A. Written by the special education administrator
   B. Written by the teacher who has the issue with the student
   C. Written by the primary teacher
   D. Written by a team

126. NCLB changed: *(Competency 31) (Rigorous)*

   A. Special education teacher placement
   B. Classroom guidelines
   C. Stricter behavioral regulations.
   D. Academic content

127. **IDEA 97 changed IDEA by:** *(Competency 31) (Rigorous)*

   A. Requiring IEPs to be in electronic format
   B. Requiring all staff working with the student to have access to the IEP
   C. Allowing past assessments to be used in triennials
   D. Requiring BIPs for many students with FBAs

128. **Which of these groups is not comprehensively covered by IDEA?** *(Competency 31) (Easy Rigor)*

   A. Gifted and talented
   B. Mentally retarded
   C. Specific learning disabilities
   D. Speech and language impaired

129. **Educators who advocate educating all children in their neighborhood classrooms and schools, who propose the end of labeling and segregation of special needs students in special classes, and who call for the delivery of special supports and services directly in the classroom may be said to support the:** *(Competency 31) (Easy Rigor)*

   A. Full service model
   B. Regular education initiative
   C. Full inclusion model
   D. Mainstream model

130. **NCLB (No Child Left Behind Act), was signed on January 8, 2002. It addresses what?** *(Competency 31) (Rigorous)*

   A. Accessibility of curriculum to the student
   B. Administrative incentives for school improvements
   C. The funding to provide services required
   D. Accountability of school personnel for student achievement

131. **Section 504 differs from the scope of IDEA because its main focus is on:** *(Competency 31) (Average Rigor)*

   A. Prohibition of discrimination on the basis of disability
   B. A basis for additional support services and accommodations in a special education setting
   C. Procedural rights and safeguards for the individual
   D. Federal funding for educational services

132. **Public Law 99-457 amended the EHA to make provisions for:** *(Competency 31) (Average Rigor)*

   A. Education services for "uneducable" children
   B. Education services for children in jail settings
   C. Special education benefits for children birth to five years
   D. Education services for medically-fragile children

133. **Under the provisions of IDEA, the student is entitled to all of these EXCEPT:** *(Competency 31) (Average Rigor)*

   A. Placement in the best environment
   B. Placement in the least restrictive environment
   C. Provision of educational needs at no cost
   D. Provision of individualized, appropriate educational program

134. **As a new special education teacher, you have the responsibility to:** *(Competency 31) (Average Rigor)*

   A. Share new law related to special education
   B. Discuss and plan intervention strategies for other teachers
   C. Stay current on national and local news
   D. Observe incoming students for possible referrals to CSE

135. **Which law specifically states that "full inclusion is not the only way for a student to reach his/her highest potential?"** *(Competency 31) (Rigorous)*

   A. IDEA
   B. IDEA 97
   C. IDEA 2004
   D. Part 200

136. **The following words describe an IEP objective EXCEPT:** *(Competency 31) (Rigorous)*

   A. Specific
   B. Observable
   C. Measurable
   D. Flexible

137. **NCLB and IDEA 2004 changed special education teacher requirements by:** *(Competency 31) (Easy Rigor)*

   A. Requiring a "highly qualified" status for job placement
   B. Adding changes to the requirement for certifications
   C. Adding legislation requiring teachers to maintain knowledge of law
   D. Requiring inclusive environmental experience prior to certification

SPECIAL EDU. CROSS-CATEGORY

138. IDEA 2004 stated that there is a disproportionate amount of minority students classified. The reason IDEA 2004 suggests is:
(Competency 31) (Average Rigor)

   A. Socioeconomic status where disproportionate numbers exist
   B. Improper evaluations; not making allowances for students who speak English as a second language
   C. Growing population of minorities
   D. Percentage of drug abuse per ethnicity

139. Guidelines for an Individualized Family Service Plan (IFSP) are described in which legislation?
(Competency 31) (Rigorous)

   A. Education of the Handicapped Act Amendments
   B. IDEA (1990)
   C. IDEA 2004
   D. ADA

140. Cheryl is a 15-year old student receiving educational services in a full-time EH classroom. The date for her IEP review is planned for two months before her 16th birthday. According to the requirements of IDEA, what must ADDITIONALLY be included in this review?
(Competency 31) (Average Rigor)

   A. Graduation plan
   B. Individualized transition plan
   C. Vocational assessment
   D. Transportation planning

141. Previous to IDEA 97, what was not accepted?
(Competency 31) (Rigorous)

   A. Using previous assessments to evaluate placement
   B. Parent refusal of CSE determination (no due process)
   C. Student input on placement and needs
   D. All of the above

142. Hector is a 10th grader in a program for the severely emotionally handicapped. After a classmate taunted him about his mother, Hector threw a desk at the other boy and attacked him. A crisis intervention team tried to break up the fight, and one teacher hurt his knee. The other boy received a concussion. Hector now faces disciplinary measures. How long can he be suspended without the suspension reviewing a possible "change of placement"? *(Competency 31) (Rigorous)*

   A. 5 days
   B. 10 days
   C. 10 + 30 days
   D. 60 days

143. The concept that a handicapped student cannot be expelled for misconduct that is a manifestation of the handicap itself is not limited to students who are labeled "seriously emotionally disturbed." Which reason does not explain this concept? *(Competency 31) (Easy Rigor)*

   A. Emphasis on individualized evaluation
   B. Consideration of the problems and needs of handicapped students
   C. Right to a free and appropriate public education
   D. Students in special education get special privileges

144. Teachers have a professional obligation to do all of the following except: *(Competency 31) (Average Rigor)*

   A. Join a professional organization, such as CEC or LDA
   B. Attend in-services or seminars related to the position
   C. Stay after school to help students
   D. Run school clubs

SPECIAL EDU. CROSS-CATEGORY 285

145. **Satisfaction of the LRE requirement means that (Competency 31) (Easy Rigor):**

   A. A school is providing the best services it can offer there
   B. The school is providing the best services the district has to offer
   C. The student is being educated in the least restrictive setting that meets his or her needs
   D. The student is being educated with the fewest special education services necessary

146. **The court case that determined that a student may not be denied education or be excluded from school when their behavior is related to their handicap was: (Competency 31) (Rigorous)**

   A. Honig v. Doe 1988
   B. School Board of Nassau County v. Arline, 1987
   C. Florence County School District v. Shannon Carter, 1993
   D. Smith v. Robinson, 1984

147. **Teaching materials that are copyrighted may: (Competency 31) (Average Rigor)**

   A. may not be reproduced
   B. May be reproduced if they are intended for that purpose.
   C. may be reproduced only for your immediate students
   D. may be reproduced for students that did not receive the texts with the other students.

148. **John has received a long term suspension for assaulting a student. John is classified as being Mentally Retarded. In the assault he threw a chair at another student. The Manifestation Determination CSE determined that John's actions were not related to his disability. According to the law then: (Competency 31) (Easy Rigor)**

   A. John may receive the same punishment that a "regular" education student would receive.
   B. John will be returned to program after the completion of 10 days.
   C. CSE will revisit placement at a later meeting.
   D. John may return to the school, but may not be returned to the class where he hurt the other student.

149. NCLB requires that the special education teacher be *Highly Qualified*. To be *Highly Qualified (HQ) a teach must:* (Competency 31) (Easy Rigor)

   A. Have the same certification as the regular education teacher in their position.
   B. Show relevant course work and professional development
   C. Have a comparable degree in the field they are working in.
   D. A and/or B and/or C.

150. The 1975, Goss v. Lopez, decision had a large impact on special education as a whole because it: *(Competency 31) (Rigorous)*

   A. required due process for all students receiving a school suspension.
   B. required a manifestation determination
   C. required districts to re-evaluate students who receive 3 suspensions a year.
   D. required school districts to give parents their due process rights when they do not agree with a CSE.

TEACHER CERTIFICATION STUDY GUIDE

Rationales for Post-Test Sample Questions

1. Jonathan has attention deficit hyperactivity disorder (ADHD). He is in a regular classroom and appears to be doing okay. However, his teacher does not want John in her class because he will not obey her when she asks him to stop doing a repetitive action such as tapping his foot. The teacher sees this as distractive during tests. John needs: *(Competency 1) (Easy Rigor)*

   A. An IEP

   B. A 504 Plan

   C. A VESID evaluation

   D. A more restrictive environment

Answer: B. A 504 Plan

John is exhibiting normal grade level behavior with the exception of the ADHD behaviors, which may need some acceptance for his academic success. John has not shown any academic deficiencies. John needs a 504 Plan to provide small adaptations to meet his needs.

2. According to IDEA, a child whose disability is related to being deaf and blind may not be classified as: *(Competency 1) (Rigorous)*

   A. Multiple disabilities
   B. Other health impaired
   C. Having mental retardation
   D. Visually Impaired

Answer: A. Multiple Disabilities

The only stated area where deaf-blindness is not accepted is in multiple disabilities.

SPECIAL EDU. CROSS-CATEGORY

TEACHER CERTIFICATION STUDY GUIDE

3. A child may be classified under the special education "umbrella" as having a traumatic brain injury (TBI) if he/she does not have which of the following causes? *(Competency 1) (Rigorous)*

   A. Stroke
   B. Anoxia
   C. Encephalitis
   D. Birth trauma

Answer: D. Birth trauma

According to IDEA and Part 200, a child may not be labeled as having traumatic brain injury if the injury is related to birth

4. Children with visual-spatial difficulties may not accomplish some developmental tasks, such as: *(Competency 1) (Rigorous)*

   A. Answering when called upon.
   B. Demonstrating characteristics of a certain letter in print
   C. A delay in achieving the "th" sound
   D. Recognition of the permanence of print

Answer: B. Demonstrating characteristics of a certain letter in print

Visual-spatial difficulties misinterpret direct compositions of objects and symbols. The characteristics of a letter are samples of items/symbols that could be wrongly misinterpreted.

5. A developmental delay may be indicated by a: *(Competency 1) (Rigorous)*

   A. Second grader having difficulty buttoning clothing
   B. Stuttered response
   C. Kindergartner not having complete bladder control
   D. Withdrawn behavior

Answer: A. Second grader having difficulty buttoning clothing

Buttoning of clothing is generally mastered by the age of four. While many children have full bladder control by age four, it is not unusual for "embarrassing accidents" to occur.

TEACHER CERTIFICATION STUDY GUIDE

6. Parents are more likely to have a child with a learning disability if: *(Competency 2) (Average Rigor)*

   A. They smoke tobacco
   B. The child is less than five pounds at birth
   C. The mother drank alcohol on a regular basis until she planned for a baby
   D. The father was known to consume large quantities of alcohol during the pregnancy

Answer: B. The child is less than five pounds at birth

Babies that are born weighing less than five pounds at birth are more likely to have a form of learning disability. The reasoning is that the babies may not have fully developed before birth.

7. Echolalia and a severe disorder of thinking and communication are indicative of: *(Competency 2.0) (Average Rigor)*

   A. Psychosis
   B. Schizophrenia
   C. Autism
   D. Paranoia

Answer: C. Autism

The behaviors listed are indicative of autism.

8. Which behavioral disorder is difficult to diagnose in children because the symptoms are manifested quite differently than in adults? *(Competency 2) (Rigorous)*

   A. Anorexia
   B. Schizophrenia
   C. Paranoia
   D. Depression

Answer: D. Depression.

Rationale: In an adult, it may be displayed as age-appropriate behavior and therefore go undiagnosed. In a child, it may be displayed as not age appropriate, so it is easier to recognize.

SPECIAL EDU. CROSS-CATEGORY

TEACHER CERTIFICATION STUDY GUIDE

9. Tom's special education teacher became concerned about her ability to deliver the adaptations and services he needs when she heard him begin to talk to someone who was not there. He also responds to questions in a nonsensical manner. Tom's teacher is concerned because she thinks he may be exhibiting symptoms of: *(Competency 2) (Easy Rigor)*

    A. Sensory perceptual disorder
    B. Mental illness
    C. Depression
    D. Tactile sensory deprivation

Answer: B. Mental illness

Tom is demonstrating delusional or hallucinogenic symptoms. These symptoms may indicate a need for psychiatric treatment within a more restrictive environment.

10. Of the following, which does not describe the term delinquency? *(Competency 2) (Average Rigor)*

    A. Behavior that would be considered criminal if exhibited by an adult
    B. Socialized aggression
    C. Academic truancy
    D. Inciting fights with verbal abuse

Answer: D. Inciting fights with verbal abuse

Socialized aggression and criminal behavior are characteristics of gang membership and delinquency. Truancy is also characteristic of this behavior. Verbal abuse, however, is not descriptive of this as it is not seen as criminal behavior

SPECIAL EDU. CROSS-CATEGORY

11. Janice is a new student in your self-contained class. She is extremely quiet and makes little, if any, eye contact. Yesterday she started to "parrot" what another student said. Today you became concerned when she did not follow directions and seemed not to even recognize your presence. Her cumulative file arrived today; when you review the health section, it will most likely state that she is diagnosed with: *(Competency 2) (Average)*

    A. Autism
    B. Central processing disorder
    C. Traumatic brain injury
    D. Mental retardation

Answer: A. Autism

Janice is exhibiting three symptoms of autism. While a child may demonstrate some of these behaviors if they are diagnosed with traumatic brain injury or mental retardation, the combination of these symptoms are more likely to indicate autism.

12. Students who engage in gang activity, are often in fights, and are often truant could be said to be: *(Competency 2) (Average Rigor)*

    A. Socially maladjusted
    B. Emotionally disturbed
    C. Learning disabled
    D. Depressed

Answer: A. Socially Maladjusted

These behaviors do not demonstrate a disability, and may be placed under the description of social maladjustment.

13. A student who has issues with truancy, gang membership, low school performance, and drug use is displaying: *(Competency 2) (Average Rigor)*

    A. Emotionally disturbed behaviors
    B. Symptoms of self-medication
    C. Average adolescent behavior
    D. Warning signs of crisis

Answer: D. Warning signs of crisis

The student is acting out by using aggression. This gives him or her a sense of belonging.

TEACHER CERTIFICATION STUDY GUIDE

14. Which of these explanations would not likely account for the lack of a clear definition of behavior disorders? *(Competency 3) (Rigorous)*

    A. Problems with measurement
    B. Cultural and/or social influences and views of what is acceptable
    C. The numerous types of manifestations of behavior disorders
    D. Differing theories that use their own terminology and definitions

Answer: B. Cultural and/or social influences and views of what is acceptable

A, C, and D are factors that account for the lack of a clear definition of some behavioral disorders. B is not a factor.

15. Mark is receiving special education services within a 12:1:1. His teacher recommends that he be placed in a more restrictive setting, such as a residential placement. She presents good reasoning. What will the committee most likely recommend? *(Competency 3) (Average Rigor)*

    A. 8:1:1
    B. BOCES school placement
    C. 1:1 Aide
    D. Return to placement

Answer: A. 8:1:1

The teacher presents well, but the committee most likely will attempt the next level down of services before placing a child in a special school setting. This is believed to be the best way of following the LRE requirement.

16. What is the highest goal a teacher should aim for while preparing a student for success? *(Competency 3) (Average Rigor)*

    A. Reading
    B. Budgeting
    C. Cooking
    D. Self-advocacy

Answer: D. Self-advocacy

When a student is able to self-advocate well, he or she is on the road to independence, with an understanding of personal limits and needs to find success in his or her endeavors.

SPECIAL EDU. CROSS-CATEGORY

TEACHER CERTIFICATION STUDY GUIDE

17. Modeling of a behavior by an adult who verbalizes the thinking process, overt self-instruction, and covert self-instruction are components of: *(Competency 3)* *(Rigorous)*

    A. Rational-emotive therapy
    B. Reality therapy
    C. Cognitive behavior modification
    D. Reciprocal teaching

Answer: C. Cognitive behavior modification

Neither A, B, nor D involves modification or change of behavior.

18. Cognitive modeling is an excellent transition to: *(Competency 3)* *(Rigorous)*

    A. Covert Self-instruction
    B. Overt self-guidance
    C. Self-monitoring
    D. self-reinforcement

Answer: B. Overt self-guidannce

When an adult models by self talking through a task, a student talking through the actions just as the teacher did would be the next educational method.

19. Across America there is a toxic substance that is contributing to the creation of disabilities in our children. What is it? *(Competency 4)* *(Average Rigor)*

    A. Children's aspirin
    B. Fluoride water
    C. Chlorine gas
    D. Lead

Answer: D. Lead

Lead poisoning is still a major factor influencing and/or causing disabilities. Today, many homes in urban, suburban, and rural neighborhoods are still working to remove lead paint.

TEACHER CERTIFICATION STUDY GUIDE

20. **Children who are characterized by impulsivity generally:** *(Competency 4) (Easy Rigor)*

    A. Do not feel sorry for their actions
    B. Blame others for their actions
    C. Do not weigh alternatives before acting
    D. Do not outgrow their problem

Answer: C. Do not weigh alternatives before acting

They act without thinking, so they either cannot think or do not think before they act

21. **A person who has a learning disability:** *(Competency 4) (Easy Rigor)*

    A. Has an IQ two standard deviations below the norm
    B. Has congenital abnormalities
    C. Is limited by the educational environment
    D. Has a disorder in one of the basic psychological processes

Answer: D. Has a disorder in one of the basic psychological processes

The definition of "learning disability" begins as "a disorder in one or more of the basic psychological processes involved in understanding or in using language, spoken or written."

22. **What is considered the most effective when teaching children with special needs new concepts in math?** *(Competency 4) (Rigorous)*

    A. Problem solving
    B. Direct instruction
    C. Repetition
    D. Ongoing assessment

Answer: A. Problem solving

Teaching problem-solving techniques relevant to the task creates the possibility for students to address the problem independently. Allowing students to problem solve in groups where peer instruction and group review can be addressed allows for higher developed understanding of the concept.

23. Mr. Ward notes that Jennifer, a 9th grade student, understands the concept for three-step equations but seems unable to do problems successfully. When he reviews Jennifer's work, he notes that her addition and subtraction is not correct. What strategy would be most appropriate? *(Competency 4)* *(Average Rigor)*

    A. Basic multiplication and addition charts
    B. Checks for understanding
    C. Private instruction on adding and subtracting
    D. Calculator usage

Answer: D. Calculator usage

If Jennifer is in 9th grade and still has difficulty adding and subtracting correctly, it is likely that this is part of her disability. The correct compensatory intervention would be a calculator and brief tutoring on how to correctly use it.

24. All of these are effective in teaching written expression EXCEPT: *(Competency 4) (Easy Rigor)*

    A. Exposure to various styles and direct instruction in those styles
    B. Immediate feedback from the teacher with all mistakes clearly marked
    C. Goal setting and peer evaluation of written products according to set criteria.
    D. Incorporating writing with other academic subjects

Answer: B. Immediate feedback from the teacher with all mistakes clearly marked

Teacher feedback is not always necessary. The student can have feedback from peers or apply skills learned to other subjects.

TEACHER CERTIFICATION STUDY GUIDE

25. Those with learning disabilities that are not physically noticeable continue to feel the stigma of the label "Special Education." Part of the reason for this is… (Competency 5) (Average Rigor)

    A. The media rarely portrays people with learning disabilities that are not physically noticeable.
    B. The label "stupid" often accompanies the label "special."
    C. There is a very low percentage of people with special needs that are not visually noticeable.
    D. The appearance of "normal" is difficult to maintain.

Answer: A. The media rarely portrays people with learning disabilities that are not physically noticeable.

Today's world is heavily influenced by media in any form. Today acceptance of many cultures, and points of view has been attained because of media influence. But, the media rarely portrays an average person with a disability who can not "rise above it" with a special skill or talent.

26. Women who smoke during pregnancy are more likely to have a child with a learning disability as their children are born with: *(Competency 6) (Easy Rigor)*

    A. low birth weight.
    B. nicotine addiction.
    C. jaundice.
    D. low oxygen intake rate.

Answer: A. low birth weight.

Women who smoke during pregnancy are predisposed to having babies born less than 5 lbs. In today's world children can survive at a lower birth rate, but birth weight is a coordinating factor for those who have been diagnosed with learning disabilities.

SPECIAL EDU. CROSS-CATEGORY

TEACHER CERTIFICATION STUDY GUIDE

27. You checked the IEP for more information when you received a new student. Unfortunately, the IEP only provided the label "Mental Retardation." You are looking for an IQ level or a level of retardation. To verify your own conclusions. The student has difficulty communicating his thoughts difficulty receiving communication. He has difficulty with tasks that require fine motor skills. He requires hand over hand assistance to wash his hands. It is likely that the student is: *(Competency 6) (Rigorous)*

   A. Mildly Retarded
   B. Moderately Retarded
   C. Severely Retarded
   D. Profoundly Retarded

Answer: C. Severely Retarded

The student has difficulty communicating and receiving communication. He may simply nod his head as a form of communicating I heard you instead of a nod for yes. His poor motor skills and limited self help skills combine to give a possible indication that severe retardation with an IQ somewhere between 20 and 40.

28. Which of the following traits is NOT typical of a student who is labeled as orthopedically impaired or as Other health Impaired? **(Competency 8) (Rigorous)**

   A. Frequent speech and language defects; communication may be prevented
   B. echolatia orthosis may be present
   C. Periods of confusion and loss of memory
   D. Emotional (psychological) problems, which require treatment

Answer: C. Periods of confusion and loss of memory

While this may be a characteristic in a student classified under Orthopedically Impaired or as Other Health Impaired (OHI), it is not typical. Answer c is typical of a person who has had a Traumatic Brain Injury (TBI).

SPECIAL EDU. CROSS-CATEGORY 298

TEACHER CERTIFICATION STUDY GUIDE

29. A good assessment of whether a child may have ADHD in your classroom would include a(n) _____.*(Competency 10) (Average Rigor)*

    A. Baseline
    B. Monetary time sampling
    C. Age-based norm criteria
    D. Construct validity

Answer: B. Monetary time sampling

Assessing ADHD should include measurements of time on task. A simple box chart of five to ten minute intervals that record on-task versus off-task behavior is a good example of this.

30. Criteria for choosing behaviors to measure by frequency include all but those that: *(Competency 10) (Average Rigor)*

    A. Have an observable beginning
    B. Last a long time
    C. Last a short time
    D. Occur often

Answer: B. Last a long time

We use frequency to measure behaviors that do not last a long time.

31. Criteria for choosing behaviors to measure by duration include all but those that: *(Competency 10) (Easy Rigor)*

    A. Last a short time
    B. Last a long time
    C. Have no readily observable beginning or end
    D. Do not happen often

Answer: A. Last a short time

We use duration to measure behaviors that do not last a short time.

SPECIAL EDU. CROSS-CATEGORY

32. The basic tools necessary to observe and record behavior may include all BUT: *(Competency 10) (Average Rigor)*

   A. Cameras
   B. Timers
   C. Counters
   D. Graphs or charts

Answer: A. Cameras

The camera gives a snapshot. It does not record behavior.

33. You are working with a functional program and have placed a student in a vocational position at a coffee house. You need to perform a task analysis of making coffee. Which task should be first in the analysis? *(Competency 10) (Average Rigor)*

   A. Filling the pot with water
   B. Taking the order
   C. Measuring the coffee
   D. Picking the correct coffee

Answer: D. Picking the correct coffee

While the student is in a coffee house, the task was to make coffee, not to wait on customers. There are different kinds of coffee (decaffeinated, regular, etc.) and they all have their appropriate canisters. The student must be able to choose the correct coffee before measuring it.

34. The extent that a test measures what it claims to measure is called: *(Competency 10) (Rigorous)*

   A. Reliability
   B. Validity
   C. Factor analysis
   D. Chi Square

Answer: B. Validity

Validity is defined as the degree to which a test measures is what it claims to measure.

TEACHER CERTIFICATION STUDY GUIDE

35. **A best practice for evaluating student performance and progress on IEPs is:** *(Competency 10) (Rigorous)*

    A. Formal assessment
    B. Curriculum-based assessment
    C. Criterion-based assessment
    D. Norm-referenced evaluation

Answer: B. Curriculum-based assessment

This is a teacher-prepared test that measures the student's progress; at the same time, it shows the teacher whether or not the accommodations are effective.

36. **Statements like "Darren is lazy," are not helpful in describing his behavior for all but which of these reasons?** *(Competency 10) (Average Rigor)*

    A. There is no way to determine if any change occurs from the information given
    B. The student—not the behavior—becomes labeled
    C. Darren's behavior will manifest itself clearly enough without any written description
    D. Constructs are open to various interpretations among the people who are asked to define them

Answer: C. Darren's behavior will manifest itself clearly enough without any written description

"Darren is lazy" is a label. It can be interpreted in a variety of ways, and there is no way to measure this description for change. A description should be measurable.

37. Marcie is often not in her seat when the bell rings. She may be found at the pencil sharpener, throwing paper away, or fumbling through her notebook. Which of these descriptions of her behavior can be described as a pinpoint? *(Competency 10) (Easy Rigor)*

   A. Is tardy
   B. Is out of seat
   C. Is not in seat when late bell rings
   D. Is disorganized

Answer: C. Is not in seat when late bell rings

Even though A, B, and D describe the behavior, C is most precise.

38. Which is NOT an example of a standard score? *(Competency 10) (Rigorous)*

   A. T-score
   B. Z-score
   C. Standard deviation
   D. Stanine

Answer: C. Standard deviation.

Answers a, b, and d are all standardized scores. Stanines are whole number scores from 1 to 9, each representing a wide range of raw scores. Standard deviation is <u>not a score</u>. It measures how widely scores vary from the mean.

39. Criteria for choosing behaviors that are in the most need of change involve all but the following: *(Competency 10) (Average Rigor)*

   A. Observations across settings to rule out certain interventions
   B. Pinpointing the behavior that is the poorest fit in the child's environment
   C. The teacher's concern about what is the most important behavior to target
   D. Analysis of the environmental reinforcers

Answer: C. The teacher's concern about what is the most important behavior to target

The teacher must take care of the criteria in A, B, and D. Her concerns are of the least importance.

40. Alternative assessments include all of the following EXCEPT: *(Competency 10) (Average Rigor)*

   A. Portfolios
   B. Interviews
   C. Teacher-made tests
   D. Performance-based tests

Answer: C. Teacher-made tests

Teacher-made tests are normally created on worksheets, not on observations. It is a standard form of evaluation.

41. The most direct method of obtaining assessment data, and perhaps the most objective, is: *(Competency 10) (Rigorous)*

   A. Testing
   B. Self-recording
   C. Observation
   D. Experimenting

Answer: C. Observation

Observation is often better than testing, due to language, culture, or other factors.

42. When a teacher is choosing behaviors to modify, the issue of social validity must be considered. Social validity refers to: *(Competency 10) (Easy Rigor)*

   A. The need for the behavior to be performed in public
   B. Whether the new behavior will be considered significant by those who deal with the child
   C. Whether there will be opportunities to practice the new behavior in public
   D. Society's standards of behavior

D. is correct.

Rationale: Validity has to do with the appropriateness of the behavior. Is it age appropriate? Is it culturally appropriate?

43. Which of these would be the least effective measure of behavioral disorders? *(Competency 10) (Average Rigor)*

   A. Alternative assessment
   B. Naturalistic assessment
   C. Standardized test
   D. Psychodynamic analysis

Answer: C. Standardized test

These tests make comparisons, rather than measure skills.

44. Which would not be an advantage of using a criterion-referenced test? *(Competency 10) (Rigorous)*

   A. Information about an individual's ability level is too specific for the purposes of the assessment
   B. It can pinpoint exact areas of weaknesses and strengths
   C. You can design them yourself
   D. You do not get comparative information

Answer: D. You do not get comparative information

Criterion-referenced tests measure mastery of content rather than performance compared to others. Test items are usually prepared from specific educational objectives and may be teacher-made or commercially-prepared. Scores are measured by the percentage of correct items for a skill (e.g., adding and subtracting fractions with like denominators).

45. Measurement of adaptive behavior should include all but: *(Competency 10) (Rigorous)*

   A. The student's behavior in a variety of settings
   B. *The student's skills displayed in a variety* of settings
   C. Comparative analysis to other students in the class
   D. Analysis of the student's social skills

Answer: C. Comparative analysis to other students in the class

Evaluating a student's adaptability requires analysis only of that person, and does not allow for comparative analysis. Comparing to people and how they interact with others or comparing skill levels is not a good measure of adaptability.

SPECIAL EDU. CROSS-CATEGORY 304

TEACHER CERTIFICATION STUDY GUIDE

46. **Grading should be based on all of the following EXCEPT:** *(Competency 10) (Average Rigor)*

    A. Clearly-defined mastery of course objectives
    B. A variety of evaluation methods
    C. Performance of the student in relation to other students
    D. Assigning points for activities and basing grades on a point total

Answer: C. Performance of the student in relation to other students

Grading should never be based on the comparison of performance to other students. It should always be based on the student's mastery of course objectives, the methods of evaluation, and the grading rubric (how points are assigned).

47. **Anecdotal records should?** *(Competency 10) (Average Rigor)*

    A. Record observable behavior
    B. End with conjecture
    C. Record motivational factors
    D. Note previously stated interests

Answer: A. Record observable behavior

Anecdotal records should only record observable behavior, describing the actions. It should avoid interests or motivational factors that may lead to possible prejudicial reviews.

48. **A good naturalistic assessment requires:** *(Competency 11) (Rigorous)*

    A. Communication notebooks
    B. Portfolios
    C. Long-range planning
    D. Diverse responses

Answer: C. Long-range planning

Naturalistic assessment must take place in a variety of settings. (It also requires instruction in a variety of settings.)

49. Otumba is a 16 year old in your class who recently came from Nigeria. The girls in your class have come to you to complain about the way he treats them in a sexist manner. When they complain, you reflect that this is also the way he treats adult females. You have talked to Otumba before about appropriate behavior. You should first? *(Competency 11) (Rigorous)*

   A. Complain to the principal
   B. Ask for a parent-teacher conference
   C. Check to see if this is a cultural norm in his country
   D. Create a behavior contract for him to follow

Answer: C. Check to see if this is a cultural norm in his country

While A, B, and D are good actions, it is important to remember that Otumba may come from a culture where woman are treated differently than they are here in America. Learning this information will enable the school as a whole to address this behavior.

50. If a child does not qualify for classification under special education, the committee shall: *(Competency 11)) (Average Rigor)*

   A. Refer the parental interventions to the 504 Plan
   B. Provide temporary remedial services for the student
   C. Recommend to the parent possible resources outside of the committee for which the child may qualify
   D. Give the parents the information about possible reviews by an exterior source

Answer: C. Recommend to the parent possible resources outside of the committee for which the child may qualify

A student may qualify for a 504 Plan or not. The student, however, may be in need of additional resources, such as outside counseling with an agency or a mentor situation similar to what Big Brother provides.

51. **What is required of a special education teacher when approaching an administrator regarding a request to change placement of a student?** *(Competency 11) (Rigorous)*

   A. Observation
   B. Objectivity
   C. Assessments
   D. Parent permission

Answer: B. Objectivity

Presenting a case for change of placement to your supervisor does not require parental permission. It requires your ability to objectively analyze the needs of the student versus current placement.

52. **Which of the following statements was not offered as a rationale for inclusion?** *(Competency 11) (Average Rigor)*

   A. Special education students are not usually identified until their learning problems have become severe
   B. Lack of funding will mean that support for the special needs children will not be available in the regular classroom
   C. Putting children in segregated special education placements is stigmatizing
   D. There are students with learning or behavior problems who do not meet special education requirements but who still need special services

Answer: B. Lack of funding will mean that support for the special needs children will not be available in the regular classroom

All except lack of funding were offered in support of inclusion.

53. What is required of a special education teacher when approaching an administrator regarding a request to change placement of a student? *(Competency 11) (Rigorous)*

   A. Observation
   B. Objectivity
   C. Assessments
   D. Parent permission

Answer: B. Objectivity

Presenting a case for change of placement to your supervisor does not require parental permission. It requires your ability to objectively analyze the needs of the student versus current placement.

54. Mr. Johnson asks his students to score each of their classmates in areas such as with whom they would prefer to play and work. A Likert-type scale with non-behavioral criteria is used. This is an example of: *(Competency16) (Rigorous)*

   A. Peer nomination
   B. Peer rating
   C. Peer assessment
   D. Sociogram

Answer: A. Peer nomination

Students are asked for their preferences on non-behavioral criteria.

55. Mrs. Taylor takes her students to a special gymnastics presentation that the P.E. coach has arranged in the gym. The students get a chance to perform some of the simple stunts. They all easily go through the movements except for Sam, who is known as the class klutz. Carl, another student of Mrs. Taylor's, helps Sam, who does not give up and finally completes the stunts. His classmates cheer him on with comments like, "Way to go!" What kind of teaching technique was implemented? *(Competency 16) (Average Rigor)*

   A. Group share
   B. Modeling
   C. Peer tutoring
   D. All of the above

Answer: D. All of the above

Sam observed the gymnastics, he was encouraged by his group of peers, and received assistance to accomplish the task from a peer.

56. Ms. Denario was planning on using graphic organizers with the new book the students would be reading. When would be a good time to use a graphic organizer? *(Competency 16) .(Average Rigor)*

   A. Before the lesson
   B. During the lesson
   C. Before, during and, after the lesson.
   D. Before and after the lesson

Answer: C. Before, during and, after the lesson.

Graphic organizers are great tools for teaching. They can be used to jump start a lesson. Using a KWL chart, and then be used throughout the lesson and after a lesson is completed another graphic organizer can be used. Graphic organizers help students with learning disabilities visually organize their thoughts and often assists them to score higher on exams.

57. Kareem's father sounds upset and is in the office demanding to see his son's cumulative recorD. You should: *(Competency 17) (Average Rigor)*

   A. Tell him that he will have to make an appointment
   B. Bring the record to a private room for him to review with either an administrator or yourself
   C. Take the record to the principal's office for review
   D. Give the record to the parent

Answer: B. Bring the record to a private room for him to review with either an administrator or yourself

Parents have the rights to see their children's cumulative records. You do not have the right to remove something so that the parent may not see it. However, it is important to remember that the documents should remain in the folder, and that the parent may need information explained or interpreted; therefore, someone should be present.

58. Standards of accuracy for a student's spelling should be based on the student's: *(Competency 17) (Rigorous)*

   A. Grade level spelling list
   B. Present reading book level
   C. Level of spelling development
   D. Performance on an informal assessment

Answer: C. Level of spelling development

Spelling instruction should include words misspelled in daily writing, generalize spelling knowledge, and support mastering objectives in progressive stages of development.

TEACHER CERTIFICATION STUDY GUIDE

59. Which of these techniques is least effective in helping children correct spelling problems? *(Competency 17) (Easy Rigor)*

   A. The teacher models the correct spelling in a context
   B. Student sees the incorrect and the correct spelling together in order to visualize the correct spelling
   C. Positive reinforcement as the child tests the rules and tries to approximate the correct spelling
   D. Copying the correct word five times

Answer: D. Copying the correct word five times

The student may not understand why it was written incorrectly or may not understand the phonetic reasoning behind the spelling..

60. Teacher feedback, task completion, and a sense of pride over mastery or accomplishment of a skill are examples of: *(Competency 18) (Average Rigor)*

   A. Extrinsic reinforcers
   B. Behavior modifiers
   C. Intrinsic reinforcers
   D. Positive feedback

Answer: C. Intrinsic reinforcers

Motivation may be achieved through intrinsic reinforcers or extrinsic reinforcers. Intrinsic reinforcers are usually intangible, and extrinsic reinforcers are usually tangible rewards from an external source.

61. Which of the following does NOT have an important effect on the spatial arrangement (physical setting) of your classroom? *(Competency 18) (Average Rigor)*

   A. Adequate physical space
   B. Ventilation
   C. Window placement
   D. Lighting adequacy

Answer: C. Window placement

Many classrooms today do not have windows, as they may be placed in the middle of a building. It is also the only factor listed that cannot be controlled or adjusted by you or the administration.

SPECIAL EDU. CROSS-CATEGORY

62. A suggested amount of time for a large-group instruction lesson for a sixth or seventh grade group would be: *(Competency 18)* *(Rigorous)*

   A. 5 to 40 minutes
   B. 5 to 20 minutes
   C. 5 to 30 minutes
   D. 5 to 15 minutes

Answer: C. 5 to 30 minutes

The recommended time for large group instruction is 5-15 minutes for grades first through fifth and 5-40 minutes for grades eighth through twelfth.

63. Cooperative learning does NOT utilize: *(Competency 18 (Average Rigor)*

   A. Shared ideas
   B. Small groups
   C. Independent practice
   D. Student expertise

Answer: C. Independent practice

Cooperative learning focuses on group cooperation; it allows for the sharing of student expertise and provides some flexibility for creative presentation of the students as they share with others.

64. Which of these techniques is least effective in helping children correct spelling problems? *(Competency 18)* *(Rigorous)*

   A. The teacher models the correct spelling in a context
   B. Student sees the incorrect and the correct spelling together in order to visualize the correct spelling
   C. Positive reinforcement as the child tests the rules and tries to approximate the correct spelling
   D. Copying the correct word five times

Answer: D. Copying the correct word five times

Copying the word is not as effective because it utilizes the least amount of positive reinforcement and correction.

TEACHER CERTIFICATION STUDY GUIDE

65. **A typical one to one teaching/tutoring model is typically found in a ....** *(Competency 18) (Average Rigor)*

   A. 12:1:1
   B. 6:1:1
   C. Inclusive classroom
   D. Resource Room

Answer: D. Resource Room

While there are more opportunities for a 1:1 teaching situation in a smaller class, it is not the norm. Typically students in a resource room setting receive 1:1 opportunities.

66. **The phonics approach to teaching children how to read utilizes what method?** *(Competency 19) (Average Rigor)*

   A. Reading for meaning
   B. Reading for letter combinations
   C. Identifying words by their position and context
   D. Word configurations

Answer: C. Identifying words by their position and context

The phonics program utilizes a "bottom-up/code emphasis" approach to reading.

67. **Marisol has been mainstreamed into a 9th grade language arts class. Although her behavior is satisfactory, and she likes the class, Marisol's reading level is about two years below grade level. The class has been assigned to read *Great Expectations* and write a report. What intervention would be LEAST successful in helping Marisol complete this assignment?** *(Competency 19) (Average Rigor)*

   A. Having Marisol listen to a taped recording while following the story in the regular text
   B. Giving her a modified version of the story
   C. Telling her to choose a different book that she can read
   D. Showing a film to the entire class and comparing and contrasting it with the book

Answer: C. Telling her to choose a different book that she can read

A, B, and D are positive interventions. C is not an intervention.

TEACHER CERTIFICATION STUDY GUIDE

68. A teacher should consider all of the following when evaluating a student's reading comprehension EXCEPT: *(Competency 19) (Average Rigor)*

A. Past experience
B. Teacher-prepared preset questions on text
C. Level of content
D. Oral language comprehension.

Answer: B. Teacher-prepared preset questions on text

Preset question will influence the evaluation of a student's reading comprehension, so a true score will not be given.

69. Task related attending skills include: *(Competency 19) (Hard)*

A. Compliance to requests
B. Writing the correct answer on the chalk board
C. Listening to the assignment
D. Repeating instructions

Answer: C. Listening to the assignment

Attending skills are used to receive a message. Compliance may have nothing to do with what was said at the moment. Repetition of instructions may be a compensatory strategy.

70. Organizing ideas by use of a web or outline is an example of which writing activity? *(Competency 20) (Easy Rigor)*

A. Revision
B. Drafting
C. Prewriting
D. Final draft

Answer: C. Prewriting

Organizing ideas come before drafting, final draft, and revision.

SPECIAL EDU. CROSS-CATEGORY 314

TEACHER CERTIFICATION STUDY GUIDE

71. Ryan is working on a report about dogs. He uses scissors and tape to cut and rearrange sections and paragraphs. He then photocopies the paper so he can continue writing. In which stage of the writing process is Ryan? *(Competency 20 (Easy Rigor)*

    A. Final draft
    B. Prewriting
    C. Revision
    D. Drafting

Answer: C. Revision

Ryan is revising and reordering before final editing.

72. Celia, who is in first grade, asked, "Where are my ball?" She also has trouble with passive sentences. Language interventions for Celia would target: *(Competency 20) (Rigorous)*

    A. Morphology
    B. Syntax
    C. Pragmatics
    D. Semantics

Answer: B. Syntax

Syntax refers to the rules for arranging words to make sentences.

73. Teaching techniques that stimulate active participation and understanding in the mathematics class include all but which of the following? *(Competency 21) (Easy Rigor)*

    A. Having students copy computation facts for a set number of times
    B. Asking students to find the error in an algorithm
    C. Giving immediate feedback to students
    D. Having students chart their progress

Answer: A. Having students copy computation facts for a set number of times

Copying does not stimulate participation or understanding.

SPECIAL EDU. CROSS-CATEGORY

TEACHER CERTIFICATION STUDY GUIDE

74. **One of the skills necessary for problem solving is:** (Competency 21) (Easy Rigor)

    A. Identifying the main idea
    B. Order of operations
    C. Algebraic comprehension
    D. Written expression

Answer: A. Identifying the main idea.

In order to solve a problem you must first be able to identify what the problem is about. This will enable you to ask what contemplate how to solve the problem.

75. **Children enter school with many skills. Generally they have all the skills below, EXCEPT:** *(Competency 21) (Rigorous)*

    A. Classifying
    B. Numerical Notation
    C. Comparing
    D. Equalizing

Answer: b Numerical Notation

Numerical notation has to do with place value. Generally students do not learn numbers greater than 10 until after they begin school.

76. **Many special education students may have trouble with the skills necessary to be successful in algebra and geometry for all but one of these reasons:** *(Competency 22 (Average Rigor)*

    A. Prior instruction focused on computation rather than understanding
    B. Unwillingness to problem solve
    C. Lack of instruction in prerequisite skills
    D. Large amount of new vocabulary

Answer: A. Prior instruction focused on computation rather than understanding

In order to build skills in math, students must be able to understand math concepts.

SPECIAL EDU. CROSS-CATEGORY 316

TEACHER CERTIFICATION STUDY GUIDE

77. Which of the following sentences will NOT test recall? *(Competency 22)(Average Rigor)*

    A. What words in the story describe Goldilocks?
    B. Why did Goldilocks go into the three bears' house?
    C. Name in order the things that belonged to the three bears that Goldilocks tried.
    D. What did the three bears learn about leaving their house unlocked?

Answer: D. What did the three bears learn about leaving their house unlocked?

Recall requires the student to produce from memory ideas and information explicitly stated in the story. Answer D requires an inference.

78. Which is not indicative of a handwriting problem? *(Competency 23) (Rigorous)*

    A. Errors persisting over time
    B. Little improvement on simple handwriting tasks
    C. Fatigue after writing for a short time
    D. Occasional letter reversals, word omissions, and poor spacing

Answer: D. Occasional letter reversals, word omissions, and poor spacing

A, B, and C are physical handwriting problems. D, however, is a problem with language development.

79. Laura is beginning to raise her hand first instead of talking out. An effective schedule of reinforcement should be: *(Competency 23) (Average Rigor)*

    A. Continuous
    B. Variable
    C. Intermittent
    D. Fixed

Answer: A. Continuous

Note that the behavior is new. The pattern of reinforcement should not be variable, intermittent, or fixed. It should be continuous.

SPECIAL EDU. CROSS-CATEGORY

TEACHER CERTIFICATION STUDY GUIDE

80. To facilitate learning instructional objectives in spelling: *(Competency 23) (Average Rigor)*

    A. They should include a grade level spelling list
    B. They should be written and shared
    C. They should be arranged in order of similarity
    D. They should be taken from a scope and sequence

Answer: C. They should be arranged in order of similarity

Spelling instruction should include words misspelled in daily writing, generalizing spelling knowledge, and mastering objectives in progressive stages of development.

81. Transfer of learning occurs when? *(Competency 25) (Rigorous)*

    A. Experience with one task influences performance on another task
    B. Content can be explained orally
    C. Student experiences the "I got it!" syndrome
    D. Curricular objective is exceeded

Answer: A. Experience with one task influences performance on another task

Consultation programs cannot be successful without people skills.

82. Teacher modeling, student-teacher dialogues, and peer interactions are part of which teaching technique designed to provide support during the initial stages of instruction? *(Competency 23) (Rigorous)*

    A. Reciprocal teaching
    B. Scaffolding
    C. Peer tutoring
    D. Cooperative learning

Answer: B. Scaffolding

Scaffolding provides support through the building of new knowledge on previous knowledge, much like one layer is placed on another.

SPECIAL EDU. CROSS-CATEGORY 318

83. Functional curriculum focuses on all of the following EXCEPT: *(Competency 23) (Rigorous)*

    A. Skills needed for social living
    B. Occupational readiness
    C. Functioning in society.
    D. Remedial academic skills

Answer: D. Remedial academic skills

Remedial academics may be applied but are not a focus. The primary goal is to achieve skills for functioning in society on an independent basis, where possible.

84. Kenny is a 9th grader enrolled in Wood Shop; he is having difficulty grasping fractions. You know that Kenny has difficulty with abstract concepts. What would be a good method to teach this concept? *(Competency 23) (Rigorous)*

    A. Pie blocks that proportionately measure whole, half, 1/4, 1/8, etc.
    B. Strips of paper that proportionately measure whole, half, 1/4, 1/8, etc.
    C. One-on-one review of the worksheet
    D. Working in the wood shop, privately showing him how to measure

Answer: B. Strips of paper that proportionately measure whole, half, 1/4, 1/8, etc.

Strips of paper can be used to teach the concept by tearing a whole sheet into proportionate pieces. They can also be used like a tape measure to measure a length of wood. This instruction would enable him to transfer knowledge easily when the topic is grasped.

85. Sam is working to earn half an hour of basketball time with his favorite P.E. teacher. At the end of each half hour, Sam marks his point sheet with an X if he reached his goal of no call-outs. When he has received 25 marks, he will receive his basketball free time. This behavior management strategy is an example of: *(Competency 24) (Average)*

    A. Self-recording
    B. Self-evaluation
    C. Self-reinforcement
    D. Self-regulation

Answer: A. Self-recording

Self-management is an important part of social skills training, especially for older students preparing for employment. Components for self-management include:

3. *Self-monitoring:* choosing behaviors and alternatives and monitoring those actions.
4. *Self-evaluation:* deciding the effectiveness of the behavior in solving the problem.
3. *Self-reinforcement:* telling oneself that one is capable of achieving success.

In this case, Sam is simply recording his behavior.

86. Mark has been working on his target goal of completing his mathematics class work. Each day he records, on a scale of 0 to 3, how well he has done his work, and his teacher provides feedback. This self-management technique is an example of: *(Competency 24) (Average Rigor)*

    A. Self-recording
    B. Self reinforcement
    C. Self-regulation
    D. Self-evaluation

Answer: D. Self-evaluation

Sam is evaluating his behavior, not

TEACHER CERTIFICATION STUDY GUIDE

87. Children with behavior disorders often do not exhibit stimulus control. This means they do not display: *(Competency 25) (Average Rigor)*

   A. Culturally correct behaviors
   B. Understanding of where and when certain behaviors are appropriate
   C. Acceptance of others
   D. Listening skills

Answer: B. Understanding of where and when certain behaviors are appropriate

Children with behavioral disorders often do not have the ability to understand what behavior is appropriate and where. Inappropriate cultural behavior, however, is often a learned response as an expression of prejudice.

88. Which of the following is NOT a feature of effective classroom rules? *(Competency 25) (Easy Rigor)*

   A. They are about four to six in number
   B. They are negatively stated
   C. Consequences are consistent and immediate
   D. They can be tailored to individual teaching goals and teaching styles

Answer: B. They are negatively stated

Rules should be positively stated, and they should follow the other three features listed.

89. When would proximity control not be a good behavioral intervention? *(Competency 25) (Easy Rigor)*

   A. Two students are arguing
   B. A student is distracting others
   C. One student threatens another
   D. Involve fading and shaping

Answer: C. One student threatens another

Threats can break into fights. Standing in the middle of a fight can be threatening to your ability to supervise the class as a whole or to get the help needed to stop the fight.

SPECIAL EDU. CROSS-CATEGORY

TEACHER CERTIFICATION STUDY GUIDE

90. Which of the following should be avoided when writing goals for social behavior? *(Competency 25) (Average Rigor)*

    A. Non-specific adverbs
    B. Behaviors stated as verbs
    C. Criteria for acceptable performance
    D. Conditions where the behavior is expected to be performed

Answer: A. Non-specific adverbs

Behaviors should be specific. The more clearly the behavior is described, the less the chance for error.

91. In a positive classroom environment, errors are viewed as: *(Competency 25) (Average Rigor)*

    A. Symptoms of deficiencies
    B. Lack of attention or ability
    C. A natural part of the learning process
    D. The result of going too fast

Answer: C. A natural part of the learning process

We often learn a great deal from our mistakes and shortcomings. It is normal. Where it is not normal, fear develops. This fear of failure inhibits children from working and achieving. Copying and other types of cheating result from this fear of failure.

92. Which of the following is NOT the best way to encourage and strengthen a social skill? *(Competency 25) (Average Rigor)*

    A. Role playing
    B. Field trips
    C. Student story telling
    D. Reading a book on the topic

Answer: D. Reading a book on the topic

All of the other answers are interactive, and involve student input on possible ethical dilemmas.

SPECIAL EDU. CROSS-CATEGORY

TEACHER CERTIFICATION STUDY GUIDE

93. **Distractive behavior, verbal outbursts, and passive aggressiveness should be addressed using:** *(Competency 25.0)* *(Rigorous)*

    A. Time-outs
    B. Response cost
    C. Planned ignoring
    D. Rule reminders

Answer: C. Planned ignoring

Planned ignoring takes away the attention the student may be seeking to receive. It is also a good way to model appropriate responses to the behavior for the other students in the room

94. **A student with a poor self-concept may manifest in all of the ways listed below EXCEPT:** *(Competency 25)* *(Average Rigor)*

    A. Withdrawn actions
    B. Aggression
    C. Consistently announcing his/her achievements
    D. Shyness

Answer: C. Consistently announcing his/her achievements

A poor self-concept is not seen in someone who boasts of his/her achievements.

95. **Mr. Brown finds that his chosen consequence does not seem to be having the desired effect of reducing the target misbehavior. Which of these would LEAST LIKELY account for Mr. Brown's lack of success with the consequence?** *(Competency 25)* *(Rigorous)*

    A. The consequence was aversive in Mr. Brown's opinion but not the students'
    B. The students were not developmentally ready to understand the connection
    C. Mr. Brown was inconsistent in applying the consequence
    D. The intervention had not previously been shown to be effective in studies

Answer: D. The intervention had not previously been shown to be effective in studies

Answers a, b, and c might work if applied in the classroom, but research is the least of Mr. Brown's options.

SPECIAL EDU. CROSS-CATEGORY

TEACHER CERTIFICATION STUDY GUIDE

96. Token systems are popular for all of these advantages EXCEPT: *(Competency 25)* **(Average Rigor)**

    A. The number needed for rewards may be adjusted
    B. Rewards are easy to maintain
    C. They are effective for students who generally do not respond to social reinforcers
    D. Tokens reinforce the relationship between desirable behavior and reinforcement

Answer: B. Rewards are easy to maintain

The ease of maintenance is not a valid reason for developing a token system.

97. An effective classroom behavior management plan includes all but which of the following? *(Competency 25)* **(Average Rigor)**

    A. Transition procedures for changing activities
    B. Clear consequences for rule infractions
    C. Concise teacher expectations for student behavior
    D. Strict enforcement

Answer: D. Strict enforcement

There are always situations where rules must be flexible. Not all of the rules need to be flexible, but allowing a student to stop a behavior with a reminder of the rule is a good way to avoid strict enforcement.

98. Teaching children skills that will be useful in their home lives and neighborhoods is the basis of: *(Competency 27)* **(Average Rigor)**

    A. Curriculum-based instruction
    B. Community-based instruction
    C. Transition planning
    D. Academic curriculum

Answer: B. Community-based instruction

Transitional training is a standard for all students labeled as having special needs after age 12. For example, students can learn how to balance a checkbook, shop, and understand how to use mass transit.

SPECIAL EDU. CROSS-CATEGORY 324

TEACHER CERTIFICATION STUDY GUIDE

99. An important goal of collaborative consultation is:

   A. Mainstream as many ESE students as possible
   B. Guidance on how to handle ESE students from the ESE teacher
   C. Mutual empowerment of both the mainstream and the ESE teacher
   D. Document progress of mainstreamed students

C. is correct.

Rationale: Empowerment of these service providers is extremely important.

100. Transition services that are mandatory to be addressed include all of the following EXCEPT: *(Competency 27) (Easy Rigor)*

   A. Instruction
   B. Community experience
   C. Development of employment
   D. Self-Advocacy

Answer: D. Self-advocacy

While the student's ability to self-advocate should be discussed it is not mandated to be reviewed.

101. You are having continual difficulty with your classroom assistant. A good strategy to address this problem would be: *(Competency 28) (Rigorous)*

   A. To address the issue immediately
   B. To take away responsibilities
   C. To write a clearly established role plan for discussion
   D. To speak to your supervisor

Answer: C. To write a clearly established role plan for discussion

If you are having difficulty with your classroom assistant, it is most likely is over an issue or issues that have happened repeatedly, and you have attempted to address them. Establishing clear roles between the two of you will provide a good step in the right direction. It may also provide you with the ability to state you have made an attempt to address the issue/issues to an administrator should the need arise.

TEACHER CERTIFICATION STUDY GUIDE

102. Which of the following is a responsibility that can NOT be designated to a classroom aide? *(Competency 28) (Average Rigor)*

    A. Small group instruction
    B. Small group planning
    C. Coordination of an activity
    D. Assist in BIP implementation

Answer: C. Coordination of an activity

Teachers are responsible for all lesson planning.

103. The key to success for the exceptional student placed in a regular classroom is: *(Competency 28) (Average Rigor)*

    A. Access to the special aids and materials
    B. Support from the ESE teacher
    C. Modification in the curriculum
    D. The mainstream teacher's belief that the student will profit from the placement

Answer: D. The mainstream teacher's belief that the student will profit from the placement

Without the regular teacher's belief that the student can benefit, no special accommodations will be provided.

104. Ability to supply specific instructional materials, programs, and methods and to influence environmental learning variables are advantages of which service model for exceptional students? *(Competency 28) (Rigorous)*

    A. Regular classroom
    B. Consultant teacher
    C. Itinerant teacher
    D. Resource room

Answer: B. Consultant teacher

Consultation is usually done by specialists.

SPECIAL EDU. CROSS-CATEGORY

TEACHER CERTIFICATION STUDY GUIDE

105. A consultant teacher should be meeting the needs of his/her students by: *(Competency 28) (Easy Rigor)*

    A. Pushing in to do small group instruction with regular education students
    B. Asking the student to show his/her reasoning for failing
    C. Meeting with the teacher before class to discuss adaptations and expectations
    D. Accompanying the student to class

Answer: A. Pushing in to do small group instruction with regular education students

Students who receive consult services are receiving minimum instructional services. They require little modification to their educational programs.

106. Students with disabilities develop greater self-images and recognize their own academic and social strengths when they are: *(Competency 28) Easy)*

    A. Included in the mainstream classroom
    B. Provided community-based internships
    C. Socializing in the hallway
    D. Provided 1:1 instructional opportunity

Answer: A. Included in the mainstream classroom

When a child with a disability is included in the regular classroom, it raises the expectations of the child's academic performance and his or her need to conform to "acceptable peer behavior."

107. When a teacher is choosing behaviors to modify, two issues must be considered. What are they? *(Competency 28) (Average Rigor)*

    A. The need for the behavior to be performed in public *and* the culture of acceptance
    B. The culture of the child *and* society's standards regarding the behavior
    C. Evidence that the behavior can be changed *and* society norms
    D. Standards of the student's community *and* school rules

Answer: B. The culture of the child *and* society's standards regarding the behavior

American society's standards may or may not be the same standards of other cultures. It may be important to check the standards of the specific behavior in the student's cultural background before attempting to modify it.

SPECIAL EDU. CROSS-CATEGORY

TEACHER CERTIFICATION STUDY GUIDE

108. A BIP (Behavior Intervention Plan) is written to teach positive behavior. Which element listed below is NOT a standard feature of the plan? *(Competency 28) (Rigorous)*

    A. Identification of behavior to be modified
    B. Strategies to implement the replacement behavior
    C. Statement of distribution
    D. Team creation of BIP

Answer: C. Statement of distribution

There is no statement on how or who shall receive the BIP on the student.

109. By November, Annette's 7th grade teacher is concerned with her sporadic attendance. What action should take place next? *(Competency 28) (Average Rigor)*

    A. Notify Child Protective Services
    B. Notify the police of non-compliance with compulsory attendance
    C. Question parents about the absences
    D. Notify the administrator

Answer: C. Question parents about the absences

The parents should be contacted initially; they may be willing to file a report with the police (PINS) or have a rational reason for the absences.

110. You have a group of 8th grade students in an English class. Sheryl sits in the back of the room by choice and rarely answers questions. You believe that she has a learning disability and begin to modify her worksheets. You are: *(Competency 28)) (Average Rigor)*

    A. Planning for success of the student
    B. Creating a self-fulfilling prophecy
    C. Developing a student-centered curriculum
    D. Testing her ability

Answer: B. Creating a self-fulfilling prophecy

If Sheryl does not answer questions orally, she may simply not be as expressive as those around her, but it does not mean that she has a learning disability. Handing this type of worksheet out could create frustration and a lack of will to work to her ability.

SPECIAL EDU. CROSS-CATEGORY

111. Parents of children with disabilities may seek your advice on several aspects regarding their children. A mother calls you and complains she can't keep her son on task and she has to keep sending her son back to the bathroom until he finishes getting prepared for the day. What advice should you give her? *(Competency 28) (Average Rigor)*

   A. Request an educational evaluation
   B. Recommend close supervision until he does all tasks together consistently
   C. Create a list of tasks to be completed in the bathroom
   D. Ask for outside coordination of services advocacy that can assist with this type of issue

Answer: C. Create a list of tasks to be completed in the bathroom

This requires the child to be independent on each task. Calling outside resources is a good idea, but it does not address the issue. The student may simply have a short-term memory loss, and may need a reminder to keep on task.

112. Which is not a goal of collaboration for a consult teacher? *(Competency 28) (Average Rigor)*

   A. To have the regular education teacher understand the student's disability
   B. Review content for accuracy
   C. Review lessons for possible necessary modifications
   D. Understanding of reasons for current grade

Answer: B. Review content for accuracy

The regular education teacher is responsible for the content. You are responsible for seeing that the child's necessary modifications are adapted.

113. You have documented proof that Janice performs higher with the use of a computer on both class work and tests. Which kind of CSE/IEP Conference should be held? *(Competency 29) (Easy Rigor)*

   A. Manifestation determination
   B. Post-school transition to insure provision of a laptop by outside services
   C. Amendment; change of program/placement
   D. Annual

Answer: C. Amendment; change of program/placement

The amendment CSE should be held to add or remove services. Adding a test modification or service is a change in program.

114. Diversity can be identified in students by: *(Competency 29) (Average Rigor)*

   A. Biological factors
   B. Socioeconomic status (SES)
   C. Ethnicity
   D. All of the above

Answer: D. All of the above

Biological factors can place students apart from one other. Students who are genetically predisposed to being muscular or being overweight are examples of this diversity. Socioeconomic status and ethnicity also play a role.

115. Kara's mother has requested a computer for her child to do class work and homework; the CSE does not agree. Kara complains to you. You should: *(Competency 29) (Easy Rigor)*

   A. Tell her you agree with her
   B. Recommend an outside source that may provide a free laptop computer
   C. Tell Kara's mother she can still fight the CSE's decision by requesting a due process hearing
   D. Tell the parent to call a lawyer

Answer: C. Tell Kara's mother she can still fight the CSE's decision by requesting a due process hearing

It is your legal obligation to let Kara's mother know that she does not have to accept the CSE decision if she does not like it. She can request a due process hearing.

116. Shyquan is in your inclusive class, and she exhibits a slower comprehension of assigned tasks and concepts. Her first two grades were Bs but she is now receiving failing marks. She has seen the resource teacher. You should: *(Competency 29) (Rigorous)*

   A. Ask for a review of current placement
   B. Tell Shyquan to seek extra help
   C. Ask Shyquan if she is frustrated
   D. Ask the regular education teacher to slow instruction

Answer: A. Ask for a review of current placement

All of the responses listed above can be deemed correct, but you are responsible for reviewing her ability to function in the inclusive environment. Shyquan may or may not know she is not grasping the work, and she has sought out extra help with the resource teacher. If the regular education class students are successful, the class should not be slowed to adjust to Shyquan's learning rate. It is more likely that she may require a more modified curriculum to stay on task and to succeed academically. This would require a more restrictive environment.

117. The integrated approach to learning utilizes all resources available to address student needs. What are the resources? *(Competency 30) (Average Rigor)*

   A. The student, his/her parents, and the teacher
   B. The teacher, the parents, and the special education team
   C. The teacher, the student, and an administrator to perform needed interventions
   D. The student, his/her parents, the teacher, and community resources

Answer: D. The student, his/her parents, the teacher, and community resources

The integrated response encompasses all possible resources, including the resources in the community.

SPECIAL EDU. CROSS-CATEGORY

TEACHER CERTIFICATION STUDY GUIDE

118. Which of these characteristics is NOT included in the IDEA definition of emotional disturbance? *(Competency 31) (Average Rigor)*

    A. General pervasive mood of unhappiness or depression
    B. Social maladjustment manifested in a number of settings
    C. Tendency to develop physical symptoms, pains, or fear associated with school or personal problems
    D. Inability to learn that is not attributed to intellectual, sensory, or health factors

Answer: B. Social maladjustment manifested in a number of settings

Social maladjustment is not considered a disability.

119. IDEA 2004 changed the IEP by? *(Competency 31) (Rigorous)*

    A. Not requiring short-term objectives
    B. Requiring an inclusive activity
    C. Requiring parents to participate in the CSE
    D. Establishing new criteria to be classified as learning disabled

Answer: A. Not requiring short-term objectives

Until IDEA 2004, short-term goals and objectives needed to be in place to see progress towards a goal.

120. According to IDEA 2004, students with disabilities are to do what? *(Competency 31 (Average Rigor)*

    A. Participate in the general education program to the fullest extent that it is beneficial for them
    B. Participate in a vocational training within the general education setting
    C. Participate in a general education setting for physical education
    D. Participate in a modified program that meets their needs

Answer: A. Participate in the general education program to the fullest extent that it is beneficial for them

B,C, and D are all possible settings related to participating in the general education setting to the fullest extent possible. This still can mean that a student's LRE may restrict him/her to a 12:1:1 for the entire school day.

SPECIAL EDU. CROSS-CATEGORY 332

TEACHER CERTIFICATION STUDY GUIDE

121. **Teachers in grades K-3 are mandated to teach what to all students using scientifically based methods with measurable outcomes?** *(Competency 31) (Average Rigor)*

    A. Math
    B. Reading
    C. Citizenship
    D. Writing

Answer: B. Reading

Reading is the mandated subject, as it is looked at as the fountain from which all learning can be secured.

122. **What legislation started FAPE?** *(Competency 31) (Average Rigor)*

    A. Section 504
    B. EHCA
    C. IDEA
    D. Education Amendment 1974

Answer: A. Section 504

FAPE stands for Free Appropriate Public Education. Section 504 of the Rehabilitation Act in 1973 is what enacted/created FAPE.

123. **The revision of Individuals with Disabilities Education Act in 1997:** *(Competency 31) (Rigorous)*

    A. Required collaboration of educational professionals in order to provide equitable opportunities for students with disabilities
    B. Removed the requirement for short-term objectives with objectives with goals
    C. Required school administrator approval for an IEP to be put into place
    D. Required FBAs and BIPs for all students that were suspended for six days

Answer: A. Required collaboration of educational professionals in order to provide equitable opportunities for students with disabilities

Teachers must collaborate professionally to render the best possible education to the student.

TEACHER CERTIFICATION STUDY GUIDE

124. Taiquan's parents are divorced and have joint custody. They have both requested to be present at the CSE. You call to make sure that they received the letter informing them of the upcoming CSE. Taiquan's father did not receive the notification and is upset. You should: *(Skill 13.06) (Rigorous)*

    A. Tell him that you could review the meeting with him later
    B. Ask him if he can adjust his schedule
    C. Tell him you can reschedule the meeting
    D. Ask him to coordinate a time for the CSE to meet with his ex-wife

Answer: C. Tell him you can reschedule the meeting

A parent should be informed if he/she is divorced, if both have joint custody, and if he/she has expressed a desire to be present at the CSE. In this case, if one of the parents wants to be at the meeting and is unable to attend, the meeting should be rescheduled.

125. According to IDEA 2004, an FBA must be: *(Competency 31) (Average Rigor)*

    A. Written by the special education administrator
    B. Written by the teacher who has the issue with the student
    C. Written by the primary teacher
    D. Written by a team

Answer: D. Written by a team

FBAs (Functional Behavioral Assessments) should be written and reviewed as a team. This approach is the most effective for improving student behavior.

126. NCLB changed: *(Competency 31) (Rigorous)*

    A. Special education teacher placement
    B. Classroom guidelines
    C. Stricter behavioral regulations.
    D. Academic content

Answer: A. Special education teacher placement

Special education teachers are now required to meet the same criteria as those of the content teachers in their area to be *highly qualified.*

SPECIAL EDU. CROSS-CATEGORY

TEACHER CERTIFICATION STUDY GUIDE

127. **IDEA 97 changed IDEA by:** *(Competency 31) (Rigorous)*

    A. Requiring IEPs to be in electronic format
    B. Requiring all staff working with the student to have access to the IEP
    C. Allowing past assessments to be used in triennials
    D. Requiring BIPs for many students with FBAs

Answer: D. Requiring BIPs for many students with FBAs

IDEA 97 created a mandate to provide interventions to change inappropriate behaviors. This increases the possibility for students to avoid the consequences of repeating the behavior.

128. **Which of these groups is not comprehensively covered by IDEA?** *(Competency 31)) (Easy Rigor)*

    A. Gifted and talented
    B. Mentally retarded
    C. Specific learning disabilities
    D. Speech and language impaired

Answer: C. Specific learning disabilities

IDEA did not cover all exceptional children.

129. **Educators who advocate educating all children in their neighborhood classrooms and schools, who propose the end of labeling and segregation of special needs students in special classes, and who call for the delivery of special supports and services directly in the classroom may be said to support the:** *(Competency 31) (Easy Rigor)*

    A. Full service model
    B. Regular education initiative
    C. Full inclusion model
    D. Mainstream model

Answer: C. Full inclusion model

All students must be included in the regular classroom.

TEACHER CERTIFICATION STUDY GUIDE

130. **NCLB (No Child Left Behind Act), was signed on January 8, 2002. It addresses what?** *(Competency 31) (Rigorous)*

    A. Accessibility of curriculum to the student
    B. Administrative incentives for school improvements
    C. The funding to provide services required
    D. Accountability of school personnel for student achievement

Answer: D. Accountability of school personnel for student achievement

All behavior is learned. This behavior is different from the norm. It is different because of something the child has experienced or learned.

131. **Section 504 differs from the scope of IDEA because its main focus is on:** *(Competency 31) (Average Rigor)*

    A. Prohibition of discrimination on the basis of disability
    B. A basis for additional support services and accommodations in a special education setting
    C. Procedural rights and safeguards for the individual
    D. Federal funding for educational services

Answer: A. Prohibition of discrimination on the basis of disability

Section 504 prohibits discrimination on the basis of disability.

132. **Public Law 99-457 amended the EHA to make provisions for:** *(Competency 31) (Average Rigor)*

    A. Education services for "uneducable" children
    B. Education services for children in jail settings
    C. Special education benefits for children birth to five years
    D. Education services for medically-fragile children

Answer: C. Special education benefits for children birth to five years

PL 99-457 amended EHA to provide special education programs for children aged three to five years, with most states offering outreach programs to identify children with special needs from birth to age three.

TEACHER CERTIFICATION STUDY GUIDE

133. **Under the provisions of IDEA, the student is entitled to all of these EXCEPT:** *(Competency 31) (Average Rigor)*

    A. Placement in the best environment
    B. Placement in the least restrictive environment
    C. Provision of educational needs at no cost
    D. Provision of individualized, appropriate educational program

Answer: A. Placement in the best environment

IDEA mandates a least restrictive environment, an IEP (individual education plan), and a free public education.

134. **As a new special education teacher, you have the responsibility to:** *(Competency 31) (Average Rigor)*

    A. Share new law related to special education
    B. Discuss and plan intervention strategies for other teachers
    C. Stay current on national and local news
    D. Observe incoming students for possible referrals to CSE

Answer: A. Share new law related to special education

Quite often, school administrators are not knowledgeable of the changes in special education laws until a court case becomes public or an angry parent approaches and tells them they are in violation of the law. You, as the special education teacher, must keep current on the law. Sharing that knowledge is a collegial responsibility, if you believe people who need to be informed of the changes are not aware of them.

135. **Which law specifically states that "full inclusion is not the only way for a student to reach his/her highest potential?"** *(Competency 31) (Rigorous)*

    A. IDEA
    B. IDEA 97
    C. IDEA 2004
    D. Part 200

Answer: C. IDEA 2004

IDEA (IDEA 2004) full inclusion stated that this was not always best for the individual student. It allows for students who need more restrictive services to be served appropriately when people who push full inclusion are confronted.

136. The following words describe an IEP objective EXCEPT:
(Competency 31) (Rigorous)

A. Specific
B. Observable
C. Measurable
D. Flexible

Answer: D. Flexible

IEPs are not flexible for interpretation. They are enforceable legal documents that must be followed or modified by the CSE team.

137. NCLB and IDEA 2004 changed special education teacher requirements by: *(Competency 31) (Easy Rigor)*

A. Requiring a "highly qualified" status for job placement
B. Adding changes to the requirement for certifications
C. Adding legislation requiring teachers to maintain knowledge of law
D. Requiring inclusive environmental experience prior to certification

Answer: A. Requiring a "highly qualified" status for job placement

NCLB and IDEA 2004 place a requirement that all teacher shall be equally qualified to teach in their content areas.

138. IDEA 2004 stated that there is a disproportionate amount of minority students classified. The reason IDEA 2004 suggests is: *(Competency 31) (Average Rigor)*

A. Socioeconomic status where disproportionate numbers exist
B. Improper evaluations; not making allowances for students who speak English as a second language
C. Growing population of minorities
D. Percentage of drug abuse per ethnicity

Answer: B. Improper evaluations; not making allowances for students who speak English as a second language

IDEA 2004 questioned the overrepresentation of students who speak English as a second language.

139. **Guidelines for an Individualized Family Service Plan (IFSP) are described in which legislation?** *(Competency 31) (Rigorous)*

   A. Education of the Handicapped Act Amendments
   B. IDEA (1990)
   C. IDEA 2004
   D. ADA

Answer: B. IDEA (1990)

Education for All Handicapped Children Act was passed in the Civil Rights era, and its amendment in 1986 provided financial incentive to educate children with disabilities who are three to five years of age. ADA is the Americans with Disabilities Act.

140. **Cheryl is a 15-year old student receiving educational services in a full-time EH classroom. The date for her IEP review is planned for two months before her 16th birthday. According to the requirements of IDEA, what must ADDITIONALLY be included in this review?** *(Competency 31) (Average Rigor)*

   A. Graduation plan
   B. Individualized transition plan
   C. Vocational assessment
   D. Transportation planning

Answer: B. Individualized transition plan

This is necessary, as the student should be transitioning from school to work.

141. **Previous to IDEA 97, what was not accepted?** *(Competency 31) (Rigorous)*

   A. Using previous assessments to evaluate placement
   B. Parent refusal of CSE determination (no due process)
   C. Student input on placement and needs
   D. All of the above

Answer: B. Using previous assessments to evaluate placement

Previous to IDEA 97, evaluation of placement always required assessments. No acceptance of previous testing was accepted. This was recognized as creating needless testing for students, as IQs generally do not change, while the student's knowledge base grows.

142. Hector is a 10th grader in a program for the severely emotionally handicapped. After a classmate taunted him about his mother, Hector threw a desk at the other boy and attacked him. A crisis intervention team tried to break up the fight, and one teacher hurt his knee. The other boy received a concussion. Hector now faces disciplinary measures. How long can he be suspended without the suspension reviewing a possible "change of placement"?
(Competency 31) (Rigorous)

   A. 5 days
   B. 10 days
   C. 10 + 30 days
   D. 60 days

Answer: B. 10 days

According to Honig versus Doe (1988), *Where the student has presented an immediate threat to others, that student may be temporarily suspended for up to 10 school days to give the school and the parents time to review the IEP and discuss possible alternatives to the current placement.*

143. The concept that a handicapped student cannot be expelled for misconduct that is a manifestation of the handicap itself is not limited to students who are labeled "seriously emotionally disturbed." Which reason does not explain this concept?
(Competency 31) (Easy Rigor)

   A. Emphasis on individualized evaluation
   B. Consideration of the problems and needs of handicapped students
   C. Right to a free and appropriate public education
   D. Students in special education get special privileges

Answer: D. Students in special education get special privileges

A, B, and C are tenets of IDEA and should take place in the least restrictive environment. D does not explain this concept.

TEACHER CERTIFICATION STUDY GUIDE

144. **Teachers have a professional obligation to do all of the following except:** *(Competency 31) (Average Rigor)*

    A. Join a professional organization, such as CEC or LDA
    B. Attend in-services or seminars related to the position
    C. Stay after school to help students
    D. Run school clubs

Answer: D. Run school clubs

Teachers are not obligated to run a school club. It is often considered volunteering of your time.

145. **Satisfaction of the LRE requirement means:** (Competency 31) (Easy Rigor)

    A. The school is providing the best services it can offer
    B. The school is providing the best services the district has to offer
    C. The student is being educated with the fewest special education services necessary
    D. The student is being educated in the least restrictive setting that meets his or her needs

Answer: D. The student is being educated in the least restrictive setting that meets his or her needs

IDEA mandates LRE, which is the least restrictive environment.

146. **The court case that determined that a student may not be denied education or be excluded from school when their behavior is related to their handicap was:** *(Competency 31) (Rigorous)*

    A. Honig v. Doe 1988
    B. School Board of Nassau County v. Arline, 1987
    C. Florence County School District v. Shannon Carter, 1993
    D. Smith v. Robinson, 1984

Answer: A. Honig v. Doe, 1988

This case verified the "stay put" provision of IDEA allows students to remain in their current educational setting pending the outcome of administrative or judicial hearings. In the case of behavior that is a danger to the student or others, the court allows school districts to apply their normal procedures for dealing with dangerous behavior, such as time-out, loss of privileges, detention, or study carrels.

SPECIAL EDU. CROSS-CATEGORY

147. Teaching materials that are copyrighted may: *(Competency 31)* *(Average Rigor)*

   A. may not be reproduced
   B. may be reproduced if they are intended for that purpose.
   C. may be reproduced only for your immediate students
   D. may be reproduced for students that did not receive the texts with the other students.

Answer: B. may be reproduced if they are intended for that purpose.

Many teacher materials come in books called reproducables. These materials may also come with a copyright. Books may not be reproduced in copy format even if only one student is missing the book. The school or district must purchase the book.

148. John has received a long term suspension for assaulting a student. John is classified as being Mentally Retarded. In the assault he threw a chair at another student. The Manifestation Determination CSE determined that John's actions were not related to his disability. According to the law then:
(Competency 31) (Easy Rigor)

   A. John may receive the same punishment that a "regular" education student would receive.
   B. John will be returned to program after the completion of 10 days.
   C. CSE will revisit placement at a later meeting.
   D. John may return to the school, but may not be returned to the class where he hurt the other student.

Answer: A. John may receive the same punishment that a "regular" education student would receive.

If a student that is labeled as having special needs is suspended for more than 10 days during the year, and it is determined by a CSE that the actions of the student did not relate to the student's disability. IDEA 2004 and IDEA 1997 specifically state that, that student may be disciplined in the same manner as his non-disabled peers.

TEACHER CERTIFICATION STUDY GUIDE

149. **NCLB requires that the special education teacher be *Highly Qualified*. To be *Highly Qualified (HQ)* a teach must:** *(Competency 31) (Easy Rigor)*

    A. Have the same certification as the regular education teacher in their position.
    B. How relevant course work and professional development
    C. Have a comparable degree in the field they are working in.
    D. A and/or B and/or C.

Answer: A and/or B and/or C.

NCLB makes requirements on the state. The state in turn may define those requirements further. The federal form allows for points to demonstrate *HQ*. So a combination of course work certifications professional development and time served teaching the subject can be utilized. BUT, it is possible your district or state may be more specific as to how you qualify as HQ.

150. **The 1975, Goss v. Lopez, decision had a large impact on special education as a whole because it:** *(Competency 31) (Rigorous)*

    A. required due process for all students receiving a school suspension.
    B. required a manifestation determination
    C. required districts to re-evaluate students who receive 3 suspensions a year.
    D. required school districts to give parents their due process rights when they do not agree with a CSE.

Answer: A. required due process for all students receiving a school suspension.

Goss v. Lopez was not a specifically special education oriented case. The decision made school districts become responsible for their own investigations and providing just cause for suspension.

References

Ager, C.L. & Cole, C.L. (1991). A review of cognitive-behavioral interventions for children and adolescents with behavioral disorders. *Behavioral Disorders,* 16(4), 260-275.

Aiken, L.R. (1985). *Psychological testing and assessment* (5th ed.). Boston: Allyn and Bacon.

Alberto, P.A. & Trouthman, A.C. (1990). *Applied behavior analysis for teachers: Influencing student performance.* Columbus, Ohio: Charles E. Merrill.

Algozzine, B. (1990). *Behavior problem management: Educator's resource service.* Gaithersburg, MD: Aspen Publishers.

Algozzine, B., Ruhl, K., & Ramsey, R. (1991). *Behaviorally disordered: Assessment for identification and instruction CED mini-library.* Renson, VA: The Council for Exceptional Children.

Ambron, S.R. (1981). *Child development* (3rd ed.). New York: Holt, Rinehart and Winston.

Anerson, V., & Black, L. (Eds.). (1987, Winter). National news: U.S. Department of Education releases special report (Editorial). *GLRS Journal* [Georgia Learning Resources System].

Anguili, R. (1987, Winter). The 1986 amendment to the Education of the Handicapped Act. *Confederation* [A quarterly publication of the Georgia Federation Council for Exceptional Children].

Ashlock, R.B. (1976). *Error patterns in computation: A semi-programmed approach* (2nd ed.). Columbus, Ohio: Charles E. Merrill.

Association of Retarded Citizens of Georgia (1987). *1986-87 Government report.* College Park, GA: Author.

Ausubel, D.P. & Sullivan, E.V. (1970). *Theory and problems of child development.* New York: Grune & Stratton.

Banks, J.A., & McGee Banks, C.A. (1993). *Multicultural education* (2nd ed.). Boston: Allyn and Bacon.

Barrett, T.C. (Ed.). (1967). *The evaluation of children's reading achievement. in perspectives in reading, No. 8.* Newark, Delaware: International Reading Association.

Bartoli, J.S. (1989). An ecological response to Cole's interactivity alternative. *Journal of Learning Disabilities,* 22 (5), 292-297.

Basile-Jackson, J. *The exceptional child in the regular classroom.* Augusta, GA: East Georgia Center, Georgia Learning Resources System.

Bauer, A.M., & Shea, T.M. (1989). *Teaching exceptional students in your classroom.* Boston: Allyn and Bacon.

Bentley, E.L. Jr. (1980). *Questioning skills* (Videocassette & manual series). Northbrook, IL: Hubbard Scientific Company. (Project STRETCH [Strategies to Train Regular Educators to Teach Children with Handicaps], Module 1, ISBN 0-8331-1906-0).

Berdine, W.H., & Blackhurst, A.E. (1985). *An introduction to special education.* (2nd ed.) Boston: Little, Brown and Company.

Blake, K. (1976). *The mentally retarded: An educational psychology.* Englewood Cliff, NJ: Prentice-Hall.

Bohline, D.S. (1985). *Intellectual and affective characteristics of attention deficit disordered children.* Journal of Learning Disabilities, 18 (10),604-608.

Boone, R. (1983). Legislation and litigation. In R.E. Schmid, & L. Negata (Eds.). *Contemporary Issues in Special Education.* New York: McGraw Hill.

Brantlinger, E.A., & Guskin, S.L. (1988). Implications of social and cultural differences for special education. In Meten, E.L. Vergason, G.A., & Whelan, R.J. *Effective Instructional Strategies for Exceptional Children.* Denver, CO: Love Publishing.

Brewton, B. (1990). Preliminary identification of the socially maladjusted. In Georgia Psycho-educational Network, Monograph #1. *An Educational Perspective On: Emotional Disturbance and Social Maladjustment.* Atlanta, GA Psychoeducational Network.

Brolin, D.E., & Kokaska, C.J. (1979). *Career education for handicapped children approach.* Renton, VA: The Council for Exceptional Children.

Brolin, D.E. (Ed). (1989). *Life centered career education: A competency based approach.* Reston, VA: The Council for Exceptional Children.

Brown, J.W., Lewis, R.B., & Harcleroad, F.F. (1983). *AV instruction: Technology, media, and methods* (6TH ed.). New York: McGraw-Hill.

Bryan, T.H., & Bryan, J.H. (1986). *Understanding learning disabilities* (3rd ed.). Palo Alto, CA: Mayfield.

Bryen, D.N. (1982). *Inquiries into child language.* Boston: Allyn & Bacon.

Bucher, B.D. (1987). *Winning them over.* New York: Times Books.

Bush, W.L., & Waugh, K.W. (1982). *Diagnosing learning problems* (3rd ed.). Columbus, OH: Charles E. Merrill.

Campbell, P. (1986). *Special needs report* [Newsletter]. 1(1), 1-3.

Carbo, M., & Dunn, K. (1986). *Teaching students to read through their individual learning styles.* Englewood Cliffs, NJ: Prentice Hall.

Cartwright, G.P., & Cartwright, C.A., & Ward, M.E. (1984). *Educating special learners* (2nd ed.). Belmont, CA: Wadsworth.

Cejka, J.M. (Consultant), & Needham, F. (Senior Editor). (1976). *Approaches to mainstreaming.* (Filmstrip and cassette kit, units 1 & 2). Boston: Teaching Resources Corporation. (Catalog Nos. 09-210 & 09-220).

Chalfant, J. C. (1985). *Identifying learning disabled students: A summary of the national task force report.* Learning Disabilities Focus, 1, 9-20.

Charles, C.M. (1976). *Individualizing instructions.* St Louis: The C.V. Mosby Company.

Chrispeels, J.H. (1991). *District leadership in parent involvement: Policies and actions in San Diego.* Phi Delta Kappa, 71, 367-371.

Clarizio, H.F. (1987). Differentiating characteristics. In Georgia Psychoeducational Network, Monograph #1, *An educational perspective on: Emotional disturbance and social maladjustment.* Atlanta, GA: Psychoeducational Network.

Clarizio, H.F. & McCoy, G.F. (1983). *Behavior disorders in children* (3rd ed.). New York: Harper & Row.

Coles, G.S. (1989). *Excerpts from the learning mystique: A critical look at disabilities.* Journal of Learning Disabilities, 22 (5), 267-278.

Collins, E. (1980). *Grouping and special students.* (Videocassette & manual series). Northbrook, IL: Hubbard Scientific Company. (Project STRETCH [Strategies to Train Regular Educators to Teach Children with Handicaps], Module 17, ISBN 0-8331-1922-2).

Craig, E., & Craig, L. (1990). *Reading In the Content Areas.* (Videocassette & manual series). Northbrook, IL: Hubbard Scientific Company. (Project STRETCH [Strategies to Train Regular Educators to Teach Children with Handicaps], Module 13, ISBN 0-8331-1918-4).

Compton, C., (1984). *A Guide to 75 Tests for Special Education.* Belmont, CA., Pitman Learning.

Council for Exceptional Children. (1976). *Introducing P.L. 94-142.* _ [Filmstrip-cassette kit manual]. Reston, VA: Author.

Council for Exceptional Children. (1987). *The Council for Exceptional Children's Fall 1987. Catalog of Products and Services.* Renton, VA: Author.

Council for Exceptional Children Delegate Assembly. (1983). *Council for Exceptional Children Code of Ethics* (Adopted April 1983). Reston, VA: Author.

Czajka, J.L. (1984). *Digest of Data on Person With Disabilities* (Mathematics Policy Research, Inc.). Washington, D.C.: U.S. Government Printing Office.

Dell, H.D. (1972). *Individualizing Instruction: Materials and Classroom Procedures.* Chicago: Science Research Associates.

Demonbreun, C., & Morris, J. *Classroom Management* [Videocassette & Manual series]. Northbrook, IL: Hubbard Scientific Company. Project STRETCH (Strategies to Train Regular Educators to Teach Children with Handicaps]. Module 5, ISBN 0-8331-1910-9).

Department of Education. *Education for the Handicapped Law Reports.* Supplement 45 (1981), p. 102: 52. Washington, D.C.: U.S. Government Printing Office.

Department of Health, Education, and Welfare, Office of Education. (1977, August 23). *Education of Handicapped Children.* Federal Register, 42, (163).

Diana vs. State Board of Education, Civil No. 70-37 R.F.P. (N.D.Cal. January, 1970).

Digangi, S.A., Perryman, P., & Rutherford, R.B., Jr. (1990). Juvenile Offenders in the 90's A Descriptive Analysis. *Perceptions*, 25(4), 5-8.

Division of Educational Services, Special Education Programs (1986). *Fifteenth Annual Report to Congress on Implementation of the Education of the Handicapped Act.* Washington, D.C.: U.S. Government Printing Office.

Doyle, B.A. (1978). Math Readiness Skills. Paper presented at National Association of School Psychologists, New York. K.J. (1978). *Teaching Students Through Their Individual Learning Styles.*

Dunn, R.S., & Dunn, K.J. (1978). *Teaching Students Through Their Individual Learning Styles: A Practical Approach.* Reston, VA: Reston.

Epstein, M.H., Patton, J.R., Polloway, E.A., & Foley, R. (1989). Mild retardation: Student characteristics and services. *Education and Training of the Mentally Retarded*, 24, 7-16.

Ekwall, E.E., & Shanker, J.L. 1983). *Diagnosis and Remediation of the Disabled Reader* (2nd ed.) Boston: Allyn and Bacon.

Firth, E.E. & Reynolds, I. (1983). Slide tape shows: A creative activity for the gifted students. *Teaching Exceptional Children.* 15(3), 151-153.

Frymier, J., & Gansneder, B. (1989). *The Phi Delta Kappa Study of Students at Risk.* Phi Delta Kappa. 71(2) 142-146.

Fuchs, D., & Deno, S.L. 1992). Effects of curriculum within curriculum-based measurement. *Exceptional Children* 58 (232-242).

Fuchs, D., & Fuchs, L.S. (1989). Effects of examiner familiarity on Black, Caucasian, and Hispanic Children. A Meta-Analysis. *Exceptional Children.* 55, 303-308.

Fuchs, L.S., & Shinn, M.R. (1989). Writing CBM IEP objectives. In M.R. Shinn, *Curriculum-based Measurement: Assessing Special Students.* New York: Guilford Press.

Gage, N.L. (1990). *Dealing With the Dropout Problems?* Phi Delta Kappa. 72(4), 280-285.

Gallagher, P.A. (1988). *Teaching Students with Behavior Disorders: Techniques and Activities for Classroom Instruction* (2nd ed.). Denver, CO: Love Publishing.

Gearheart, B.R. (1980). *Special Education for the 80s.* St. Louis, MO: The C.V. Cosby Company.

Gearhart, B.R. & Weishahn, M.W. (1986). *The Handicapped Student in the Regular Classroom* (2nd ed.). St Louis, MO: The C.V. Mosby Company.

TEACHER CERTIFICATION STUDY GUIDE

Gearhart, B.R. (1985). *Learning Disabilities: Educational Strategies* (4th ed.). St. Louis: Times Mirror/ Mosby College of Publishing.

Georgia Department of Education, Program for Exceptional Children. (1986). *Mild Mentally Handicapped* (Vol. II), Atlanta, GA: Office of Instructional Services, Division of Special Programs, and Program for Exceptional Children. Resource Manuals for Program for Exceptional Children.

Georgia Department of Human Resources, Division of Rehabilitation Services. (1987, February). Request for Proposal [Memorandum]. Atlanta, GA: Author.

Georgia Psychoeducational Network (1990). *An Educational Perspective on: Emotional Disturbance and Social Maladjustment.* Monograph #1. Atlanta, GA Psychoeducational Network.

Geren, K. (1979). *Complete Special Education Handbook.* West Nyack, NY: Parker.

Gillet, P.K. (1988). Career Development. Robinson, G.A., Patton, J.R., Polloway, E.A., & Sargent, L.R. (eds.). *Best Practices in Mild Mental Disabilities.* Reston, VA: The Division on Mental Retardation of the Council for Exceptional Children.

Gleason, J.B. (1993). *The Development of Language* (3rd ed.). New York: Macmillan Publishing.

Good, T.L., & Brophy, J.E. (1978). *Looking into Classrooms* (2nd Ed.). New York: Harper & Row.

Hall, M.A. (1979). Language-Centered Reading: Premises and Recommendations. *Language Arts*, 56, 664-670.

Halllahan, D.P. & Kauffman, J.M. (1988). *Exceptional Children: Introduction to Special Education.* (4th Ed.). Englewood Cliffs, NJ; Prentice-Hall.

Hallahan, D.P. & Kauffman, J.M. (1994). *Exceptional Children: Introduction to Special Education* (6th ed.). Boston: Allyn and Bacon.

Hammill, D.D., & Bartel, N.R. (1982). *Teaching Children With Learning and Behavior Problems* (3rd ed.). Boston: Allyn and Bacon.

Hammill, D.D., & Bartel, N.R. (1986). *Teaching Students with Learning and Behavior Problems* (4th ed.). Boston and Bacon.

Hamill, D.D., & Brown, L. & Bryant, B. (1989) *A Consumer's Guide to Tests in Print.* Austin, TX: Pro-Ed.

Haney, J.B. & Ullmer, E.J. ((1970). *Educational Media and the Teacher.* Dubuque, IA: Wm. C. Brown Company.

Hardman, M.L., Drew, C.J., Egan, M.W., & Wolf, B. (1984). *Human Exceptionality: Society, School, and Family.* Boston: Allyn and Bacon.

Hardman, M.L., Drew, C.J., Egan, M.W., & Worlf, B. (1990). *Human Exceptionality* (3rd ed.). Boston: Allyn and Bacon.

Hargrove, L.J., & Poteet, J.A. (1984). *Assessment in Special Education.* Englewood Cliffs, NJ: Prentice-Hall.

Haring, N.G., & Bateman, B. (1977). *Teaching the Learning Disabled Child.* Englewood Cliffs, NJ: Prentice-Hall.

Harris, K.R., & Pressley, M. (1991). The Nature of Cognitive Strategy Instruction: Interactive strategy instruction. *Exceptional Children*, 57, 392-401.

Hart, T., & Cadora, M.J. (1980). The Exceptional Child: Label the Behavior [Videocassette & manual series], Northbrook, IL: Hubbard Scientific Company. (Project STRETCH [Strategies to Train Regular Educators to Teach Children with Handicaps], Module 12, ISBN 0-8331-1917-6). HART, V. (1981) *Mainstreaming Children with Special Needs.* New York: Longman.

Henley, M., Ramsey,R.S., & Algozzine, B. (1993). *Characteristics of and Strategies for Teaching Students with Mild Disabilities.* Boston: Allyn and Bacon.

Hewett, F.M., & Forness, S.R. (1984). *Education of Exceptional Learners.* (3rd ed.). Boston: Allyn and Bacon.

Howe, C.E. (1981) *Administration of Special Education.* Denver: Love.

Human Services Research Institute (1985). *Summary of Data on Handicapped Children and Youth.* (Digest). Washington, D.C.: U.S. Government Printing Office.

Johnson, D.W. (1972) *Reaching Out: Interpersonal Effectiveness and Self-Actualization.* Englewood Cliffs, NJ: Prentice-Hall.

Johnson, D.W. (1978) *Human Relations and Your Career: A Guide to Interpersonal Skills.* Englewood Cliffs, NJ: Prentice-Hall.

Johnson, D.W., & Johnson, R.T. (1990). *Social Skills for Successful Group Work. Educational Leadership.* 47 (4) 29-33.

Johnson, S.W., & Morasky, R.L. *Learning Disabilities* (2nd ed.) Boston: Allyn and Bacon.

Jones, F.H. (1987). *Positive Classroom Discipline.* New York: McGraw-Hill Book Company.

Jones, V.F., & Jones, L. S. (1986). *Comprehensive Classroom Management: Creating Positive Learning Environments.* (2nd ed.). Boston: Allyn and Bacon.

Jones, V.F. & Jones, L.S. (1981). *Responsible Classroom Discipline: Creating Positive Learning Environments and Solving Problems.* Boston: Allyn and Bacon.

Kauffman, J.M. (1981) *Characteristics of Children's Behavior Disorders.* (2nd ed.). Columbus, OH: Charles E. Merrill.

Kauffman, J.M. (1989). *Characteristics of Behavior Disorders of Children and Youth.* (4th ed.). Columbus, OH: Merrill Publishing.

Kem, M., & Nelson, M. (1983). *Strategies for Managing Behavior Problems in the Classroom.* Columbus, OH: Charles E. Merrill.

Kerr, M.M., & Nelson, M. (1983) *Strategies for Managing Behavior Problems in the Classroom.* Columbus, OH: Charles E. Merrill.

Kirk, S.A., & Gallagher, J.J. (1986). *Educating Exceptional Children* (5th ed.). Boston: Houghton Mifflin.

Kohfeldt, J. (1976). Blueprints for construction. *Focus on Exceptional Children.* 8 (5), 1-14.

Kokaska, C.J., & Brolin, D.E. (1985). *Career Education for Handicapped Individuals* (2nd ed.). Columbus, OH: Charles E. Merrill.

Lambie, R.A. (1980). A systematic approach for changing materials, instruction, and assignments to meet individual needs. *Focus on Exceptional Children,* 13(1), 1-12.

Larson, S.C., & Poplin, M.S. (1980). *Methods for Educating the Handicapped: An Individualized Education Program Approach.* Boston: Allyn and Bacon.

Lerner, J. (1976) *Children with Learning Disabilities.* (2nd ed.). Boston: Houghton Mifflin.

Lerner, J. (1989). *Learning Disabilities,: Theories, Diagnosis and Teaching Strategies* (3rd ed.). Boston: Houghton Mifflin.

Levenkron, S. (1991). *Obsessive-Compulsive Disorders.* New York: Warner Books.

Lewis, R.B., & Doorlag, D.H. (1991). *Teaching Special Students in the Mainstream.* (3rd ed.). New York: Merrill.

Lindsley, O. R. (1990). Precision Teaching: By Teachers for Children. *Teaching Exceptional Children, 22.* (3), 10-15.

Linddberg, L., & Swedlow, R. (1985). *Young Children Exploring and Learning.* Boston: Allyn and Bacon.

Long, N.J., Morse, W.C., & Newman, R.G. (1980). *Conflict in the Classroom: The Education of Emotionally Disturbed Children.* Belmont, CA: Wadsworth.

Losen, S.M., & Losen, J.G. (1985). *The Special Education Team.* Boston: Allyn and Bacon.

Lovitt, T.C. (1989). *Introduction to Learning Disabilities.* Boston: Allyn and Bacon.

Lund, N.J., & Duchan, J.F. (1988)/ *Assessing Children's Language in Naturalist Contexts.* Englewood Cliffs, NJ: Prentice Hall

Male, M. (1994) *Technology for Inclusion: Meeting the Special Needs of all Children.* (2nd ed.). Boston: Allyn and Bacon.

Mandelbaum, L.H. (1989). Reading. In G.A. Robinson, J.R., Patton, E.A., Polloway, & L.R. Sargent (eds.). *Best Practices in Mild Mental Retardation.* Reston, VA: The Division of Mental Retardation, Council for Exceptional Children.

Mannix. D. (1993). *Social Skills for Special Children.* West Nyack, NY: The Center for Applied Research in Education.

Marshall, et al. vs. Georgia U.S. District Court for the Southern District of Georgia. C.V. 482-233. June 28, 1984.

Marshall, E.K., Kurtz, P.D., & Associates. *Interpersonal Helping Skills.* San Francisco, CA: Jossey-Bass Publications.

Marston, D.B. (1989) A curriculum-based measurement approach to assessing academic performance: What it is and why do it. In M. Shinn (Ed.). *Curriculum-Based Measurement: Assessing Special Children*. New York: Guilford Press.

McDowell, R.L., Adamson, G.W., & Wood, F.H. (1982). *Teaching Emotionally Disturbed Children.* Boston: Little, Brown and Company.

McGginnis, E., Goldstein, A.P. (1990). *Skill Streaming in Early*

Childhood: Teaching prosocial skills to the preschool and kindergarten child. Champaign, IL: Research Press.

McLloughlin, J.A., & Lewis, R.B. (1986). *Assessing Special Students* (3rd ed.). Columbus, OH: Charles E. Merrill.

Mercer, C.D. (1987). *Students with Learning Disabilities.* (3rd. ed.). Merrill Publishing.

Mercer, C.D., & Mercer, A.R. (1985). *Teaching Children with Learning Problems* (2nd ed.). Columbus, OH: Charles E. Merrill.

Meyen, E.L., Vergason, G.A., & Whelan, R.J. (Eds.). (1988). *Effective Instructional Strategies for Exceptional Children.* Denver, CO: Love Publishing.

Miller, L.K. (1980). *Principles of Everyday Behavior Analysis* (2nd ed.). Monterey, CA: Brooks/Cole Publishing Company.

Mills Vs. The Board Of Educaton Of The District Of Columbia, 348F. Supp. 866 (D.C. 1972).

Mopsick, S.L. & Agard, J.A. (Eds.) (1980). Cambridge, MA: Abbott Associates.

Morris, C.G. (1985). *Psychology: An Introduction* (5th ed.). Englewood Cliffs, NJ: Prentice-Hall.

Morris, J. (1980). *Behavior Modification.* [Videocassette and manual series]. Northbrook, IL: Hubbard Scientific Company. (Project STRETCH [Strategies to Train Regular Educators to Teach Children with Handicaps,] Module 16, Metropolitan Cooperative Educational Service Agency.).

Morris, J. & Demonbreun, C. (1980). *Learning Styles* [Videocassettes & Manual series]. Northbrook, IL: Hubbard Scientific Company. (Project STRETCH [Strategies to Train Regular Educators to Teach Children with Handicaps], Module 15, ISBN 0-8331-1920-6).

Morris, R.J. (1985). *Behavior Modification with Exceptional Children: Principles and Practices.* Glenview, IL: Scott, Foresman and Company.

Morsink, C.V. (1984). *Teaching Special Needs Students in Regular Classrooms.* Boston: Little, Brown and Company.

Morsink, C.V., Thomas, C.C., & Correa, V.L. (1991). *Interactive Teaming, Consultation and Collaboration in Special Programs.* New York: MacMillan Publishing.

Mullsewhite, C.R. (1986). *Adaptive Play for Special Needs Children: Strategies to Enhance Communication and Learning.* San Diego: College Hill Press.

North Central Georgia Learning Resources System/Child Serve. (1985). *Strategies Handbook for Classroom Teachers.* Ellijay, GA.

Patton, J.R., Cronin, M.E., Polloway, E.A., Hutchinson, D., & Robinson, G.A. (1988). Curricular considerations: A life skills orientation. In Robinson, G.A., Patton, J.R., Polloway, E.A., & Sargent, L.R. (Eds.). *Best Practices in Mental Disabilities.* Des Moines, IA: Iowa Department of Education, Bureau of Special Education.

Patton, J.R., Kauggman, J.M., Blackbourn, J.M., & Brown, B.G. (1991). *Exceptional Children in Focus* (5th ed.). New York: MacMillan.

Paul, J.L. (Ed.). (1981). *Understanding and Working with parents of Children with Special Needs.* New York: Holt, Rinehart and Winston.

Paul, J.L. & Epanchin, B.C. (1991). *Educating Emotionally Disturbed Children and Youth: Theories and Practices for Teachers.* (2nd ed.). New York: MacMillan. Pennsylvania Association For Retarded Children Vs. Commonwealth Of Pennsylvania, 334 F. Supp. 1257 (E.D., PA., 1971), 343 F. Supp. 279 (L.D. PA., 19972).

Phillips, V., & Mccullough, L. (1990). Consultation based programming: Instituting the Collaborative Work Ethic. *Exceptional Children.* 56 (4), 291-304.

Podemski, R.S., Price, B.K., Smith, T.E.C., & Marsh, G.E., IL (1984). *Comprehensive Administration of Special Education.* Rockville, MD: Aspen Systems Corporation.

Polloway, E.A., & Patton, J.R. (1989). *Strategies for Teaching Learners with Special Needs.* (5th ed.). New York: Merrill.

Polloway, E.A., Patton, J.R., Payne, J.S., & Payne, R.A. 1989). *Strategies for Teaching Learners with Special Needs,* 4th ed.). Columbus, OH: Merrill Publishing.

Pugach, M.C., & Johnson, L.J. (1989a). The challenge of implementing collaboration between general and special education. *Exceptional Children, 56* (3), 232-235.

Pugach, M.C., & Johnson, L.J. (1989b). Pre-referral interventions: Progress, Problems, and Challenges. *Exceptional Children, 56* (3), 217-226.

Radabaugh, M.T., & Yukish, J.F. (1982). *Curriculum and Methods for the Mildly Handicapped.* Boston: Allyn and Bacon.

Ramsey, R.S. (1981). Perceptions of disturbed and disturbing behavioral characteristics by school personnel. (Doctoral Dissertation, University of Florida) Dissertation Abstracts International, 42(49), DA8203709.

Ramsey, R.S. (1986). Taking the practicum beyond the public school door. *Journal of Adolescence.* 21(83), 547-552.

Ramsey, R.S., (1988). *Preparatory Guide for Special Education Teacher Competency Tests.* Boston: Allyn and Bacon, Inc.

Ramsey, R.S., Dixon, M.J., & Smith, G.G.B. (1986) *Eyes on the Special Education: Professional Knowledge Teacher Competency Test.* Albany, GA: Southwest Georgia Learning Resources System Center.

Ramsey R.W., & Ramsey, R.S. (1978). Educating the emotionally handicapped child in the public school setting. *Journal of Adolescence.* 13(52), 537-541.

Reinheart, H.R. (1980). *Children I Conflict: Educational Strategies for the Emotionally Disturbed and Behaviorally Disordered.* (2nd ed.). St Louis, MO: The C.V. Mosby Company.

Robinson, G.A., Patton, J.R., Polloway, E.A., & Sargent, L.R. (Eds.). (1989a). *Best Practices in Mental Disabilities.* Des Moines, IA Iowa Department of Education, Bureau of Special Education.

Robinson, G.A., Patton, J.R., Polloway, E.A., & Sargent, L.R. (Eds.). (1989b). *Best Practices in Mental Disabilities.* Renton, VA: The Division on Mental Retardation of the Council for Exceptional Children.

Rothstein, L.F. (1995). *Special education Law* (2nd ed.). New York: Longman Publishers.

Sabatino, D.A., Sabation, A.C., & Mann, L. (1983). *Management: A Handbook of Tactics, Strategies, and Programs.* Aspen Systems Corporation.

Salvia, J., & Ysseldyke, J.E. (1985). *Assessment in Special Education* (3rd. ed.). Boston: Houghton Mifflin.

Salvia J., & Ysseldyke, J.E. (1991). *Assessment* (5th ed.). Boston: Houghton Mifflin.

Salvia, J. & Ysseldyke, J.E. (1995) *Assessment* (6th ed.). Boston: Houghton Mifflin.

Sattler, J.M. (1982). *Assessment of Children's Intelligence and Special Abilities* (2nd ed.). Boston: Allyn and Bacon.

Schloss, P.J., Harriman, N., & Pfiefer, K. (in press). Application of a sequential prompt reduction technique to the independent composition performance of behaviorally disordered youth. <u>Behavioral Disorders.</u>

Schloss, P.J.., & Sedlak, R.A.(1986). *Instructional Methods for Students with Learning and Behavior Problems.* Boston: Allyn and Bacon.

Schmuck, R.A., & Schmuck, P.A. (1971). *Group Processes in the Classroom.* Dubuque, IA: William C. Brown Company.

Schubert, D.G. (1978). Your teaching - the tape recorder. *Reading Improvement, 15*(1), 78-80.

Schulz, J.B., Carpenter, C.D., & Turnbull, A.P. (1991). *Mainstreaming Exceptional Students: A Guide for Classroom Teachers.* Boston: Allyn and Bacon.

Semmel, M.I., Abernathy, T.V., Butera G., & Lesar, S. (1991). Teacher perception of the regular education initiative. *Exceptional Children, 58* (1), 3-23.

Shea, T.M., & Bauer, A.M. (1985). *Parents and Teachers of Exceptional Students: A Handbook for Involvement.* Boston: Allyn and Bacon.

Simeonsson, R.J. (1986). *Psychological and Development Assessment of Special Children.* Boston: Allyn and Bacon.

Smith, C.R. (1991). *Learning Disabilities: The Interaction of Learner, Task, and Setting.* Boston: Little, Brown, and Company.

Smith, D.D., & Luckasson, R. (1992). *Introduction to Special Education: Teaching in an Age of Challenge.* Boston: Allyn and Bacon.

Smith, J.E., & Patton, J.M. (1989). *A Resource Module on Adverse Causes of Mild Mental Retardation.* (Prepared for the President's Committee on Mental Retardation).

Smith, T.E.C., Finn, D.M., & Dowdy, C.A. (1993). *Teaching Students With Mild Disabilities.* Fort Worth, TX: Harcourt Brace Jovanovich College Publishers.

Smith-Davis, J. (1989a April). *A National Perspective on Special Education.* Keynote presentation at the GLRS/College/University Forum, Macon, GA.

Stephens, T.M. (1976). *Directive Teaching of Children with Learning and Behavioral Disorders.* Columbus, OH Charles E. Merrill.

Sternburg, R.J. (1990). *Thinking Styles: Key to Understanding Performance.* Phi Delta Kappa, 71(5), 366-371.

Sulzer, B., & Mayer, G.R. (1972). *Behavior Modification Procedures for School Personnel.* Hinsdale, IL: Dryden.

Tateyama-Sniezek, K.M. (1990.) Cooperative Learning: Does it improve the academic achievement of students with handicaps? *Exceptional Children,* 57(2), 426-427.

Thiagarajan, S. (1976). Designing instructional games for handicapped learners. *Focus on Exceptional Children.* 7(9), 1-11.

Thomas, O. (1980). *Individualized Instruction* [Videocassette & manual series]. Northbrook, IL: Hubbard Scientific Company. (Project STRETCH [Strategies to Train Regular Educators to Teach Children with Handicaps]. Module 14, ISBN 0- 8331-1919-2).

Thomas, O. (1980). *Spelling* [Videocassette & manual series]. (Project STRETCH [Strategies to Train Regular Educators to Teach Children with Handicaps]. Module 10, ISBN 0-83311915-X).

Thornton, C.A., Tucker, B.F., Dossey, J.A., & Bazik, E.F. (1983). *Teaching Mathematics to Children with Special Needs.* Menlo Park, CA: Addison-Wesley.

Turkel, S.R., & Podel, D.M. (1984). Computer-assisted learning for mildly handicapped students. *Teaching Exceptional Children.* 16(4), 258-262.

Turnbull, A.P., Strickland, B.B., & Brantley, J.C. (1978). *Developing Individualized Education Programs.* Columbus, OH: Charles E. Merrill.

U.S. Department Of Education. (1993). *To Assure the Free Appropriate Public Education of all Children with Disabilities. (Fifteenth annual report to Congress on the Implementation of The Individuals with Disabilities Education Act.).* Washington, D.C.

Walker, J.E., & Shea, T.M. (1991). *Behavior Management: A Practical Approach for Educators.* New York: MacMillan.

Wallace, G., & Kauffman, J.M. (1978). *Teaching Children with Learning Problems.* Columbus, OH: Charles E. Merrill.

Wehman, P., & Mclaughlin, P.J. (1981). *Program Development in Special Education.* New York: McGraw-Hill.

Weintraub, F.J. (1987, March). [Interview].

Wesson, C.L. (1991). Curriculum-based measurement and two models of follow-up consultation. *Exceptional Children.* 57(3), 246-256.

West, R.P., Young, K.R., & Spooner, F. (1990). Precision Teaching: An Introduction. *Teaching Exceptional Children.* 22(3), 4-9.

Wheeler, J. (1987). *Transitioning Persons with Moderate and Severe Disabilities from School to Adulthood: What Makes it Work?* Materials Development Center, School of Education, and Human Services. University of Wisconsin-Stout.

Whiting, J., & Aultman, L. (1990). *Workshop for Parents.* (Workshop materials). Albany, GA: Southwest Georgia Learning Resources System Center.

Wiederholt, J.L., Hammill, D.D., & Brown, V.L. (1983). *The Resource Room Teacher: A Guide to Effective Practices* (2nd ed.). Boston: Allyn and Bacon.

Wiig, E.H., & Semel, E.M. (1984). *Language Assessment and Intervention for the Learning Disabled.* (2nd ed.). Columbus, OH: Charles E. Merrill.

Wolfgang, C.H., & Glickman, C.D.(1986). *Solving Discipline Problems: Strategies for Classroom Teachers* (2nd ed.). Boston: Allyn and Bacon.

Ysselkyke, J.E., Algozzine, B., (1990). *Introduction to Special Education* (2nd ed.). Boston: Houghton Mifflin.

Ysseldyke, J.E., Algozzine, B., & Thurlow, M.L. (1992). *Critical Issues in Special Education* (2nd ed.). Boston: Houghton Mifflin Company.

Yssedlyke, J.E., Thurlow, M.L., Wotruba, J.W., Nania, Pa.A (1990). Instructional arrangements: Perceptions From General Education. *Teaching Exceptional Children, 22*(4), 4-8.

Zargona, N., Vaughn, S., &7 Mcintosh, R. (1991). Social Skills Interventions and children with behavior problems: A review. *Behavior Disorders, 16*(4), 260-275.

Zigmond, N., & Baker, J. (1990). Mainstream experiences for learning disabled students (Project Meld): Preliminary report. *Exceptional Children, 57*(2), 176-185.

Zirpoli, T.J., & Melloy, K.J. (1993). *Behavior Management.* New York: Merrill.

XAMonline, INC. 21 Orient Ave. Melrose, MA 02176

Toll Free number 800-509-4128

TO ORDER Fax 781-662-9268 OR www.XAMonline.com

ARIZONA Teacher Certification -AEPA- 2008

PO#   Store/School:

Address 1:

Address 2 (Ship to other):

City, State Zip

Credit card number _____-_____-_____-_____   expiration _____

EMAIL _____

PHONE   FAX

ISBN	TITLE	Qty	Retail	Total
978-1-58197-747-9	AEPA EARLY CHILDHOOD EDUCATION 36			
9781-58197-749-3	AEPA BASIC SKILLS 96, 97, 98			
978-1-58197-738-7	AEPA ELEMENTARY EDUCATION 01			
978-1-58197-703-5	AEPA ENGLISH 02			
978-1-58197-731-8	AEPA SOCIAL STUDIES 03			
978-1-58197-732-5	AEPA BIOLOGY 07			
978-1-58197-722-6	AEPA CHEMISTRY 08			
978-1-58197-748-6	AEPA PHYSICS 09			
978-1-58197-642-7	AEPA MIDDLE SCHOOL MATHEMATICS 37			
978-1-58197-641-0	AEPA MATHEMATICS 10			
978-1-58197-746-2	AEPA HEALTH 18			
978-1-58197-734-9	AEPA LIBRARY-EDUCATIONAL MEDIA 12			
978-1-58197-729-5	AEPA ART SAMPLE TEST 13			
978-1-58197-735-6	AEPA SPANISH 15			
978-1-58197-743-1	AEPA HISTORY 05			
978-1-58197-736-3	AEPA FRENCH SAMPLE TEST 16			
978-1-58197-739-4	AEPA SPECIAL EDUCATION - EMOTIONAL DISABILTIES 24			
978-1-58197-770-7	AEPA SPECIAL EDUCATION: CROSS-CATEGORY 22			
978-1-58197-745-5	AEPA CONSTITUTION OF THE UNITED STATES AND ARIZONA 33			
978-1-58197-740-0	AEPA POLITICAL SCIENCE/AMERICAN GOVERNMENT 06			
978-1-58197-291-7	AEPA PROFESSIONAL KNOWLEDGE - ELEMENTARY & SECONDARY 91, 92			
			SUBTOTAL	
	Ship 1 book $8.70, 2 books $11.00		Ship	$8.70
			TOTAL	